International Development Policy:
Aid, Emerging Economies and Global Policies

International Development Policy

Previous and forthcoming titles

AFRICA: 50 YEARS OF INDEPENDENCE, NO. 1
Geneva: Graduate Institute Publications, 2010, ISSN print 1663-9383
ISSN online 1663-9405 I ISBN 978-2-940415-27-4.

ENERGY AND DEVELOPMENT, NO. 2
Basingstoke/Geneva: Graduate Institute Publications/Palgrave Macmillan, 2011,
ISBN 978-0-230-28248-3.

RELIGION AND DEVELOPMENT, NO. 4
Basingstoke/Geneva: Graduate Institute Publications/Palgrave Macmillan, 2013.

THE GRADUATE INSTITUTE GENEVA
Graduate Institute of International and Development Studies
Institut de hautes etudes internationales et du développement
Graduate Institute Publications
P.O. Box 136
CH – 1211 Geneva 21

publications@graduateinstitute.ch
http://www.graduateinstitute.ch/publications

INTERNATIONAL DEVELOPMENT POLICY: AID, EMERGING ECONOMIES AND GLOBAL POLICIES

Editor-in-Chief

Gilles Carbonnier
Professor of Development Economics, The Graduate Institute, Geneva

Coordinator

Marie Thorndahl
The Graduate Institute, Geneva

Editorial Board

Jean-Louis Arcand
Professor of Development Economics, The Graduate Institute, Geneva

Francis Cheneval
Professor of Political Philosophy, University of Zurich

Suren Erkman
Director, Institute of Land Use Policies and Human Environment, University of Lausanne

Daniel Fino
Director, Executive Master in Development Policies and Practices (DPP),
The Graduate Institute, Geneva

Till Foerster
Professor of Social Anthropology, Institute of Social Anthropology, University of Basel

Jean-Claude Huot
General-Secretary, Swiss Catholic Lenten Fund, Lausanne

Katharina Michaelowa
Professor of Political Economy and Development, Institute of Political Science,
University of Zurich; Director, Centre for Comparative and International Studies, Zurich

Gérard Perroulaz
Research Fellow, Economist, The Graduate Institute, Geneva

Dominique Rossier
Senior Lecturer and Head of Africa Section, Executive Master in
Development Policies and Practices (DPP), The Graduate Institute, Geneva

Cédric Tille
Professor of International Economics, The Graduate Institute, Geneva

James Zhan
Director, Division on Investment and Enterprise, United Nations Conference on
Trade and Development (UNCTAD)

Research Assistant Emmanuel Dalle Mulle

Figures layout Catherine Fragnière

Infographic section Emmanuel Dalle Mulle, y-b design www.ybdigital.com

Translator Syntax Übersetzungen AG

Cover photo AFP/Ahmad Zamroni

Visit the *International Development Policy* and associated documents online
http://poldev.revues.org

First published 2012 by
PALGRAVE MACMILLAN

Palgrave Macmillan in the UK is an imprint of Macmillan Publishers Limited,
registered in England, company number 785998, of Houndmills, Basingstoke,
Hampshire RG21 6XS.

Palgrave Macmillan in the US is a division of St Martin's Press LLC,
175 Fifth Avenue, New York, NY 10010.

Palgrave Macmillan is the global academic imprint of the above companies
and has companies and representatives throughout the world.

Palgrave® and Macmillan® are registered trademarks in the United States,
the United Kingdom, Europe and other countries.

ISBN: 978-1-137-00340-9   paperback

This book is printed on paper suitable for recycling and made from fully
managed and sustained forest sources. Logging, pulping and manufacturing
processes are expected to conform to the environmental regulations of the
country of origin.

A catalogue record for this book is available from the British Library.

Library of Congress Cataloging-in-Publication Data

10 9 8 7 6 5 4 3 2 1
22 21 19 18 17 16 15 14 13 12

Printed and bound in Great Britain by
CPI Antony Rowe, Chippenham and Eastbourne

CONTENTS

PART 2: REVIEW
MAJOR DEVELOPMENT POLICY TRENDS

LIST OF FIGURES

LIST OF TABLES

PREFACE

International Development Policy is a critical source of analysis of development policy and international cooperation trends for scholars, policymakers, development professionals and journalists. It offers a diverse range of academic views from both industrialised countries and emerging economies. Each book presents in-depth coverage of a chosen theme, and focuses on the latest debates and innovations in finance, trade and development.

The 2012 issue analyses the shift from traditional development assistance toward global public policies. It examines how rising global challenges – ranging from climate change to worldwide pandemics – and the emergence of new aid actors profoundly affect international development cooperation, altering its architecture and approaches. It questions how far bilateral and multilateral aid agencies succeed in mainstreaming global issues within their operations. With specific attention to Brazil, China and South Africa, it assesses how emerging and traditional foreign aid donors address competing objectives, often using diverging rationales.

The *International Development Policy* is edited by the Graduate Institute of International and Development Studies, an institution of research and higher education dedicated to the study of world affairs. Located in Geneva at the heart of an international centre of multilateral governance, the Graduate Institute benefits from a rich legacy linked not only to the founding of the international system and the League of Nations in the 1920s, but also to the emergence of the developing world in the 1960s.

http://graduateinstitute.ch/publications
http://poldev.revues.org

We extend our thanks to the Swiss Agency for Development and Cooperation (SDC) for its financial support.

NOTES ON CONTRIBUTORS

Marine Buissonnière
Director of the Public Health Program at the Open Society Foundations. From 2003 to 2007, she served as Secretary-General of Médecins Sans Frontières International, where she oversaw coordination and cooperation between the 19 sections that make up the MSF movement. She has also held key positions for MSF in Korea, Japan, China and the Palestinian Territories.

Christophe Bellmann
Programmes Director at the International Centre for Trade and Sustainable Development (ICTSD). He has previously worked for the Swiss Coalition of Development Organisations. He also was a Research Associate at the Economic Commission for Latin America and the Caribbean in Santiago.

Maurizio Carbone
Professor of International Development and Jean Monnet Professor of EU External Relations, School of Social and Political Sciences at the University of Glasgow. He has previously taught at the University of Pittsburgh, Carnegie Mellon University and Duke University. He has held visiting research positions at the University of Cambridge, Sciences Po Paris, the European University Institute and Université Libre de Bruxelles. He has published extensively on the external relations of the European Union, foreign aid and the politics of international development.

Gilles Carbonnier
Professor of Development Economics at the Graduate Institute of International and Development Studies and Editor-in-Chief of *International Development Policy*. His research and teaching focus on international development cooperation, humanitarianism, energy, the governance of natural resources and the political economy of war. Before joining the Graduate Institute, he gained over 18 years of professional experience in multilateral trade negotiations, development cooperation and humanitarian action.

Thomas Richard Davies
Lecturer in International Politics at City University, London, where he runs the Project on the Evolution of International Non-Governmental Organizations. He is the author of *The Possibilities of Transnational Activism* (Martinus Nijhoff, 2007), and he is currently completing a manuscript on the general history of international non-governmental organisations since the eighteenth century.

Jonathan Hepburn
Agriculture Programme Manager, International Centre for Trade and Sustainable Development (ICTSD). Before joining ICTSD, he represented Oxfam International at the World Bank and the International Monetary Fund (IMF) in Washington, and led Oxfam's global campaign on aid, debt and the Millennium Development Goals. He previously worked on trade, development and human rights issues at the Quaker United Nations Office in Geneva.

Meibo Huang
Professor of Economics and Director of the China Institute for International Development of Xiamen University. She holds a PhD in Economics and has been associated with the Economics School, Xiamen University, since 1991. Professor Huang's current research focuses on international monetary cooperation, regional economic integration and China's foreign aid.

Bruce Jenks
Senior non-resident Fellow at Harvard University Kennedy School of Government. He currently lectures at the Geneva Graduate Institute of International and Development Studies and at the Columbia University School of International and Public Affairs. He served as Assistant Secretary-General at the United Nations Development Programme until 2010, and was responsible for the UNDP's resource mobilisation, and its relations with the Executive Board, donors, UN agency partners, the World Bank, OECD/DAC, the private sector and civil society.

Michel Mordasini
Assistant Director General and Head of the Global Cooperation Domain, Swiss Agency for Development and Cooperation. He was the Swiss Executive Director on the Board of the World Bank Group from 2006 to March 2011. Overall, he has more than 30 years of development cooperation experience.

Robert Muggah
Fellow at the Instituto de Relações Internacionais, Pontifícia Universidade Católica do Rio de Janeiro. There, he directs several projects on humanitarian action in non-war settings, civilian rosters for peace support operations, and urban violence. Dr Muggah also works closely with the OECD, UN and World Bank in Latin America, the Caribbean, Africa, the Middle East, South and South-East Asia and the South Pacific. IIe received his DPhil from the University of Oxford and an MPhil from the Institute of Development Studies, University of Sussex.

Ugo Panizza
Chief of the Debt and Finance Analysis Unit at the Division on Globalization and Development Strategies of UNCTAD and Lecturer in Econometrics and Development Politics at the Graduate Institute of International and Development Studies, Geneva. Prior to joining UNCTAD, Mr Panizza was Senior Economist at the Inter-American Development Bank (1998–2006). He also worked for the World Bank and taught at the University of Torino and the American University of Beirut. His research interests include international finance, sovereign debt, banking, political economy and public sector labour markets.

Eduarda Passarelli Hamann
Brazilian lawyer, with MA and PhD in international relations. Her areas of interest include peace operations, Brazilian foreign policy, South–South cooperation and related subjects. Dr Hamann is currently a senior researcher at Instituto Igarapé and a consultant at the World Bank. She has previously worked for Viva Rio, QUNO-Geneva and Canal Futura. She also has teaching experience in renowned Brazilian universities (Pontifícia Universidade Católica do Rio de Janeiro, Fundação Getulio Vargas and Universidade Candido Mendes).

Peiqiang Ren
PhD student of World Economics, Department of International Economics and Trade, Economics School, Xiamen University, China. His previous area of research interest was international trade, and his PhD thesis focuses on the management of China's foreign aid.

Elizabeth Sidiropoulos
National Director of the South African Institute of International Affairs (SAIIA), an independent foreign policy think-tank based in Johannesburg. She has headed the Institute since 2005. Before her current appointment she was Director of Studies at SAIIA from 1999 to April 2005. She is the editor-in-chief of the *South African Journal of International Affairs*. Her research focus is South Africa's foreign policy, global governance and the role of emerging powers in Africa.

Andy Sumner
Research Fellow in the Vulnerability and Poverty Reduction Team at the Institute of Development Studies, Sussex, UK, and a Visiting Fellow at the Centre for Global Development, Washington, DC. He is a cross-disciplinary economist. His research relates to poverty, inequality and human well-being, with particular reference to poverty concepts and indicators, global trends and MDG/post-MDG debates.

Marie Wilke
International Trade Law Programme Officer at the International Centre for Trade and Sustainable Development (ICTSD). Previously she worked for the United Nations Conference on Trade and Development (UNCTAD) and for the German Federal Ministry of Economics and Technology. She holds a law degree from Hanse Law School and an LLM in Public International Law from Helsinki University (summa cum laude).

LIST OF ACRONYMS AND ABBREVIATIONS

ABC   Agência Brasileira de Cooperação (Brazilian Agency for Cooperation)
ACP   African Caribbean and Pacific (countries)
ADB   Asian Development Bank
AFDB   African Development Bank
AFP   Agence France Presse
ANND   Arab NGO Network for Development
ARF   African Renaissance Fund
ARV   Antiretroviral Drug
AMC   Advanced Market Commitments
AMS   Aggregate Measure of Support
ANC   African National Congress
AU   African Union

BINGO   Business-Interest Not-for-Profit Organisation
BMGF   Bill and Melinda Gates Foundation
BNDES   Brazilian Development Bank
BRAC   Bangladesh Rural Advancement Committee
BRIC   Brazil-Russia-India-China
BTA   Bilateral Trade Agreement

CANVAS   Centre for Applied Non-Violent Action and Strategies
CAS   Chinese Academy of Sciences
CDI   Commitment to Development Index
CDM   Clean Development Mechanism
CEPR   Centre for Economic Policy Research (UK)
CEXIM   China Export and Import Bank
CIF   Climate Investment Fund
CNAT   National Commission for Technical Assistance (Brazil)
CPS   Country Partnership Strategies
CSO   Civil Society Organisation
CWFS   Committee on World Food Security

DAC   Development Assistance Committee
DAFC   Department of Aid to Foreign Countries (China)
DBSA   Development Bank of Southern Africa
DCD   Development Cooperation Directorate (OECD)
DDA   Doha Development Agenda

DFID	Department for International Development (UK)
DG	Directorate-General (EU)
DIRCO	Department of International Relations and Cooperation (South Africa)
DNDI	Drugs and Neglected Disease Initiative
DSB	Dispute Settlement Body
DSU	Dispute Settlement Understanding (WTO)
EC	European Commission
ECOSOC	Economic and Social Council (UN)
EPOC	Environmental Policy Committee (OECD)
EPTA	Expanded Programme for Technical Assistance
EU	European Union
FAO	Food and Agriculture Organization
FOGS	Functioning of the GATT System
FTAA	Free Trade Area of the Americas
GAFSP	Global Agriculture and Food Security Program
GATT	General Agreement on Tariffs and Trade
GCAP	Global Call to Action against Poverty
GDP	Gross Domestic Product
GEF	Global Environment Facility
GFATM	Global Fund to Fight AIDS, Tubercolosis and Malaria
GFRP	Global Food Crisis Response Program
GIZ	Deutsche Gesellschaft für Internationale Zusammenarbeit (German Development Agency)
GMM	Generalised Method of Moments
GNI	Gross National Income
GOARN	Global Outbreak Alert and Response Network
GPG	Global Public Good
GPPI	Global Public Policy Institute (Berlin)
GRI	Global Reporting Initiative
GSTP	Global System of Trade Preferences
HIV/AIDS	Human Immunodeficiency Virus/Acquired Immune Deficiency Syndrome
IAC	InterAcademy Council
IAP	InterAcademy Panel
IBSA	India-Brazil-South Africa
ICC	International Criminal Court
ICTSD	International Centre for Trade and Sustainable Development
IDPM	Institute of Development Policy Management (University of Antwerp)
IDS	Institute of Development Studies (UK)
IEG	Independent Evaluation Group (World Bank)
IFM	Innovative Financing Mechanism
IFPMA	International Federation of Pharmaceutical Manufacturers & Associations

IMF	International Monetary Fund
INCAF	International Network on Conflict and Fragility
INGO	International Non-Governmental Organisation
IPCC	Intergovernmental Panel on Climate Change
IPEA	Istituto de Pesquisa Econômica Aplicada (Institute of Applied Economic Research)
IT	Information Technology
ITEC	Indian Technical and Economic Cooperation
ITO	International Trade Organization
LDC	Least Developed Country
LIC	Low-Income Country
LMIC	Lower Middle-Income Country
MDG	Millennium Development Goal
M&A	Monitoring and Evaluation
MFN	Most Favoured Nation
MIC	Middle-Income Country
MINUSTAH	United Nations Stabilization Mission in Haiti
MOF	Ministry of Finance (China)
MOFA	Ministry of Foreign Affairs (China)
MOFCOM	Ministry of Commerce (China)
MTR	Marginal Tax-Rate
NAM	Non-Aligned Movement
NGO	Non-Governmental Organisation
NEPAD	New Partnership of African Development
ODA	Official Development Assistance
ODI	Overseas Development Institute (UK)
OECD	Organisation for Economic Cooperation and Development
PALAMA	Public Administration Leadership and Management Academy
PCD	Policy Coherence for Development
PEPFAR	United States President's Emergency Plan for AIDS Relief
PINCI	Pakistan, India, Nigeria, China and Indonesia
PINGO	Public Interest Non-Governmental Organisation
PPP	Purchasing Power Parity
PRC	People's Republic of China
RTA	Regional Trade Agreement
RtoP	Responsibility to Protect
SACU	Southern African Customs Union
SAIIA	South African Institute of International Affairs
SADPA	South African Development Partnership Agency
SDC	Swiss Agency for Development and Cooperation
SECO	State Secretariat for Economic Affairs

SENAI	National Service for Industrial Apprenticeship (Brazil)
SG	Secretary General (of the United Nations)
SID	Society for International Development
SSC	South–South Cooperation
SSDC	South–South Development Cooperation
TB	Tubercolosis
TRICO	Trilateral Cooperation Fund (South Africa and Germany)
UK	United Kingdom
UMIC	Upper Middle-Income Country
UN	United Nations
UNCTAD	United Nations Conference on Trade and Development
UNDP	United Nations Development Programme
UNEF	United Nations Emergency Force
UNESCO	United Nations Educational, Scientific and Cultural Organization
UNFCCC	United Nations Framework Convention on Climate Change
UIA	Union of International Associations
WEF	World Economic Forum
WHO	World Health Organization
WBCSD	World Business Council for Sustainable Development
WTO	World Trade Organization

PART 1: DOSSIER

AID, EMERGING ECONOMIES AND GLOBAL POLICIES

1
REFRAMING AID IN A WORLD WHERE THE POOR LIVE IN EMERGING ECONOMIES

Gilles Carbonnier, Andy Sumner

Abstract

This special issue of *International Development Policy* analyses the major shifts affecting traditional development assistance, particularly with regard to global public policy and the emerging economies. In this introductory chapter, the authors examine the changing development landscape and the shifting geography of poverty to question the role of aid organisations in middle-income economies (MICs). They argue that continued donor engagement in these richer countries is warranted for two reasons. First, and in the best interest of lower-income countries (LICs), traditional donors and MICs must cooperate in the design and implementation of global policies to protect global public goods. Second, foreign aid agencies can assist MICs in reducing poverty at home. They must, however, tread lightly in this political endeavour that often implies supporting domestic drivers of change in pushing for tax reform and improved public service delivery. The authors focus in particular on the pivotal role of the emerging middle classes and civil society organisations in MICs. Finally, they introduce policy coherence for sustainable development as a shared framework for MICs and high-income countries (HICs) to effectively address the poverty and global public goods agendas.

Acknowledgements

Special thanks for research assistance to Rich Mallett, Ricardo Santos, Pui Yan, Henrique Conca Bussacos, Nicki Goh, and Emmanuel Dalle.

1. Introduction

The landscape for aid is undergoing a major international rethink (Evans, 2010). Many are grappling with the question of how aid can be done better – for example, via an aid transparency and accountability revolution (Barder, 2009) or conditional cash transfers and output-based aid (Birdsall and Savedoff, 2010). Others are stepping back from the aid paradigm altogether and beginning to explore possible alternatives to international development cooperation. They argue that contemporary aid effectiveness debates have missed the point by focusing solely on the quality or quantity of aid, rather than discussing wider structural issues (see e.g. Fischer, 2010).

The very definition of what aid is and what it hopes to achieve are increasingly on the table for discussion, and the scope for a new kind of development assistance – an Aid 2.0 – is increasingly evident.[1] The global development landscape is currently undergoing significant changes. In this chapter, we focus on three of them that will largely contribute to determining the future of aid.

First, there is a shift in the geography of poverty. The traditional remit of development assistance has long been to alleviate poverty and promote socioeconomic development in poor countries. Yet, today, the vast majority of the world's poor do not live in the poorest countries, but in middle-income ones (MICs). Over the past 15 years, many developing economies have grown substantially and graduated from low-income (LICs) to MICs. In these richer economies, international development assistance typically accounts for a very limited share of gross domestic product (GDP) and government revenue. Hence aid tends to play only a marginal role in MICs. The transfer of official development assistance (ODA) to these countries has been put into question because of their capacity to finance their own development without foreign aid. Poverty alleviation increasingly depends on domestic policies in the MICs themselves, which requires addressing inequality through political engagement rather than technical approaches.

Second, there is a mushrooming of new aid donors. Over the past few years, large MICs such as Brazil, China, India and South Africa have become significant donors themselves: non-traditional donor states (meaning non-members of the Development Assistance Committee – DAC) accounted for about US$10 billion a year in 2010 – a doubling since 2005. The emergence of these bilateral donors together with the rise of large private donors erodes the *de facto* oligopoly exerted by the DAC members. Increasing donor competition opens new doors to address development challenges but it may also diminish the power of aid conditionality.

Third, the international cooperation agenda increasingly centres on the provision of global public goods or the fight against global public bads. This has resulted in the mushrooming of new financing and delivery modalities and of innovative finance mechanisms, most notably in the area of public health and climate change. Bilateral and multilateral aid agencies – willingly or unwillingly – focus ever more on financing, implementing and monitoring global public policies whose scope and objectives go well beyond poverty reduction. Such global public policies address biodiversity, peace and security, public health, energy security, financial stability, migration, environmental degradation and other issues that are critical not only for developing countries, but for donors as well.

---

1   For early suggestions on Aid 2.0 see these examples: www.owen.org/blog/3397 and www.how-matters.org/2010/08/05/development-aid-2-0 (accessed on 11 October 2011).

There are of course additional shifts in the development landscape with a direct bearing on the future of aid, most notably:

- Stringent environmental and energy constraints fundamentally challenge the dominant development model centred on maximisation of economic growth. Increased competition over scarce resources and environmental degradation calls for a paradigm shift in the relationship between human activity and the biosphere and lower carbon development, at least in MICs and high-income countries (HICs).
- Shifts in regional comparative advantages and patterns of integration in the world economy pose new risks and opportunities, especially for Africa. Much ODA is focused on this continent. Africa will double its population by 2050 (UN-DESA Population Division, 2011) making it relatively labour abundant and land scarce, while at the same time East Asia is experiencing a demographic transition that will contribute to increasing labour costs. This means that sub-Saharan Africa may fare a better chance of developing labour-intensive industrial activities than up to now.
- The unfolding of a series of crises from 2008 on – from food and energy to private finance, banking, sovereign debt and public finance – has put the aid system under great strain as support for aid erodes in the North in the face of public spending cuts. Many traditional donors are set to reduce their aid budgets, which puts into question earlier pledges made.
- Dealing with fragile states remains a major challenge, compounded by the increasing frequency of disasters in war-torn and post-conflict settings. Mixing development with defence and diplomacy has produced uneven results at best, which calls for reconsidering the role of aid in stabilisation and state-building.

Against this background, this special issue of *International Development Policy: Aid, Emerging Economies and Global Policies* focuses on shifts from traditional ODA towards global public policy. It assesses the specific contributions of multilateral and bilateral agencies as well as of non-state actors in the global public goods agenda, and addresses the emergence of non-DAC donors as significant aid and global players.

In this introductory chapter, we start by looking at the new geography of poverty, which raises the question of the role of aid organisations in MICs. We discuss two major reasons for international aid organisations to stay in MICs. The first is to engage them in the design and implementation of global policies required to protect global public goods, arguably in the best interest of LICs and of DAC members themselves. The second is to assist MICs in combating poverty at home, which often relies on redistributive policies that include social security and tax reform as well as improved, targeted public services. As part of this political endeavour, foreign aid agencies must tread a fine line in supporting domestic drivers of change that play a pivotal role in pushing this agenda forward. In this chapter, we focus in particular on the emerging middle classes and civil society organisations. We conclude by arguing that policy coherence for sustainable development offers a common framework for MICs and DAC donors to effectively address poverty alleviation and the provision of global public goods.

2. Aid in a world where poor people live in MICs

If one accepts the core business of development aid is poverty reduction, where the poor live is an important question. Sumner (2010, 2011a,b,c) shows that most of the world's poor no longer live in LICs, i.e. countries classified as such by the World Bank on the basis of gross national income (GNI) per capita (see Table 1.1). In 1990, over 90 per cent of the world's poor lived in LICs. Twenty years on, MICs account for three-quarters of the world's poor. Sumner (see above), and Kanbur and Sumner (2011a,b), note that most of the world's poor live in a small number of countries: of the 28 economies that graduated from LIC to MIC status over the last decade, there is a concentration of world poverty in five of them, which the authors refer to as the PINCIs: China (graduated 1999), Pakistan (graduated 2008), India (graduated 2007), Nigeria (2008), and Indonesia (re-graduated in 2003). The data show that the graduation process translated in less poverty reduction and more inequality than might be expected. As a result, donors need to rethink their poverty reduction strategies and policies since there are fewer very poor countries and most of the world's poor live in MICs.

Table 1.1 – Global distribution of world poverty by country classifications, 1990 vs. 2007 (in percentage of world poor*)

| | Author's estimates based on PovCalNet (World Bank, 2011a) Non-adjusted base years | | | | Author's estimates based on PovCalNet (World Bank, 2011a) Adjusted base years | | | |
| | 1990 or nearest available year | | 2007 or nearest available year | | 1990 | | 2007 | |
	Millions	%	Millions	%	Millions	%	Millions	%
LICs	1596.1	94.5	305.3	24.1	1632.5	93.1	342.7	29.1
MICs[2]	93.2	5.5	960.4	75.9	121.4	6.9	836.0	70.9
Total	1689.3	100.0	1265.7	100.0	1753.9	100.0	1178.7	100.0
Fragile and conflict-affected states[3]	–	–	286.2	22.6	–	–	272.6	23.1
China and India	1137.9	67.4	673.0	53.2	1123.6	64.1	561.33	47.6
PINCIs[4]	1352.0	80.0	852.7	67.4	1339.5	76.4	709.20	60.2

* People living with less than US$1.25/day.
Source: Sumner (2011b) based on data processed from PovCalNet (World Bank, 2011a).

Aid dependence tends to be particularly high in LICs where ODA may account for a significant proportion of GDP and government revenues. Figure 1.1 shows that the share of ODA to each income group has been evolving in different

---

2   Low-income (LIC) and middle-income country (MIC) status is based on World Bank country classifications for World Bank financial years 1992 and 2011 (which are based on gross national product per capita Atlas data for two years earlier to each financial year).
3   FCAS (Fragile and Conflict-Affected States) definition = 43 countries of combined three lists as per OECD (2010b).
4   Pakistan, India, Nigeria, China and Indonesia.

directions between 1960 and 2009, yet with a sharp decline in the share accruing to the lower middle-income countries (LMICs) between 1960 and the mid-1970s, and again from 2007 onward, to the benefit of the LICs in general, and the group of least developed countries (LDCs) in particular. This category is defined by the United Nations (UN) as those countries that 'are highly disadvantaged in their development process and risk, more than others, failure to come out of poverty'. This classification is based on three criteria: low-income per capita, weak human development and high economic vulnerability. Since being an LDC does not exclusively depend on per capita income, surprisingly a third of all LDCs are also MICs, raising question marks about how difficult it is to graduate from the LDC category (Guillaumont and Guillaumont Jeanneney, 2010).[5]

Figure 1.1 – Breakdown of ODA recipient countries by income groups, 1960–2010 (in percentage of total ODA)

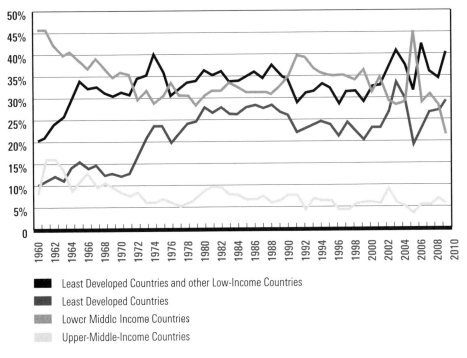

■ Least Developed Countries and other Low-Income Countries
■ Least Developed Countries
▨ Lower Middle Income Countries
▨ Upper-Middle-Income Countries

Source: OECD/DAC (2011).

---

5   The income dimension is measured by an average income per person over three years; human development is primarily captured by weak human resources, as measured by indicators of nutrition, mortality of children aged five years or under, secondary school enrolment, and adult literacy rate; economic vulnerability is captured by population size, remoteness, export diversification, share of agriculture, forestry and fisheries in the economy, instability of agricultural production and of exports, and homelessness resulting from natural disasters. In 2011, 14 MICs were classified as least developed countries (LDCs) in the list of aid recipient countries established by the Development Assistance Committee (DAC) of the Organisation for Economic Cooperation and Development (OECD): Angola, Bhutan, Djibouti, Equatorial Guinea, Kiribati, Lesotho, Sao Tomé and Principe, Samoa, Senegal, Sudan, Timor-Leste, Tuvalu, Vanuatu, and Yemen. Note that a country can also refuse to be classified as LDCs.

So are MICs just poor countries by another name? Overall, it is evident that MICs have higher standards of living than LICs and are far less aid dependent (see Table 1.2). The average, population weighted, GNI per capita – by Atlas or Purchasing Power Parity (PPP) methods – in LMICs is quadruple that of LICs. Even LMICs have much lower ODA dependency data than LICs. The removal of China and India or the PINCIs raises the aid dependency indicators but to levels still far lower than that of the LICs group.

Table 1.2 – Economic indicators in LICs, LMICs and UMICs (population weighted)

Indicator	Years	LICs	LMICs	LMICs minus China and India	LMICs minus China, India, Pakistan, Nigeria and Indonesia	UMICs
GNI per capita (Atlas, current US$)	2009	494.5	2276.3	1851.4	2112.7	7480.3
GNI per capita (PPP, current US$)	2009	1156.5	4703.6	3769.0	4370.0	12,494.9
Net ODA received (% of GNI)	2008	12.3	0.6	1.5	2.2	0.2
Net ODA received (% of gross capital formation)	2008	51.3	2.0	5.8	7.8	0.9

Source: Sumner (2011c) based on data processed from World Bank (2011b).

There can be several reasons for traditional aid donors to stay engaged in MICs (Kanbur and Sumner, 2011a,b). First, pockets of extreme poverty and vulnerability arguably call for aid no matter where they occur. Besides, the Indonesian example shows that a country that graduated to the MIC status can easily relapse in the LIC category as a result of a financial crisis or an external shock. Second, negative externalities of MICs' growth, such as climate change, may affect the poor in LICs and provide an argument for directing development assistance toward public goods in MICs. Third, by partnering with MICs, Western donors can gain relevant knowledge for development assistance to LICs, for instance in setting up effective social safety nets in the framework of triangular aid programmes. Fourth, there may be a moral argument to provide development assistance given that MICs are still part of global power relations that may disadvantage them to some extent until those global relationships change (e.g. trade and finance patterns). Yet policy coherence for development should prevail over foreign aid if countries of the Organisation for Economic Cooperation and Development (OECD) seriously wish to address these issues (see concluding section below).

3. Global public goods and MICs

Foreign aid can play a catalytic or incentivising role in MICs (Glennie, 2011, 18), in particular with regard to the provision of global public goods. For instance, several donor agencies are supporting multi-stakeholder initiatives that involve governments, businesses and civil society organisations. The objective is to influence the behaviour of key actors through a mix of market and political incentives and to pave the way for the emergence of global norms that can lead to new policies and regulatory frameworks (Carbonnier, Brugger and Krause 2011).

Global public goods are particularly important with respect to donor engagement with MICs. Forging and developing partnerships with MICs is increasingly critical for effective collective action. Engaging developmentally with MICs is thus seen not only as an end in itself (i.e. achieving poverty reduction in those countries), but also, and perhaps more importantly, as a means to promote global public goods. We can therefore conceptualise global public goods in three ways: as a policy framework for engagement with MICs; as meeting the long-term interests of HICs as well as MICs and LICs; and as fundamentally contingent on the actions and cooperation of MICs not as mere aid recipients but as active stakeholders in addressing the issues at stake both domestically and internationally.

In their seminal book *Global Public Goods: International Cooperation in the 21st Century*, Kaul et al. (1999, 2–3) define global public goods benefits as public (non-rivalry and non-excludability in consumption) and quasi-universal in terms of countries, people and generations. The main rationale behind providing global public goods is to regulate or compensate for the negative effects of global public 'bads', which generate negative externalities across borders (Coyne and Ryan, 2008, 5), such as air pollution, civil war and violent conflict, pandemics, international terrorism and financial crises.

Global public goods tend to be underprovided due to three gaps in public policy making: a jurisdictional gap with a discrepancy between the global boundaries of major policy concerns and the national boundaries of policymaking; a participation gap between a *de facto* multi-stakeholder world which is not reflected in international cooperation processes that remain largely intergovernmental; and an incentive gap where individual countries lack the incentive to address their international spillovers and cooperate on the global public goods agenda (Kaul et al., 1999, 450–1). The adequate supply of global public goods often rests also on the resolution of conflicting interests at the national level, as shown by negotiations on climate change.

Since global public goods cannot be supplied by governments acting unilaterally, cooperation is needed. Donor assistance has only recently started to be focused on supplying global public goods. Te Velde et al. (2002) find that donors with large aid budgets tend to be those that also have a larger share of global public goods in their aid portfolios. In the case of aid projects in the energy sector, Michaelowa and Michaelowa (2011) show, however, that the number of bilateral projects promoting energy efficiency and renewables followed an erratic path over the past three decades, with an increase immediately before international environmental summits followed by a decrease when the political and media attention shifts to other priorities, and with a certain sensitivity to oil price booms.

Aid agencies are small but important players in the global public goods agenda. Yet they have a hard time trying to 'walk the talk' (Mordasini, this issue): the implementation of global public policies has been more than disappointing when compared to the stated ambitions and strategic objectives. The author remarks that, based on available evidence, the mainstreaming of the global public goods agenda in operational practice has been limited so far, mainly to progresses in identifying and costing global risks and their impact on developing countries. Mordasini (this issue) argues that significant reforms of multilateral and bilateral aid agencies have to take place at the institutional, organisational and operational levels in order to start addressing seriously the pressing challenges facing the developing world.

The UN and its agencies obviously have a central role in the production of global public goods, be it with regard to peace and security, human rights, development or the environment. Jenks (this issue) forcefully argues that the ability of the UN to produce significant outcome in the global public goods agenda relies on its continued capacity to generate universal norms and widely shared values. This in turn requires strong leadership and a strong capacity to leverage a broad variety of networks and new, innovative financing mechanisms.

3.1. New funding mechanisms and new donors

Funding global public policies to preserve global public goods has stimulated the emergence of different funding sources and aid channels. Innovative financing mechanisms (IFMs) and climate financing are two particular areas that received increasing interest both in policy and academic arenas (see e.g. de Ferranti, 2006; Jones, 2010; Ketkar and Ratha, 2009; Lob-Levyt and Affolder, 2006; McCoy, 2009).

Innovative financing is about a previously un(der)utilised means of financing development-related initiatives which differs in some way to the standard, 'traditional' system built on government-to-government, donor-to-recipient relationships. Innovative financing is also about creating incentives for new actors to engage with development funding, often through set-ups based on market principles and closely involving private firms, foundations and individuals. As one such example, the brand (PRODUCT)[RED] is a means of financing the Global Fund to Fight AIDS, Tuberculosis and Malaria through the licensing of its trademark to various companies including Apple, American Express and Giorgio Armani. It was founded in 2006 by Bono and Bobby Shriver to 'provide a way for companies to tap into demand by so-called "conscience consumers" without having to develop their own brand...[C]ompanies can... make more money, and do good at the same time' (de Ferranti et al., 2008, 100).

Many IFMs relate to global public goods and involve at least regional, cross-border collaborations, and focus in particular on climate change and public health:

- Brown (2009) outlines five categories of proposals, including the auctioning of assigned amount of emission allowances and the creation of carbon market-based levies, such as the 2 per cent clean development mechanism (CDM) levy to raise funds for the Kyoto Protocol's Adaptation Fund. Other proposals include imposing levies on international maritime transport and on air travel, developing a uniform global tax on CO_2 emissions and the issuance of bonds on international markets. These proposals are all means of creating new mechanisms to generate resources for addressing climate adaptation and some mitigation activities that are (or are meant to be) separate and additional to existing ODA (Brown et al., 2010).

- Aside from the more well-known new institutional approaches to global health, such as the GAVI Alliance Fund, examples of innovative financing include the Millennium Vaccine Initiative which has channelled US$1 billion in tax credits to corporations in order to promote delivery of existing vaccines and accelerate development of new vaccines for developing countries (Stansfield et al., 2002); the Debt2Health (Task Force on Innovative International Financing for Health Systems, 2009); and the International Health Partnership Plus (IHP+), which aims to strengthen national health systems.

The emergence of new powerful private actors in the global health scene, most notably the Bill and Melinda Gates Foundation, together with innovative multi-stakeholder governance structures and IFMs has radically altered the global health landscape over the past two decades, with a wider impact on the international development cooperation architecture as a whole. Traditional public health actors including the World Health Organization have lost their leadership while global and national health policies are largely funded and influenced by private actors (Buissonière, this issue). This raises many complex transparency and accountability issues and requires specific attention to make sure that health policy priorities in developing countries respond to the actual health requirements of the poor and vulnerable (see Buissonière in this issue). Some argue that output and outcome legitimacy are of the essence, but need to be complemented by an accountability-based approach to legitimacy that carefully differentiates between different forms of governance, with a variety of actors playing distinctive roles and assuming differentiated responsibilities. The legitimacy of norms setters and global policymakers in the absence of a worldwide, democratic polity has been repeatedly put into question and deserves more scrutiny. The UN Organization seems obviously well placed for the job (see Jenks in this issue), but with an uneven representation at the Security Council and other central bodies.

In this context, development assistance is becoming a strategic foreign policy instrument for major emerging economies. Indeed, three chapters in this issue that focus on Brazil, China and South Africa respectively demonstrate that these countries construe foreign aid as a strategic policy instrument in two respects: first in relation to LICs in the framework of South–South cooperation agreements, and second to advance their interests within the global governance system and in the elaboration of global public policies. Brazil's foreign policy is increasingly aligned to a South–South cooperation agenda in the pursuit of much broader objectives including trade, investment, technology and the extension of Brazil's influence in bilateral and multilateral frameworks (Muggah and Passarelli Hamann, this issue). In the same vein, South Africa's foreign aid and overall international engagement can be best understood by looking at the country's ambitions in terms of global governance (Sidiropoulos, this issue). As for China, a close examination of the evolution of the country's foreign aid and its institutional anchoring within the Chinese state apparatus provides critical insight to understand how far and why the Chinese approach to development assistance diverges from that of traditional DAC donors (Meibo Huang and Pen, this issue). All these countries have also developed a rapid response capacity not only to be prepared for disasters at home, but to be able to contribute to the international response to major humanitarian crises around the globe.

The rise of new institutional and private donors and of innovative financial mechanisms requires a reconsideration of both the very definition of ODA and the current discourse on foreign aid and international cooperation, going beyond the traditional OECD-DAC perspectives.

4. From foreign aid to domestic taxes and social service delivery

Beyond the global public goods agenda discussed in the section above, is there any additional reason why development agencies should keep working in countries that have graduated from LIC to MIC status? The question is particularly relevant for many MICs that today enjoy sound fiscal and balance-of-payments positions. To the extent that most of the poor live in MICs and that poverty reduction remains their primary objective, traditional donors have little choice but to continue working in the new MICs. But they need to adapt their interventions to the evolving reality of these countries that have grown richer. Tackling poverty often means addressing inequality, exclusion and redistribution, all of which requires political engagement rather than technical approaches. It may for instance involve assistance in the design and implementation of progressive tax reform that raises complex political economy issues.

Within the MICs the potential for achieving poverty reduction through redistribution varies but can be significant. Ravallion (2010) has estimated the marginal tax rates (MTRs) on the 'rich' (those earning more than US$13 per day) required in order to end poverty in MICs. While the MTRs needed to end poverty are less than 10 per cent in many of the 'old' MICs, in many new MICs they would have to be much higher. This is particularly due to large populations of poor relative to the number of 'rich' people in many new MICs. In India, for example, the poverty gap would require an MTR on the 'rich' of over 100 per cent.

Ravallion (2010) argues that most countries with an average per capita income over US$4000 would require very small additional taxation to end poverty. As an example, Palma (2011) notes that Brazil's *Bolsa Familia* social programme distributes US$50 per month to 11 million families at a cost of only 0.5 per cent of GDP in 2005. Similarly Soares et al. (2009) find that, thanks to 'outstanding' targeting, conditional cash transfer programmes in Brazil, Mexico and Chile have cost less than 1 per cent of GDP and have accounted for 15 to 21 per cent of the reduction in inequality. In short, the capacity to redistribute is an important issue for poverty alleviation in MICs. Donors have long understood that pushing for change, for instance via a progressive tax reform, requires the buy-in from the emerging middle classes whose contribution is central to the redistributive endeavour. Thus a better understanding of the redistributive preferences of the new middle classes in MICs is critical for donors.

4.1. The middle classes

Despite differences in defining the middle classes, general trends suggest that the middle class has been expanding fast in MICs. The African Development Bank (AFDB, 2011) and the Asian Development Bank (ADB, 2010) respectively estimate the African middle class at 313 million or one in three Africans (34 per cent of the population) and the middle classes in developing Asia at 1.9 billion or 56 per cent of the population (defining the middle classes as earning US$2–US$20 a day per capita). The growth in the size of the middle class is largely driven by a number of Asian countries whose populations are graduating out of poverty into the middle classes. However, it is much wider than just India and China.

Table 1.3 – Comparable estimates of the size of the middle classes, 1990 vs. 2008 (people living with US$2–US$20/day, household survey data)

	Millions		% of population	
	1990	2008	1990	2008
Africa	151.4	288.1	27	33
Sub-Saharan Africa	66.0	129.9	24	33
Developing Asia	565.3	1894.9	21	56
China*	180.1	817.1	16	63
India*	152.0	274.1	18	25
Latin America and Caribbean	250.3	349.7	71	77

* 2005 data.
Sources: AFDB (2011, 21) for regional data, ADB (2010, 6) for China and India 2005 data, PolcavNet for China and India 1990 data.

The OECD (2010a) discusses in detail the preferences of the middle classes for income redistribution and redistributive fiscal policy. It notes that if public services are of low quality, the middle classes are more likely to consider themselves a loser in the fiscal bargain and less willing to contribute to financing the public sector. Other factors that determine preferences include: personal experiences of social mobility, national and regional cultural and social values, the impact of (higher) taxation on leisure consumption, levels of tertiary education and attitudes toward prevailing levels of meritocracy. Support for redistribution is undermined by low institutional capacity in tax administration and the quality of state services, and by pessimistic views over social mobility.

4.2. Civil society organisations

The majority of donors acknowledge that economic growth alone is not sufficient to reduce poverty. Fighting poverty in MICs entails supporting such processes that have the potential to reduce rather than reinforce patterns of exclusion and inequality. This involves building *long-term* and *consistent* relationships with selected recipient organisations pursuing poverty reduction and social change agendas. It requires donors to involve themselves more intimately with domestic political processes, something they have tended to be unsure about doing in the past (Eyben et al., 2004, 14–15). There can obviously be various domestic actors and organisations pushing for progressive social change, defined as being conducive to poverty reduction. Women's organisations, social movements, workers' unions, professional associations, rights-based organisations and independent media can all play important roles in the mission to promote progressive agendas.

There is little point in pretending that this does not cross over into the political domain – indeed, this constitutes an explicitly political approach infused with liberal values. For example, Hearn (1999) finds that civil society organisations (CSOs) committed to the promotion of liberal democracy and economic liberalism are the most popular with donors. Donors also tend to link up with global citizenship movements, underpinned by universal human rights. This trend has been reinforced by the internationalisation of Western development NGOs, their transformation into multinational and networked organisations, their shift from development aid projects to political advocacy, seeking to influence the dominant development discourse and the design of global development policies. More recently, it gave rise to international NGOs headquartered in the South (Davies, this issue).

Suffice to say here, efforts to support Southern-based CSOs are not new. Howell and Pearce (2000, 75) remarked more than a decade ago that there was considerable funding for projects to strengthen CSOs in developing countries, and there has been much discussion on the UK aid agency's 'drivers-of-change' approach with numerous case studies (DFID, 2005). The World Bank also made the strengthening and participation of civil society in policymaking processes a core element of the poverty reduction strategy papers (Molenaers and Renard, 2002). Over the past ten years, CSOs have become a pivotal actor in multi-stake-holder initiatives, often at the risk of being overburdened with too many tasks and unrealistic expectations (see Carbonnier, Brugger and Krause, 2011, 257–9).

There are, of course, numerous risks and potential problems associated with externally funded CSOs. For example, to what degree will external assistance influence or manipulate an organisation's agenda? Do CSOs risk having their views and actions delegitimised by accepting foreign assistance, either directly from foreign governments or from international non-governmental organisations (INGOs)? The fact that aid seeks to support political change runs the risk of being regarded as a renewed colonial enterprise by Western states. Is this less the case when local CSOs are supported by INGOs? Robinson and Friedman (2007) investigate how far external donor funding influences the policy engagement and outcomes of a selection of CSOs in Uganda and South Africa. They find that the source of funding, whether internally generated or externally supplied, does not seem to be a significant factor in explaining their differential policy impact (Robinson and Friedman, 2007, 659).

Howell (2000, 7–8) outlines three broad and overlapping approaches that donors have traditionally adopted in order to support and develop CSOs: institution and capacity building, partnerships and coalitions, and financial sustainability. The latter reflects the centrality of non-governmental organisations' (NGOs) and CSOs' material bases. The performance and impact of many, if not most, of them tend to be constrained by insufficient resources. The opportunities for Southern-based NGOs and CSOs to fundraise domestically are limited due to their countries' high poverty levels and low levels of economic development.

These constraints may diminish slightly but remain prevalent in countries that just acquired MIC status, and Aldaba et al. (2000, 678) argue that one way to ensure NGO sustainability in a 'beyond aid scenario' is taking better advantage of domestic funding options. Robinson and Friedman (2007, 665) also encourage the adoption of strategies designed to identify and institution-alise local sources of funding and suggest three measures that donors can take to strengthen the organisational capacity of CSOs: replace short-term project support with long-term programme grants and technical assistance; provide specialised assistance aimed at strengthening capacity for policy analysis and advocacy; and encourage host governments to remove restrictive controls and simplify NGO registration procedures, thus promoting a more supportive policy environment for CSOs. Several MICs having a rather autocratic and centralised political culture, donors put high expectations on local civil society organisations, supporting them to address politically sensitive issues such as rent-seeking and patronage and exerting checks on the political elite.

Several authors question the democratic legitimacy of non-state actors in the global policy arena, and that of self-mandated NGOs and CSOs in particular. Thanks to the support they get from donors, these organisations are often financially stronger and enjoy a higher degree of institutionalisa-tion than domestic political parties and, at times, even state institutions. They may substitute both the government in providing essential public services and political parties in voicing opposition. How can international aid agencies avoid weakening nascent democracies in this context? Supporting political parties with ODA remains taboo and would be difficult to justify. But aid organisations could do more to strengthen legislative and judiciary bodies, starting with national and regional parliaments, which often lack the resources and capacities to function properly (Carbonnier, Brugger and Wagner, 2011).

5. Conclusion

Development cooperation is in a state of flux with new actors, new policy requirements beyond national borders and a shift in global poverty away from the poorest countries. By some estimates, there will only be about 20 or so remaining LICs in 2025, most of which will be fragile states in sub-Saharan Africa. Many of the MICs will not need ODA resource transfer. Indeed, many will be donors themselves, as is already the case of Brazil, China and South Africa, India being about to establish its own foreign aid agency (Patel, 2011). The changing dynamic entails a need to rethink aid and redesign the aid system from a focus on poor countries to poor people, tailored to different contexts.

Looking ahead, the aid system will be one with major tensions: traditional aid agencies may focus more on equity, governance and progressive change while MICs may be more interested in 'policy coherence for development' (PCD). Aid often has much less impact on MIC economies than do donor countries' policies on international migration, trade, finance, security, agriculture, investment or research and technology. For example, Berthelemy et al. (2009) find that for countries with a per capita income of less than US$7300 (PPP 2000 prices), a tightening of migration policy is equivalent to a reduction of the level of aid by about 24 per cent. Therefore, they conclude that a trade-off exists between aid and migration.

Over the last two decades, there has been much progress on policy coherence in terms of conceptual clarification, analysis and reporting,[6] and more publicity given to the concept itself.[7] Developmental NGOs and some bilateral aid agencies are taking a firmer stand on a broad range of policies that are critical to global development. In practice, however, PCD is often wrongly equated with inter-ministerial coordination and there has not been much improvement in the design and implementation of more coherent policies. Some contend that the policy coherence agenda has been pushed forward by development aid agencies in an attempt to obscure their failure to make aid more effective, as a rhetorical attempt to put the responsibility for low aid effectiveness on others (Carbone, this issue).

Obviously, total policy coherence will never be achieved. Incoherence is deeply ingrained in policymaking, reflecting the variety of conflicting interests in any society. PCD should thus not be seen as a realistic objective to be achieved at any cost. It should rather serve as a heuristic tool for informed democratic deliberation in donor countries when debating policy options. This is a precondition for minimising the most blatant inconsistencies between domestic policies and development objectives and will help to adopt compensatory or corrective measures where appropriate. Another conceptual flaw is that PCD has been regarded as relevant for (Western) donor countries only, whereas it is actually highly relevant for MICs as well and could help spur progress in international and domestic debates on global public policies, as well as for MICs developing their own foreign aid programmes.

To have a substantive impact, PCD should become part and parcel of policymaking in both MICs and HICs, and be geared toward sustainability. 'Policy coherence for sustainable development' may provide a common framework for both country groupings in the design and implementation of global public policies required to come to grips with the pressing worldwide challenges facing all of us.

REFERENCES

ADB (Asian Development Bank) (2010) 'The Rise of Asia's Middle Class', in *Key Indicators for Asia and the Pacific 2010* (Mandaluyong City: ADB).

AFDB (African Development Bank) (2011) *The Middle of the Pyramid: Dynamics of the Middle Class in Africa*, Market Brief (Tunis: African Development Bank).

Aldaba, F., P. Antezana, M. Valderrama and A. Fowler (2000) 'NGO Strategies beyond Aid: Perspectives from Central and South America and the Philippines', *Third World Quarterly*, 21(4), pp. 669–83.

Barder, O. (2009) *Beyond Planning: Markets and Networks for Better Aid*, Working Paper no. 185 (Washington, DC: Center for Global Development).

Berthelemy, J-C., M. Beuran and M. Maurel (2009) 'Aid and Migration: Substitutes or Complements?', *World Development*, 37(10), pp. 1589–99.

---

6   For instance, the regular peer review mechanism by OECD/DAC members increasingly focuses on policy coherence for development (PCD).

7   See, for example, the annual Commitment to Development Index (CDI) at http://www.cgdev.org/section/initiatives/_active/cdi/ (accessed on 11 October 2011).

Birdsall, N. and W. Savedoff (2010) *Cash on Delivery: A New Approach to Foreign Aid* (Washington, DC: Center for Global Development).

Brown, J. (2009) *Carbon Finance in Africa*, paper prepared for the Special Session on Climate Change of the African Partnership Forum, Addis Ababa, 3 September, http://www.africapartnershipforum.org/dataoecd/29/56/43551050.pdf (accessed on 11 October 2011).

Brown, J., N. Cantore and D.W. te Velde (2010) *Climate Financing and Development: Friends or Foes?*, paper commissioned by The ONE Campaign (London: Overseas Development Institute – ODI).

Carbonnier, G., F. Brugger and J. Krause (2011) 'Global and Local Policy Responses to the Resource Trap: Can Civil Society Live Up to the Expectations?', *Global Governance*, 17(2), pp. 247–64.

Carbonnier, G., F. Brugger and N. Wagner (2011) 'Oil, Gas and Minerals: The Impact of Resource-dependence and Governance on Sustainable Development', CCDP Working Paper no. 8 (Geneva: The Graduate Institute).

Coyne, C.J. and M.E. Ryan (2008) *Foreign Intervention and Global Public Bads*, unpublished paper, http://ssrn.com/abstract=1160434 (accessed on 11 October 2011).

de Ferranti, D.M. (2006) *Innovative Financing Options and the Fight Against Global Poverty: What's New and What's Next?* (Washington, DC: Brookings Institution).

de Ferranti, D.M., C.C. Griffin, M-L. Escobar, A. Glassman and G. Lagomarsino (2008) *Innovative Financing for Global Health: Tools for Analyzing the Options* (Washington, DC: Brookings Institution).

DFID (Department for International Development) (2005) *Using Drivers of Change to Improve Aid Effectiveness* (London; DFID).

Evans, A. (2010) *Aid Effectiveness post-2010 – A Think Piece on Ways Forward* (London: ODI).

Eyben, R. and S. Lister with Dickinson, B., J. Olivie and L. Tejada (2004) *Why and How to Aid 'Middle Income Countries'*, Working Paper no. 231 (Brighton: Institute of Development Studies – IDS).

Fischer, A. (2010) 'Towards genuine universalism within contemporary development policy', *IDS Bulletin*, 41(1), pp. 36–44.

Glennie, J. (2011) *The Role of Aid to Middle-Income Countries: A Contribution to Evolving EU Development Policy*, Working Paper no. 33 (London: ODI).

Guillaumont, P. and S. Guillaumont Jeanneney (2010) 'Big Push Versus Absorptive Capacity: How to Reconcile the Two Approaches', in Mavrotas, E. (ed.) *Foreign Aid for Development, Issues,*

Challenges and the New Agenda (Oxford: Oxford University Press).

Hearn, J. (1999) *Foreign Aid, Democratisation and Civil Society in Africa: A Study of South Africa, Ghana and Uganda*, Discussion Paper no. 368 (Brighton: IDS).

Howell, J. (2000) 'Making Civil Society from the Outside: Challenges for Donors', *European Journal of Development Research*, 12(1), pp. 3–22.

Howell, J. and J. Pearce (2000) 'Civil Society: Technical Instrument or Social Force for Change?', in Lewis, D. and T. Wallace (eds) *New Roles and Relevance: Development NGOs and the Challenge of Change* (Bloomfield: Kumarian), pp. 75–87.

Jones, S. (2010) 'Innovating Foreign Aid – Progress and Problems', *Journal of International Development*, DOI: 10.1002/jid.1758.

Kanbur, R. and A. Sumner (2011a) *Poor Countries or Poor People? Development Assistance and the New Geography of Global Poverty*, Charles H. Dyson School of Applied Economics and Management Working Paper (Ithaca: Cornell University).

Kanbur, R. and A. Sumner (2011b) *Poor Countries or Poor People? Development Assistance and the New Geography of Global Poverty*, Centre for Economic Policy Research (CEPR) Working Paper (London: CEPR).

Kaul, I., I. Grunberg and M.A. Stern (1999) 'Defining Global Public Goods', in *Global Public Goods: International Cooperation in the 21st Century* (New York: United Nations Development Programme – UNDP), pp. 2–19.

Ketkar, S. and D. Ratha (2009) *Innovative Financing for Development* (Washington, DC: World Bank).

Lob-Levyt, J. and R. Affolder (2006) 'Innovative Financing for Human Development', *The Lancet*, 367(9514), pp. 885–7.

McCoy, D. (2009) 'The High Level Taskforce on Innovative International Financing for Health Systems', *Health Policy and Planning*, 24(5), pp. 321–3.

Michaelowa, A. and K. Michaelowa (2011) 'Old Wine in New Bottles? Does Climate Policy Determine Bilateral Development Aid for Renewable Energy and Energy Efficiency?', in Graduate Institute of International and Development Studies, *International Development Policy: Energy and Development* (Basingstoke: Palgrave Macmillan), pp. 60–87.

Molenaers, N. and R. Renard (2002) *Strengthening Civil Society from the Outside? Donor-Driven Consultation and Participation Processes in Poverty Reduction Strategies (PRSP): The Bolivian Case*, Institute of Development Policy Management (IDPM) discussion paper no. 5 (Antwerp: IDPM).

OECD (Organisation for Economic Cooperation and Development) (2010a) *Latin American Economic Outlook 2011, How Middle-Class is Latin America?* (Paris: OECD).

OECD (2010b) *Resource Flows to Fragile and Conflict-Affected States* (Paris: OECD).

OECD/DAC (Development Assistance Committee) (2011) *Creditor Reporting System Database* (Paris: OECD).

Patel, N. (2011) 'India to Create Central Foreign Aid Agency', *The Guardian*, 26 July, http://www.guardian.co.uk/global-development/2011/jul/26/india-foreign-aid-agency (accessed on 11 October 2011).

Palma, J.G. (2011) 'Homogeneous Middles vs. Heterogeneous Tails, and the End of the "Inverted-U": It's All About the Share of the Rich', *Development and Change* 42(1), pp. 87–153, DOI: 10.1111/j.1467-7660.2011.01694.x.

Ravallion, M. (2010) 'Do Poorer Countries have Less Capacity for Redistribution?', *Journal of Globalization and Development*, 1(2), DOI: 10.2202/1948-1837.1105.

Robinson, M. and S. Friedman (2007) 'Civil Society, Democratization, and Foreign Aid: Civic Engagement and Public Policy in South Africa and Uganda', *Democratization*, 14(4), pp. 643–68.

Soares, S., R. Guerreiro Osorio, F. Veras Soares, M. Medeiros and E. Zepeda (2009) 'Conditional Cash Transfers in Brazil, Chile and Mexico: Impacts upon Inequality', *Estudioes Economicos*, no. Extra 1, pp. 207–24, http://dialnet.unirioja.es/servlet/articulo?codigo=3006356 (accessed on 1 December 2011).

Stansfield, S.K., M. Harper, G. Lamb and J. Lob-Levyt (2002) *Innovative Financing of International Public Goods for Health*, Consultation on Microeconomics and Health (CMH) Working Paper no. WG2(22) (Geneva: CMH, World Health Organization).

Sumner, A. (2010) *Global Poverty and the New Bottom Billion*, IDS Working Paper no. 349 (Brighton: IDS).

Sumner, A. (2011a) *The New Bottom Billion: What if Most of the World's Poor Live in Middle-Income Countries?*, Center for Global Development (CGD) Policy Brief (Washington, DC: CGD).

Sumner, A. (2011b) *Where Do the Poor Live? An Update* (IDS: Brighton).

Sumner, A. (2011c) *What is a Poor Country if the World's Poor Live in Middle-Income Countries?* (IDS: Brighton).

Task Force on Innovative International Financing for Health Systems (2009) *Raising and Channeling Funds*, Working Group 2 Report (Geneva/Washington, DC: International Health Partnership).

te Velde, D.W., O. Morrissey and A. Hewitt (2002) 'Allocating Aid to International Public Goods', in Ferroni, M. and A. Mody (eds) *International Public Goods: Incentives, Measurement, and Financing* (Washington, DC: World Bank), pp. 81–118.

UN-DESA (Department of Economic and Social Affairs of the United Nations) Population Division (2011) *World Population Prospects: The 2010 Revision* (Geneva/New York: UN-DESA).

World Bank (2011a) *PovcalNet, An Online Poverty Analysis Tool*, http://iresearch.worldbank.org/PovcalNet/povcalNet.html (accessed on 1 December 2011).

World Bank (2011b), *World Development Indicators*, http://data.worldbank.org/data-catalog/world-development-indicators (accessed on 1 December 2011).

2
IMPLEMENTING GLOBAL PUBLIC POLICIES: ARE THE AID AGENCIES WALKING THE TALK?

Michel Mordasini

Abstract

Beyond much rhetoric and stated ambition in recent years, the implementation of global public policies has been weak so far. There is a huge gap between the official discourse and the reality. This chapter focuses on the role, commitment and performance of aid agencies as 'small' but important suppliers of global public goods. While acknowledging some advances in the right direction (broad international recognition and improved costing of the global risks, consensus on the high vulnerability of the low-income countries and the need to act urgently, and substantial financing commitments) the author argues, based on available evidence from evaluations and effectiveness reviews, that only limited progress has been made in the aid delivery model and that the poor have not yet gained much from these undertakings. The chapter makes the case that significant institutional, organisational and operational reforms must take place urgently in aid agencies. The international community, moreover, must address the high fragmentation and proliferation of the aid architecture, in order to set the stage for a credible response to the global challenges facing developing countries.

1. Introduction

Over the past two decades, a fast expanding globalisation has translated into rapid world growth with increased economic, social and ecological interdependence across nations. But it has also caused or exacerbated significant cross-border and global externalities. Awareness of this new reality has shifted over time from narrow specialised circles to a much larger audience; the information technology (IT) revolution has expanded dramatically the access to information of the world citizen.

Today a broad recognition exists on the nature and scope of global public risks, and their impact on development. Climate change is one such challenge which transcends national boundaries and requires concerted worldwide collective action to reduce global greenhouse gases and to support climate-resilient and low-carbon investments in developing countries. There is also a growing international consensus on the urgency to act. Without a vigorous shift to a more resource-efficient and low carbon economy, the world will be confronted by 2050 with a massive further threat to already stressed ecosystems. This could jeopardise the development priorities of the international community. Lifting people out of poverty and achieving sustainable growth will therefore increasingly have to be intertwined with making steady progress in addressing global risks. Indeed, the poor do bear the brunt of more frequent natural disasters, increased water scarcity or hazards to health and agriculture; research and analytical work have now provided solid evidence confirming early empirical findings.

The threat of pandemics, the weakening of the international financial system, a resurging of protectionism, the harm to the environment or the severe risks related to climate change and conflicts require actions beyond the capability and resources of individual countries. What is needed are internationally agreed, sustainable solutions that take into account the interests of the developing countries. In this regard, consultations and negotiations are happening on the international scene to formulate global public policies in order to respond to the challenges. But how much of this effervescence is making a difference to the poor?

Based on available evidence and recent evaluation work by the World Bank, the Organisation for Economic Cooperation and Development (OECD) Development Assistance Committee (DAC) and some bilateral donors, this chapter aims at highlighting the results achieved in the implementation of the ambitious official discourse on global public policies, and at suggesting necessary changes for aid agencies to be more consistent and effective in translating their policy commitments into their work.

2. Significant advance towards action

The United Nations (UN) system and its specialised international agencies have a pre-eminent role and responsibility to steer the political process to reach international consensus on global public policies and norms. But as illustrated by the ongoing multilateral trade or climate change negotiations, such exercises are complex and often take many years before a comprehensive agreement is reached. In the meantime, a 'wait-and-see' approach would be disastrous, weakening dramatically the credibility and impact of the international efforts to reduce world poverty and to promote sustainable development.

In this context, it is noteworthy that most multilateral and bilateral aid agencies – consistent with their mandate and building on their close dialogue with developing countries – have engaged early in the discussion on the relevance and potential impact of global public policies for development and for the poor. Although they are and will remain only 'small' actors in addressing global challenges, aid agencies are playing a major role to inform the debate and to initiate pragmatic support to developing countries. This is reflected through substantive information, publication and advocacy undertaken by bilateral aid agencies within their own countries, interacting with Parliament, civil society and the public at large. Similarly, the World Development Reports on 'Development and Climate Change' (World Bank, 2010) and on 'Conflict, Security and Development' (World Bank, 2011) are contributing concretely to the international debate on global risks, by assessing the dramatic consequences for the developing countries, and by identifying and costing possible responses.

2.1. Aid agencies have taken steps to adjust their cooperation strategies

Even in the absence of comprehensive international agreements, aid agencies have been chartering a new cooperation course, focused on today's urgent development needs yet more mindful of the long-term global risks. This has translated into a notable shift in the formulation of their cooperation strategies in recent years, with a clearer commitment towards mainstreaming global issues into policies and programmes, while ensuring full alignment of their operations with the national development priorities of the partner countries.

The World Bank decided, in 2007, to integrate selected global public good concerns into all aspects of its work. The Bank's country teams were expected to integrate this new dimension into the Bank's country strategies and operations, in close dialogue with the partner countries. Moreover, the Bank was to expand its strategic participation into global programmes, to explore new financing modalities, to promote informed and constructive debate on global issues, and to increase its support to the delivery of regional public goods (World Bank, 2007). Most bilateral aid agencies have embarked on similar undertakings. The OECD has recently confirmed a significant move by many bilateral aid agencies towards addressing global issues in their strategy and policy formulation, as part of a renewed effort to meet the Millennium Development Goals (MDGs); multilateral partnerships seem also to benefit from a renewed interest, most prominently by the US in their new development agenda emphasising multi-lateralism (OECD/DCD, 2011).

2.2. Substantial financial resources have been pledged

Despite uneven progress in the negotiation on global public policies, a considerable amount of aid has been pledged to help developing countries meeting global risks. A dozen major partnerships to deliver global and regional goods have been established in the past decade, while multi-donors trust funds have skyrocketed to play a crucial role towards the same purpose; most recent data available indicate that in 2007–08 trust funds accounted for about 11 per cent of total official development assistance (ODA) (IEG, 2011b). Billions of dollars have been announced in support of global initiatives including the Global Fund to Fight AIDS, Tuberculosis and Malaria (GFATM), the Global Environment Facility (GEF), the Global Agriculture and Food Security Program (GAFSP) or the Climate Investment Funds (CIF). During the period 2002–10, the World Bank has contributed to leverage US$57.5 billion under such arrangements. In the context of the climate change, in 2010–12, donors have pledged US$30 billion for fast-starting operations in support of both adaptation and mitigation; they have also committed to mobilising US$100 billion per year from public and private sources by 2020.

Beyond traditional aid channels, new actors are playing an increasingly influential role. Emerging economies such as China, India or Brazil are becoming significant new donors with aid volumes representing already about 8–9 per cent of total ODA flows (ECOSOC, 2008). Private entrepreneurs and philanthropic foundations, as well as civil society organisations, are active partners for delivering regional and global public goods in developing countries. Moreover, new financing mechanisms have also been introduced to facilitate the funding of high priority global public goods, often bereft of a solid international normative framework. For example, the Advance Market Commitments (AMC) is an innovative way to address market failures and to incentivise companies to create and manufacture vaccines primarily needed in poor countries; donors commit money to guarantee the price of vaccines once they have been developed, thus creating the potential for a viable future market. Catastrophic risk insurance facilities and carbon finance provide new means to poor countries facing respectively short-term liquidity constraints in the aftermath of disasters or funding for medium-term investments in relation to mitigation and adaptation to climate change.

2.3. Some concrete results do emerge

The commitment of aid agencies to address global risks and to support preventive or remedial measures has delivered some visible results in recent years. As an illustration, the GFATM has made a significant contribution in providing life-saving antiretroviral therapy for people living with human immunodeficiency virus (HIV), tuberculosis treatment and insecticide-treated nets to prevent the transmission of malaria; the GFATM estimates that, every day, its funded programmes save at least 4400 lives and prevent thousands of new infections (GFATM, 2011). Similarly, in 2009, the strong and well-coordinated collective international response under the global programme for H1N1 and avian influenza control successfully contained a severe pandemic which was the first such worldwide occurrence in decades.

The surge in food prices in 2008–09 represented another major threat to the fight against poverty. Joint efforts by the international community averted a major crisis, providing rapidly considerable resources and policy support to affected poor countries. The Global Food Crisis Response Program (GFRP) mobilised more than US$2 billion, and the World Bank estimates that these resources helped nearly 40 million vulnerable people in 44 countries.

Recent reports by the Independent Evaluation Group of the World Bank have confirmed that partnership programmes and multi-donors trust funds have emerged in the last decade as the principal vehicle to deliver global and regional public goods. Relevant and effective, these instruments have permitted to involve new development actors (emerging donors, private sector and philanthropic foundations, civil society organisations) with a stronger focus on achieving the MDGs. This pooled grant financing for global public goods has also played a major role in filling a gap in the multilateral system to promote innovative efforts and investments also in middle-income countries; indeed the latter – which are home to many of the world's most important environmental assets and of most poor – are otherwise not eligible for such concessional funding from multilateral development banks. Overall, the partnership programmes and trust funds are effectively stimulating the delivery of global public goods, as reflected by the CIF (US$6.5 billion) which is expected by the World Bank to leverage US$45 billion of private and public investments in clean technology and renewable energy, forestry and climate resilience.

In specific areas, such as the adaptation to climate change, several aid agencies have embarked on pilot operations with their partner countries. But at the same time, traditional projects and programmes in relevant sectors such as food security, water or environmental protection have received renewed attention with increased funding.

3. But have the poor gained much from these undertakings?

Beyond the rhetoric, ambitious pledges and some pilot- or crisis-responses to address global risks and challenges, there is only scant, weak and anecdotal evidence so far on the actual impact of these efforts in the fight against poverty and for sustainable development. While acknowledging significant outputs under some global partnership programmes such as the fight against pandemics, it remains difficult so far to link directly these results to a dramatic progress towards the MDGs and to change the life, condition and prospects of the 'bottom billion'.

This relates partly to the deficient quality of the results framework and monitoring and evaluation systems which have been reported in the external evaluations of several global programmes (e.g. Macro International Inc., 2009; IEG, 2011a). But this situation also reflects on the very nature of most 'vertical' programmes. Unprecedented amount of funding and attention to needy and well-targeted causes have achieved impressive outputs; but the longer-term results are still difficult to measure. Many open questions remain regarding the limited sustainability of these programmes, their excessive project versus programme approach, the possible distortion of national priorities, the eventual disruption of national delivery systems, the insufficient focus on capacity-building or the negative spillover on non-targeted populations.

More than one decade after the release of the United Nations Development Programme (UNDP) Report on the Global Public Goods (Kaul et al., 1999), it remains extremely difficult to assess the actual implementation progress and outcome of global public policies; only few evaluations have been released so far by aid agencies. This being said, the available evidence tends to confirm *a rather modest overall benefit to the poor*. The vulnerability of developing countries to international food price crisis, land degradation or water scarcity has not been reduced in the recent years; health hazards, protectionism and natural disasters remain persistent threats to national and sustainable development strategies. Why is it so?

3.1. Implementation of policy intentions has lagged behind

Aid agencies have taken concrete and pragmatic steps to respond to needs of developing countries facing global risks; these well-targeted efforts have benefited millions of affected and vulnerable people worldwide. On the other hand, the stated intentions and commitments of the aid agencies towards global public goods were more ambitious. Beyond the support to specific projects and partnerships, they had the ambition to mainstream these global themes into their regular country strategies and operations. On this front, the aid agencies have clearly underperformed. In most agencies one observes a striking lack of specifics on how to translate the new corporate priorities into policy actions. Indeed, country directors and their teams rarely avail of the incentives and instruments to advance an agenda that is complex or may not immediately appeal to their counterparts. Nor do they receive the necessary internal budgets to be able to do so effectively. Little has also happened in the strengthening of the accountability systems, internal skills and knowledge sharing mechanisms that could create a stronger capability and momentum. In short, as reflected in most OECD/DAC Peers Reviews conducted in 2010 and early 2011, aid agencies appear to be still poorly equipped to bridge the gap between expectations related to global needs and the regular development cooperation.[1]

At the World Bank, recent reviews of development effectiveness have also highlighted this disappointing reality (IEG, 2008, 2009a). They indicate that the treatment of global public goods in Country Assistance Strategies has not significantly expanded over time; thematic networks have not provided the cross-country research, expertise and support needed to foster global public goods at individual country level; even the explicit mentioning of global public goods has been found to be diluted when passing from the thematic network anchors to the regional strategies. The global programmes have often failed to demonstrate how they bring added value to country programmes and the Bank's operations.

The country-based allocation and delivery model, which is an uncontested pillar of international development cooperation, presents also specific challenges for advancing the cause of global public policies. Indeed, this model – which rightly gives primacy to the partners' national decision making on policies and programmes – provides an adequate platform to promote global public goods with significant benefits to be captured at country level (i.e. fight against communicable diseases). But it fails to provide a robust basis to address other global public goods with less immediate returns at national level (i.e. cleaner air or protecting the earth's climate). This dimension has still to be reflected upon by the aid agencies.

3.2. Weak ownership and governance affect the outcome

External evaluations of global partnerships and trust funds often highlight the strong qualitative correlation between effectiveness of the programmes' governance and the achievement of their objectives. In a recent review of 17 such programmes, the Independent Evaluation Group found that 13 had moderate to significant shortcomings in relation to accountability, efficiency, transparency or fairness (IEG, 2011a). The insufficient involvement of the partner countries in the formulation and coordination of the responses to global risks has increasingly been recognised as affecting efficiency, performance and outcome; this was one important finding of the five-year evaluation of the GFATM (Macro International Inc., 2009). Evidence confirms that delivery mechanisms with shared governance have performed much more effectively. In this regard, aid agencies need to be more consistent in the application of the internationally

---

1 Development Assistance Committee peer reviews are available at: http://www.oecd.org/document/41/0,3746,en_2649_34603_46582825_1_1_1_1,00.html (accessed on 31 August 2011).

agreed principles of aid effectiveness, and ensure that mechanisms to deliver global public goods fully adhere to these principles.

But one has also to admit that many partner countries, and particularly middle-income countries, remain cautious – and even reluctant – when engaging on the issue of global public policies. While most developing countries agree that climate change is one of the biggest long-term risks to their sustainable development, many of them underline their 'no-choice' obligation to continue to privilege measures that deliver immediate benefits to the poor, such as accelerated access to jobs, electricity or basic social services. Trade-offs in the allocation of scarce public finance and foreign aid are indeed extremely difficult to decide upon; many governments insist on addressing short-term pro-poor needs versus investing for a more sustainable future growth. This situation translates into a further constraint to a rapid implementation of global public policies. In this regard, developing countries themselves have a shared responsibility for the mixed outcome of these efforts.

3.3. Actual funding for global public goods has stalled

Despite impressive pledges, the actual aid flows to developing countries to face global risks are more disappointing, on three fronts. First, the additionality of the resources is being questioned; although the total volume of ODA has reached a historical level in 2010, many donor countries have not matched their financial pledges to global public goods with a full respect of their commitment to increasing their ODA. This implies much room for the reallocation of resources, from the traditional poverty-reduction agenda to new priorities around global public goods. This trend is a source of potential misunderstanding between donors and aid recipients, the former aiming at fulfilling their international engagement to face global challenges while the latter being concerned with a perceived new constraint on aid, based on donors' self-interest.

Second, there has been no noticeable shift, during the past decade, in the share of total multilateral aid in ODA. The strong emergence of global public goods has not translated into an increased relative role of multilateral organisations, despite their established mandate and competence. While substantial flows of aid have been channelled through multi-donors partnerships or trust fund arrangements, the core contributions to multilateral institutions have fallen to a low of 28 per cent of total ODA in 2009, from a peak of 33 per cent in 2001 (OECD, 2011).

Third, several pledges are simply failing to materialise; the commitment made by the G-8 in 2009 at L'Aquila to mobilise US$20 billion for the GAFSP is a case in point, with less than one billion having been raised by July 2011 (GAFSP, 2011). The current slow and limited progress in the design of the Green Climate Fund casts already some doubts on the capacity of the international community to deliver in time on the commitments made in Copenhagen and Cancun.

3.4. Aid architecture has grown more complex

The emergence of new public and private donors in recent years is rather good news, particularly when it means more funding for poor countries. But this proliferation of development actors adds complexity to the aid architecture which is already confronted with a more worrying trend, resulting from the recent fast growing recourse by donors to partnerships and multi-donors trust funds arrangements. This evolution reflects the dissatisfaction of donors with traditional aid mechanisms, due to limitation in bilateral aid and perceived gaps in the operation of existing multilateral institutions. Overall, these new trends lead to more fragmentation of aid and an increased management complexity, with significant potential problems that require careful attention.

Involved in 120 partnerships and more than 1000 active main trust funds, dealing with 200 government or private donors, the World Bank is the quintessence of this new complexity. Positive is the confirmation that the Bank is recognised as an efficient and attractive partner for development. But the situation is also a source of concern. Internally, the Bank has demonstrated great difficulty to steer this proliferation of funding sources towards efficiency and effective use. Recent independent evaluations have highlighted the deficient integration of these instruments into the Bank's sector and country strategies, and have called for increased strategic direction and oversight by the Bank's management (IEG, 2011a,b).

This situation represents a huge additional challenge for the developing countries. When considering the global health sector, more than 100 major development partners and institutions are presently involved worldwide. Only some of them are formally committed towards the Paris Declaration principles (ownership, alignment, harmonisation, managing for results and mutual accountability). For poor countries, the situation entails significant costs and risks. Large contributions by vertical funds may derail national health strategies and priorities, by distorting or by-passing the budgetary process, and disrupting the national health delivery system due to fierce competition for scarce health workers. In addition, a plethora of funding sources imposes high transaction costs and heavy reporting requirements to already constrained national management capacities.

4. Addressing the unfinished agenda, moving forward

Over the past decade, there has been a clear and increasingly consensual identification and recognition of the nature and scope of the global public ills and risks, and their potentially dramatic impact on the developing countries. Even more impressive has been the progressive mastery across the world in formulating and shaping the strategies and some mechanisms to address the challenges, and in providing precise estimates of the means required. Much political and academic rhetoric has celebrated the gradual emergence of global public policies and the related strong commitments to action.

But implementation has lagged behind.

While most of the disappointment can be attributed to the slow progress in the international negotiations on global public policies, aid agencies have nevertheless a shared responsibility, having so far delivered rather poorly on some of their stated key intentions. Yes, some actions and concrete responses to global challenges have happened; huge resources have been mobilised to support well-targeted partnerships and multi-donors trust funds during the past decade. Millions of poor and vulnerable people have benefited from these operations. But these results still fall short of the necessary strategic and systemic transformations required for achieving a more sustainable development which can ensure a broader access to global public goods and improved living conditions to mankind. Building on the success achieved so far, and despite frustrating stalemate or slow progress in international negotiations, aid agencies have to significantly revamp their efforts to deliver global public policies. There are two main areas for further action: mainstreaming global public policies into operations and revisiting the international aid architecture.

4.1. Mainstreaming is urgently required

Global public policies relate to the whole process towards sustainable development, and they should therefore not be addressed in separate, fragmented actions. When embarking on the track of adaptation to climate change, the developing countries have to reflect in a very holistic manner on the multiple dimensions of managing the challenge, from reforming agriculture and forest management to addressing water scarcity, food security, energy or transport. Similarly, to be relevant and effective on the global public goods, the aid agencies need to position their support in such a broad perspective. For this purpose, the traditional country-based cooperation model remains an appropriate platform for defining a work programme for sustainable development with the partner countries, as long as there is a reasonable convergence on the national and global interests and the time horizon for taking action. Otherwise, priority could be focused on supporting advocacy and research on these global public goods with no immediate capture at national level, as a contribution to better inform national debate in developing countries.

Dedicated staff with solid thematic, technical and management competences to advance global public themes has to be mobilised. But experience has shown that aid agencies must also address other factors necessary to trigger a successful mainstreaming, such as adequate staff incentives, skills development, results-based approaches and strong accountability systems. Moreover, special attention should be given to ensure a closer than usual linkage between the operational and thematic units, in order for the aid agency to capitalise its full potential of knowledge, experience and competence in shaping its support to the complex needs of developing countries facing global risks. This is an ambitious agenda, beyond 'business as usual'. It is comforting to note that already some concrete steps are being undertaken by some aid agencies.

Indeed, the World Bank has recently embarked on significant internal reforms, including the review of its organisational matrix, the delivery instruments and its human resources policies. These reforms will address some of the key requirements for a better mainstreaming of global public policies into the country strategies and operations. In this regard, some recent Country Partnership Strategies (CPS) of the World Bank clearly show an improving practice in mainstreaming global public concerns. This is, for example, the case in the new CPS Costa Rica (2012–15) which is geared to support the long-term country goal of reaching carbon neutrality by 2021. Similarly, the CPS Bangladesh (2011–14) and the latest progress report on the implementation of the CPS Indonesia clearly address the necessary further efforts to adjust and expand the Bank's support towards environmental sustainability and disaster risk mitigation. These developments are positive signs of more consistent progress across the institution in better integrating global challenges into the Bank's traditional support to 'sustainable growth'.

Some bilateral agencies have also taken steps to better articulate their operational response to the global risks being faced by developing countries. In this regard, the recent reorganisation of the Swiss Agency for Development and Cooperation (SDC) presents an interesting option for the way forward. This reorganisation is indeed delivering a strong message as regards Switzerland's commitment to global public policies. While thematic networks have now been merged within the operational units, four global programmes (climate change, water, food security, migration) have been launched; country strategies are starting to better integrate all those dimensions. With specific budgetary allocations (representing 17 per cent of total SDC bilateral aid in 2010), dedicated staff, and a responsibility to ensure a broad sector monitoring, the global programmes aim at providing a policy added value to the regular projects portfolio. This is being achieved through fast-tracking innovative operations, programmes and partnerships with a view to enhance Swiss contribution and delivery to support developing countries facing major global challenges. Two examples: (i) the SDC is actively involved in a project which aims at addressing the critical challenge of water security in the Middle East through the development of collaborative solutions for sustainable regional water management; (ii) in China, the SDC supports a coordinated Swiss response to the invitation by the Ministry of Environment Protection to join in the drafting of national and provincial laws on climate change as well as in the revision of the clean air legal framework.[2] This SDC internal transformation builds on a robust signal given by the Swiss Parliament in February 2011, when it approved a dramatic increase of Swiss ODA (to reach 0.5 per cent of gross national income by 2015) and attributed most additional resources for interventions related to water and climate change, as well as to multilateral aid. An ambitious management for results is being put in place to ensure detailed reporting and full accountability *vis-à-vis* the Parliament.

The formulation and implementation of policies and operations to tackle climate change, to fight communicable disease, to improve food security or to address water scarcity – as part of a national strategy for sustainable development and poverty reduction – require massive efforts by the developing countries. To support this undertaking, aid agencies have to adjust their business and delivery model. Mainstreaming global public policies into cooperation strategies and building effective global-country linkages do not happen automatically. It is a complex process that implies substantial changes in the traditional business-delivery model for aid. In this regard, it is noteworthy that the OECD succeeded to formulate in 2009, in a joint effort of its development and environment committees under the lead of the Netherlands and Switzerland, substantive policy guidance on integrating climate change adaptation into development cooperation (OECD et al., 2009).

Nevertheless, as already indicated, institutional, organisational and operational reforms remain crucial to reach the goal. The key changes for

---

2   See http://www.deza.admin.ch/en/Home/Activities (accessed on 8 November 2011).

moving from the 'business as usual' model cannot be underestimated; they imply considerable commitment and political will. They should focus in particular on: (i) effectively integrating global challenges into country cooperation strategies; (ii) formulating, in close dialogue with partners, a comprehensive aid programme which encompasses an optimal mix of instruments (ending 'silo' approaches) and innovation; (iii) decentralising responsibilities and capabilities to country offices; (iv) deepening thematic skills and competence for selected sectors; (v) providing adequate staff incentives; (vi) strengthening performance management and accountability. Moving forward, the credibility of aid agencies on the global public goods agenda will be concretely tested in their capacity to deliver such internal reforms.

4.2. Also needed: a new aid architecture

Recent trends in international aid delivery are causes of concern and require careful attention. The aid architecture has indeed moved towards a model of 'hyper-collective' action, with a proliferation of development partners and an increased aid fragmentation (Severino and Ray, 2010). Practice also varies widely in implementing principles of sound aid delivery. The coordination and effectiveness of collective efforts have become more challenging, affecting the potential benefit to the poor. How to manage this increased complexity, in order to ensure proper coordination, transparency and accountability for results? Much is at stake for the developing countries, with high potential risks and costs.

The better provision of global public goods requires a more open and comprehensive collaboration between aid agencies and development partners at large. The international community must therefore continue improving its aid delivery. In this context, the role of existing multilateral institutions could be revisited, to better capitalise their competence and experience. But they have first to adapt to the new paradigm. For example, multilateral development banks are primarily implementation agencies; their role could usefully evolve towards a stronger focus on establishing and piloting global collaborative platforms, incentivising good management and partnership practices, while mobilising resources for global responses. If no such alternative emerges, then the pressure for creating new organisations or mechanisms – in an already overpopulated international architecture – will persist, delivering only suboptimal systems for funding global public policies. The ongoing discussion on the design of the Green Climate Fund is a case in point; the outcome of the negotiation will tell on the readiness and capacity of the international community to address the challenge.

The matter is not so much to find a mundane consensus on how to shape this or that new funding mechanism. What is really at stake is the capacity of the international community to define and support a relevant and effective response to address and mitigate the very serious global public bads that affect already today, and may devastate in the future, the poor in the low-income countries. Implementing global public policies should become truly an urgent priority for the world. To expand the supply of global public goods for a more prosperous, fairer, safer and more sustainable world, drastic actions are now needed! Fragmentation and deficient coordination and alignment of efforts will definitely not foot the bill.

REFERENCES AND FURTHER READING

Bird, N., J. Brown and L. Shatalek (2011) *Design Challenges for the Green Climate Fund* (London: Overseas Development Institute/Heinrich Boell Stiftung, Policy Brief 4).

Cabral, L. and J. Weinstock (2010) *Brazilian Technical Cooperation for Development: Drivers, Mechanics and Future Prospects* (London: Overseas Development Institute) http://www.odi.org.uk/about/staff/details.asp?id=32&name=lidia-cabral (accessed on 30 August 2011).

Conseil fédéral suisse (2010) 'Message du 17 septembre 2010 concernant l'augmentation des moyens pour le financement de l'aide publique au développement', 10.085, *Feuille fédérale* (2010: 6145). http://www.parlament.ch/f/suche/pages/geschaefte.aspx?gesch_id=20100085 (accessed on 30 August 2011).

DFID (Department for International Development) and UKaid (2011) *Multilateral Aid Review, Ensuring Maximum Value for Money for UK Aid through Multilateral Organizations* (London: DFID/UKaid).

ECOSOC (United Nations Economic and Social Council) (2008) *Trends in South-South and Triangular Development Cooperation. Background Study for the Development Cooperation Forum* (New York: United Nations), http://www.un.org/en/ecosoc/docs/pdfs/south-south_cooperation.pdf (accessed 30 on August 2011).

GAFSP (Global Agriculture and Food Security Program) (2011) *Funding*, http://www.gafspfund.org/gafsp/content/funding (accessed on 30 August 2011).

GFATM (Global Fund to Fight AIDS, Tubercolosis and Malaria) (2011) *Fighting Aids, Tubercolosis and Malaria*, http://www.theglobalfund.org/en/about/diseases/ (accessed on 30 August 2011).

IEG (Independent Evaluation Group) (2008) *Annual Review of Development Effectiveness 2008: Shared Global Challenges* (Washington, DC: The World Bank).

IEG (2009a) *Annual Review of Development Effectiveness 2009: Achieving Sustainable Development* (Washington, DC: The World Bank).

IEG (2009b) *Improving Effectiveness and Outcomes for the Poor in Health, Nutrition and Population. An Evaluation of WBG Support since 1997* (Washington, DC: The World Bank).

IEG (2010) *Climate Change and the WBG, Phase II: The Challenge of Low-Carbon Development* (Washington, DC: The World Bank).

IEG (2011a) *The World Bank's Involvement in Global and Regional Partnership Programs: An Independent Assessment* (Washington, DC: The World Bank).

IEG (2011b) *Trust Fund Support for Development: An Evaluation of the World Bank's Trust Fund Portfolio* (Washington, DC: The World Bank).

Isenman, P., C. Wathne and G. Baudienville (2010) *Global Funds: Allocation Strategies and Aid Effectiveness* (London: Overseas Development Institute).

Kaul, I., I. Grunberg and M.A. Stern (1999) *Global Public Goods. International Cooperation in the 21st Century* (New York: Oxford University Press).

Macro International Inc. (2009) *The Five-Year Evaluation of the Global Fund to Fight AIDS, Tuberculosis and Malaria, Synthesis of Study Areas 1, 2 and 3* (Geneva: Macro International Inc./GFATM).

Oates, N., D. Conway and R. Calow (2011) *The Mainstreaming Approach to Climate Change Adaptation: Insights from Ethiopia's Water Sector* (London: Overseas Development Institute, Background Note).

OECD (Organisation for Economic Cooperation and Development) (2009) *Managing Aid. Practices of DAC Member Countries*, Better Aid (Paris: OECD).

OECD (2011) *2011 DAC Report on Multilateral Aid*, DCD/DAC(2011)21/FINAL (Paris: OECD).

OECD, DAC (Development Assistance Committee) and EPOC (Environment Policy Committee) (2009) *Policy Guidance on Integrating Climate Change Adaptation into Development Cooperation* (Paris: OECD).

OECD/DCD (Development Cooperation Directorate) (2011) *Policy Changes in the DAC Members' Development Cooperation, 2010* (Paris: OECD).

SDC (Swiss Agency for Development and Cooperation) and SECO (State Secretariat for Economic Affairs) (2010) *Report on Effectiveness, Swiss Development Cooperation in the Agricultural Sector* (Bern: SDC/SECO).

Severino, J.M. and O. Ray (2010) *The End of ODA (II): The Birth of Hypercollective Action*, Working Paper 218 (Washington, DC: Center for Global Development).

World Bank (2007) *Global Public Goods: A Framework for the Role of the World Bank*, DC2007-0020 (Washington, DC: The World Bank).

World Bank (2010) *World Development Report 2010: Development and Climate Change* (Washington, DC: The World Bank).

World Bank (2011) *World Development Report 2011: Conflict, Security, and Development* (Washington, DC: The World Bank).

Websites

The Climate Investment Fund: http://www.climateinvestmentfunds.org

The Global Agriculture and Food Security Program: http://www.gafspfund.org

The Global Environmental Facility: http://www.thegef.org/gef

The Global Fund to Fight AIDS, Tubercolosis and Malaria: http://www.theglobalfund.org

3

THE UNITED NATIONS AND GLOBAL PUBLIC GOODS: HISTORICAL CONTRIBUTIONS AND FUTURE CHALLENGES

Bruce Jenks

Abstract

This chapter explores the thesis that the United Nations' (UN) most important contribution to the production of global public goods has been its role in creating the space and capacity to generate shared values. Starting with the UN Charter itself, the chapter traces the evolution of this contribution through different historical phases. It analyses the impact of globalisation on the role of the UN; in particular it identifies the quality of porousness as a product of globalisation which is critical to understanding the current challenges faced by the UN as well as central to the global public goods agenda. Through this lens the author briefly reviews the evolution of the UN's role in the fields of peace and security, human rights and development cooperation. He concludes by identifying eight levers for change that will determine the UN's ability to contribute significantly to the global public goods: the generation of norms and shared values, the quality of leadership, improved governance, innovative financing, institutional realignment, the further consolidation of legal instruments, focus, and the power of networks.

1. Introduction

The concept of 'Global Public Goods' is often used by economists to analyse issues related to their under-supply and to devise mechanisms and incentives that would correct this problem. Global public goods can also be understood more broadly as encompassing issues which the international community recognises both as important and as requiring international action. Our core argument revolves around the proposition that the United Nations (UN) Charter itself was conceived as a global public good and that the UN's contribution to the production of global public goods has evolved historically. We argue that in today's globalised world, the core value of the UN is its capacity to embed intergovernmental relations in a broad set of norms and values. This is all the more the case because today's world is characterised by two significant and newly emerging features. The first is that global public goods increasingly will need to be produced by creating shared values and will depend less on enlightened leadership. Second, in today's world, solutions increasingly will be found beyond the exclusive grasp of intergovernmental negotiation and rather as a result of broadly based, inclusive, multi-stakeholder dialogue.

2. The Charter of the UN as a global public good

The value proposition embodied in the Charter for the UN was markedly different than the principles underlying the League of Nations. The League of Nations was established to ensure that the mistakes that led to the First World War would not be repeated. The First World War was seen to have been the result of misinformation and miscommunication – a war that could have been avoided. The League was created to provide a forum where states could discuss and settle matters on the basis of shared information. The League was a club of states served by a passive secretariat. The secretariat was not seen as an independent force and the Secretary-General of the League, Eric Drummond, never addressed the Assembly of the League.

The experience of the Second World War demanded a more ambitious vision. The Charter envisages the United Nations as something more than a mechanism to prevent misunderstandings between states. Specifically, Articles 97–101 of the Charter provide political space in which the Secretary-General (SG) can take significant initiatives. It is above all Article 99 which breaks radical new ground in authorising the SG to bring to the attention of the Security Council any matter which in his opinion may threaten the maintenance of international peace and security. Article 100 also merits careful consideration. Article 100 states that in the performance of their duties the SG and the staff should not receive any instructions from any government or from any other authority external to the organisation. They should refrain from any action that might reflect on their position as international officials responsible only to the organisation. For this Article to have meaning, it presupposes the existence of a concept of internationalism – of the international interest and of the interests of an organisation that is distinct from its member states.

Dag Hammarskjöld expresses the view in his 1961 Oxford Speech that no one in 1945 realised the extent to which the SG would be required to take positions on highly controversial matters. Faced with the competing centres of authority that Hammarskjöld faced in the Congo, he saw three options. The SG could refer the matter back to be determined by the Security Council. Or the SG could refuse to take action because this forced him to abandon neutrality. Or the SG could exercise his judgment to resolve the issues on a truly international basis without obtaining the formal decision of the political organs. The first course of action was doomed to failure because there was no agreement, the second course of action simply accepted failure. Only the third course of action was responsible. The consequences of this conclusion for the functions of the SG are transformational in character.

The expectations placed on the Charter in Hammarskjöld's understanding go well beyond that envisaged by the so-called rationalist school (Martin, 1999, 55). Institutions, according to this model, do not modify underlying state interests but by changing the informational environment, they change state strategies in such a way that self-interested states find it easier to cooperate with each other. In this perspective, institutions change patterns of state behaviour not by changing fundamental state goals but by changing strategies and beliefs by influencing the informational environment. The provisions of the Charter and the powers entrusted to the SG go well beyond the minimalist concept of value creation envisaged in the rationalist model. The expectations placed on the role of the SG in the Charter make the Charter a radical and unique instrument in the advancement of international cooperation. The functions of the SG as provided for in the Charter are an invitation to leadership.

The UN as an experiment in international cooperation needs to be understood historically as a living instrument. In different periods, the substance of this experiment in international cooperation has been understood very differently. We can clearly identify three phases.

3. The building blocks to peace

The concept of functionalism inspired the design of the UN system that was created at the end of the war. David Mitrany (Mitrany, 1943) argued that the world would be able to unite against commonly perceived problems and that existing conditions had created 'self-determining' needs of a technical nature that transcended political and constitutional issues. He argued that if international organisations concentrated on providing those needs they might succeed in instilling habits of cooperative behaviour between peoples from different countries that could in the long run subvert national allegiances and put an end to classical national rivalries. Furthermore the needs would determine the form that international cooperation would take – hence Mitrany's dictum that 'form would follow function'. The experience of the war had created a 'unity beyond politics'. Functionalism is a reflection of its age: it is based on the assumption that a common will existed in the wake of the Nazi experience to go beyond traditional political rivalries.

The UN system was designed around the concept of communities of practice that would create the building blocks to peace through their pursuit of common goals and interests. The International Labour Organization (ILO) had already been established in 1919 as a forum for issues related to labour and social justice. The Food and Agriculture Organization (FAO), the United Nations Educational, Scientific and Cultural Organization (UNESCO), the World Health Organization (WHO) and a succession of other agencies were all created to allow communities of practice to build networks. These networks would create the building blocks for an authorising environment that would be informed by common interests in functional cooperation. Their strength was that they reflected a broad range of social forces and not just the government ministry involved.

The vision of a multi-stakeholder system defining and promoting common interests around communities of practice found expression in the early years in the political economy of the system. When the Expanded Programme for Technical Assistance (EPTA), the predecessor of the United Nations Development Programme (UNDP), was launched in 1949, it was envisaged as a programme that would provide support through the established communities of practice. Hence, the financing available to the EPTA was distributed on the basis of percentage shares to the different specialised agencies so that they could manage programmes in countries. A system whose formal governance arrangements were reserved for governments produced a financial architecture not based on countries at all but on the role of communities of practice in contributing to social and economic progress.

In three respects, the experience of the war was transformative in creating new space for constructing global common interests. First, the experience of the war convinced leaders that more than just a mechanism for dialogue between states was required because it was clear that war was not just the product of misunderstandings or misinformation. As reflected in the Charter, this led to the articulation of the possibility of an international interest being vested in the SG and in the concept of the international civil service. Second, the idea of communities of interest that would reach across boundaries and define common interests became embedded as a fundamental – a core – characteristic of the UN system. Third, the formal system might be governed by states but its driving force was much broader.

Building a sustainable peace required expanding the space for international leadership, drawing on social forces to put in place and strengthen the building blocks to peace and providing an inclusive form of governance that reached out to multiple stakeholders. The lynchpin of this vision remained the sovereignty of states, but it was a sovereignty embedded in broader values and principles. Anti-Nazism provided a common framework for the pursuit of these common values. This was the architecture that was constructed by the founders of the UN. It was not an idealistic project. Rather, it was highly pragmatic, responding to the urgent need for action resulting from the destruction of the war.

4. The pursuit of mutual restraint

The convergence of the reality of the Cold War, the emerging needs of developing countries and the process of decolonisation led to a transformation in the authorising environment in which the UN worked. Only a radical realignment in the UN's values and mission with this new authorising environment would secure their continued relevance. The space for international leadership drawing on broad social forces and reaching out to multiple stakeholders was challenged directly by the logic of both the Cold War and decolonisation. The Cold War, by dividing the world into two camps, severely curtailed the room for international leadership, notwithstanding the independent approaches pursued, for example, by the Non-Aligned, the Nordics and Switzerland. Finding middle ground and common interests would be met with deep suspicion and outright hostility. Decolonisation meant that at that moment in history, service to the member states was pitted against an internationalism only too easily identifiable as residual colonialism. And so the international development agenda became focused on the fundamental process of national development. Throughout the UN system there is a fundamental and radical shift from a vision of international leadership to one of service to member states.

The first victim of this realignment was the concept of the role and functions of the SG. The Soviet Union questioned the very validity of the concept of an impartial, independent international force. This was a world in which all belonged to one of the two camps. There was no space in between. Khrushchev accordingly proposed that the leadership of the UN be replaced by a triumvirate representing the interests of the Western, Socialist and Non-Aligned blocs. The secretariat would revert to being of an intergovernmental character.

Even within these constraints, Hammarskjöld with remarkable imagination found ways to carve out some political space in which to make a difference. The development of the concept of the SG's 'Good Offices' and Hammarskjöld's Peking formula provide good examples (Franck and Nolte, 1993). It was in a similar vein that Hammarskjöld and Pearson invented the concept of peace-keeping – a concept that is not to be found in the Charter (Weiss and Thakur, 2010). It is instructive that it was at a time of minimum cooperation between the great powers that the political space was engineered to develop the concept of peace-keeping. It was made possible by creating a force that was the polar opposite of what had been envisaged in the Charter. The concept embedded in the Security Council was the collaboration of the Great Powers to enforce peace and security. The condition for the creation of United Nations Emergency Force (UNEF) was that the Great Powers would be excluded from its composition. UNEF was established with the tolerance of the Great Powers, not their participation (Kennedy, 2006).

Notwithstanding these examples of international leadership, the period from the late 1940s onwards saw the principle of state sovereignty strongly affirmed and throughout the UN system the concept of service to member states became dominant. This is reflected in realignments in governance arrangements, in the evolution of the architecture of the UN's development system and in shifts in thinking on the substance of development.

In the absence of common values, international cooperation became defined by the exercise of restraint imposed by the primacy accorded to the principles of sovereignty and non-interference. This was a period when the promotion of mutual restraint was identified as being in the best interests of the international community. As Scott Barrett (2007) has pointed out, mutual restraint can be a valuable global public good.

5. The UN and global public goods in an age of porousness

The decades following the mid-1980s saw the convergence of a number of key elements: the acceleration of globalisation, the maturation of the process of decolonisation, the end of the Cold War, the emergence of major new economies and a significant redistribution of power between states on the one hand and markets and individuals on the other (private sector, civil society, social media, etc.). Together these have transformed expectations with regard to the role of the UN in fostering shared values and contributing to international cooperation.

Of particular interest is the idea that globalisation has given rise to a new quality of porousness in the exercise of state sovereignty. Philip Bobbitt (2008) has analysed what he describes as the emergence of a new constitutional order, the replacement by the market state of the nation state. The nation state was characterised by complete freedom internally on the one hand and the legal equality of states externally on the other. These two conditions defined the meaning of sovereignty. The UN was established in a world of nation states and in Bobbitt's words, the UN Charter forms the basic constitutional framework for the society of nation states as a whole. By contrast with this, in market states, the state must compete with global and domestic actors, the private sector and civil society. The external reality is no longer characterised by legal equality but by *ad hoc* alliances responding to threats and opportunities. In the world of nation states, the distinctions between domestic and external and between public and private are clear. In the market state they became blurred.

A slightly different insight into the same issue is provided by Anthony Giddens (2000) who argues that today states face risks and dangers rather than enemies as such. He distinguishes between what he calls 'manufactured risk' and 'external risk'. External risk comes from the outside. Manufactured risk is created by the impact of our developing knowledge upon the world. The concept of manufactured risk gives rise to, and is a reflection of, a condition of porousness. The growth of social media provides another important dimension to the reality of porousness. It blurs the perimeter of organisations and the lines between the official and the unofficial (Shirky, 2008).

Anne-Marie Slaughter (2004) captures the idea of porousness through her analysis of what she describes as the disaggregated state. Whereas in the nation state interests are pursued through the central machinery of the state, in a market state those interests are pursued through the disaggregated state. States still exist and are the central players but they are disaggregated. Government officials have two complementary functions, one external and one internal, rather than there being two sets of officials, one dealing with an internal portfolio and one dealing with all external portfolios. The core characteristic of sovereignty would shift from autonomy from outside interference to capacity to participate in trans-governmental networks. Slaughter argues that a disaggregated world order requires the reinventing of international organisations. The UN would not be seen as a monolith but as a complex set of networked agencies.

The language of global public goods is the language of the age of porousness. The age of the nation state was the age when external affairs were the prerogative of one ministry which financed external commitments. The interactions between a state and its external partners were managed through one central point. Global public goods should be financed from sector budget lines which would not be distinguishable from the vantage point of whether they are internal or external in character. The financing of global public goods is an expression of the quality of porousness in decision-making in the age of market states. When the defence budget finances international peace-keeping, the health budget finances international surveillance, and the environment budget finances mitigation measures, then sovereignty is being exercised through collaboration, not self-sufficiency. Global public goods represent the internalisation of international cooperation within the logic of national decision-making.

National interests and the capacity of states remain at the core of any viable or foreseeable international system today. But state power needs to work in different ways. The porousness of sovereignty requires it to be expressed differently. State capacity can no longer be self-supporting; effective capacity requires being connected. This requires reaching out to the broader stakeholder communities that represent the social forces that have generated porousness. The challenge for international leadership, as the World Economic Forum's (WEF) Global Redesign Initiative pointed out, is to embed intergovernmental relations in the broader set of values and norms coming from these social forces.

Historically, only great disasters have provided space for states to coalesce around a broader set of values. Only in the face of extreme external threats do states choose to embed their cooperation in a more robust formal framework of rules and institutions. Porousness represents a challenge of the same magnitude but it is fundamentally different in character. The challenge arises not from an external threat but from the impact of globalisation on the relationship of states to the societies they govern. What we have variously described as the movement from nation to market states, from external to manufactured risk, from unitary to disaggregated states, from vertically led to horizontally implemented intergovernmental relations, this requires a response every bit as urgent as that which has been engendered historically by great external threats.

The beginning of the UN's response to this challenge can be seen through the UN's efforts to chart a new course in many areas of its work. We turn to three areas where globalisation has had a deep impact on the mission of the UN: security, development cooperation and human rights. We could just as easily make the same case by turning to the emergence of the concept of global health in the 1990s or the emerging consensus and all its implications on the idea of human responsibility for climate change. In each instance the case for international leadership has dramatically reasserted itself as a necessary part of finding solutions because of the character of the challenges faced.

6. Security

The major realignment in the authorising environment that developed in the 1980s and 1990s led to an unprecedented expansion in the UN's role in security (Commission on Global Governance, 1995; Carnegie Commission on Preventing Deadly Conflict, 1997; Commission on Human Security, 2003). The end of the Cold War saw a rapid increase in intra-state conflict characterised by the collapse of effectively functioning states. The civil wars of the 1980s and 1990s have been succeeded by the more generalised violence characteristic of fragile states today (World Bank, 2011). The acceleration of globalisation drew attention to these state failures not as marginal cases but as potentially the weakest links in an increasingly integrated world. The twin triggers of the end of the Cold War and globalisation opened up space for robust international leadership. The facts bear out this analysis. For example, between 1988 and 1992, disputes involving UN peace-building or prevention action increased from 11 to 28 and peace-keeping deployments tripled from 5 to 17.

The demand for international leadership to cope with intra-state conflict and failed states seriously blurred the distinction between the concepts of internal and external security (MacFarlane and Khong, 2006). It led to a significant expansion in the concept and understanding of security. It entailed guerrilla wars with no clear front lines. It led to conflicts where civilians were the main victims. It resulted in humanitarian crises that demanded world attention. On the ground it demanded coherence between political, military, humanitarian and development interventions.

These realities led to an evolution in the mission and character of peace-keeping operations. Three generations of peace-keeping operations have been identified (Doyle and Sambanis, 2007). The first called for the interposition of force after a truce has been reached. It was the creation of Hammarskjöld's thin blue line, extracting space where none seemed to exist. It was fit for purpose in a world where superpower rivalry clearly restricted the role the UN could play. Neutrality, non-use of force, consent and monitoring: these were the concepts that informed operations. The second generation of peace-keeping continued to rely on the consent of the parties, but engaged in activities that were once thought to be solely the prerogative of states. It was this second generation that flourished in the 1980s and 1990s, for example in Mozambique, El Salvador and Cambodia, with the increase in intra-state conflicts and the consequent fudging of the line between domestic and international concerns. A third generation of peacekeepers started operating with Chapter VII of the Charter mandates without comprehensive agreement having been reached. These types of operations, for example in Somalia and Iraq, intruded into aspects of domestic sovereignty that not that long ago would have been way beyond the limits deemed acceptable by the authorising environment.

The evolution in the principles and practice of peace-keeping represented in these three generations constitute an enormous expansion in the political space and the expectation for international leadership. The logic of second and third generation peace-keeping led to peace-building as a major component of the UN's mission. Peace-building is a logical expression of the blurring of the external and the internal, the military with the civilian (UN Peacebuilding Commission, 2010).

Prevention represents yet another dimension to the expansion of the UN's mission relating to security (Ramcharan, 2007). The rise of intra-state conflicts as the dominant form of conflict, the expansion of the concept of security, the resulting fudging of lines between state sovereignty and international intervention – this could only in time have the consequence of making international leadership in prevention inevitable. The articulation of prevention as a mission of the UN can be traced back to Hammarskjöld's efforts to prevent third world conflicts from inflaming Cold War tensions and to the vision presented by Boutros Boutros-Ghali (1992) to the Security Council in 1992. In a succession of reports Kofi Annan developed further these concepts (United Nations Secretary-General, 2001, 2006), focusing on the need to develop a culture of prevention.

The blurring of state sovereignty issues in the case of failed states, the development of new roles and objectives for peace-keeping operations on the ground, the development of peace-building, and the increased focus on the need for preventive diplomacy represent a significant shift in the mission of the UN. The porousness endemic in the exercise of sovereignty in failed states gives birth to new norms.

7. Development cooperation

A second area where globalisation and the end of the Cold War have had a deep impact on the mission of the UN is in the area of development cooperation. In the Cold War aid was seen as an instrument of foreign policy and as a reward for members of the respective alliance. This was reinforced by a sense in the immediate post-colonial era that the emerging countries were entitled to a transfer of resources. This was not a performance-based system. But the system was highly effective in delivering what it was measured against – that is volume of resources transferred. In the decades from 1950 to 1990, aid volume approximately doubled every decade. As an integral component of foreign policy, the allocation of these resources in national budgets had a strong constituency in donor governments. Aid was an instrument of foreign policy and therefore integral to the national interest.

The end of the Cold War and the acceleration of globalisation changed the entire rationale for the allocation of aid. In the early 1990s the international development community anticipated enormous growth in aid budgets as a result of the 'peace dividend' that would accompany the end of the Cold War. In reality, the end of the primary foreign policy rationale for foreign aid led to its rapid decline – by 2000, global aid in nominal terms was almost exactly the same as it had been around 1990. This meant a substantial decrease in real terms and compared in nominal terms with the doubling that had occurred during the decades of the Cold War.

Against this background, the mission and rationale for development cooperation had to be radically redefined. It was the series of global conferences held during the 1990s, culminating in the 2000 Millennium Summit, that crystallised the emergence of a new common development agenda. The shift to defining clear goals and setting measurable targets was the inevitable consequence of the need to provide a new rationale for development cooperation. In the absence of a clear foreign policy goal, performance and measuring impact became critical to remaking the case for aid. For the first time, targets were constructed as legitimate global development goals around issues that voters in donor countries could relate to and support. This shift, which was conscious and deliberate, was first clearly reflected in the approval by the OECD/DAC of its document 'Shaping the 21st Century' (DAC, 1996) which for the first time spelt out seven selected goals for further progress in the next 15–20 years. In turn this found its way to the adoption by the millennial summit of the Millennium Development Goals (MDGs).

The MDGs constitute a radically new framework for defining the mission of the international development community. In particular they make the progress made at the national level measurable against a set of benchmarks that represent a global consensus about desirable outcomes. The acceptance of the use of verifiable, empirical data to measure national progress and performance is a significant step in giving space for a concept of international responsibility and accountability to grow.

8. Human rights

The speed of the adoption of the concept of human rights at the UN was remarkable. The Charter included significant provisions relating to human rights, complemented by the adoption of the Universal Declaration on Human Rights in 1948.

The changes in the authorising environment in the late 1980s and early 1990s had major implications for the human rights agenda. On the one hand, the increasing blurring of the distinction between internal and external security and the rise in intra-state conflict opened up new space for human rights interventions. On the other, the new focus of development cooperation on objectives and human development also brought human rights considerations to the fore. The Global Conference on Human Rights held in Vienna in 1993 served to convene a broad coalition of social forces providing momentum behind this agenda, among other things creating the post of United Nations High Commissioner for Human Rights.

This has only developed further since the mid-1990s. Experience in northern Iraq, Somalia, and then Bosnia and Rwanda drew attention to the issue of human rights. A multitude of high profile commissions and panels put a global spotlight on the need for a new level of international responsibility to be exercised leading to the adoption by the General Assembly in its 2005 Summit Declaration of the concept of the responsibility to protect (United Nations General Assembly, 2005). The success of human rights in being accepted as the standard of international morality has been described as one of the most improbable stories of the twentieth century. The provisions of the Charter, the Universal Declaration on Human Rights, the Statute of the International Criminal Court (ICC) and the adoption by the General Assembly of the international responsibility to protect constitute together a powerful endorsement of the expectation of international leadership in this sphere.

9. The UN: eight levers of change

Porousness provides a historic opportunity for the UN system to embed intergovernmental relations once again in broader values. Only this time these broader values come not from the sense of urgency that comes from an intergovernmental crisis but from the emergence of dynamic new social forces using powerful new technologies operating at lightning speed. The contribution that the UN makes to the production of global public goods in the future will depend on its success in applying eight levers of change.

9.1. Shared values

With the decreasing willingness and in some cases ability of the US to provide unilateral leadership, generating the processes and conditions that lend themselves to shared values becomes increasingly critical. In this regard the UN's role in generating norms is a vital lever of change. The UN's work on the MDGs and Responsibility to Protect (RtoP) provide good examples. These two norms, MDGs and RtoP, are having a major impact on the practice of international cooperation by embedding inter-state relations in a broader set of shared values.

A critical ingredient in the creation of shared values is the process of marshalling evidence. During the last decade the accumulation of scientific data by the Intergovernmental Panel on Climate Change (IPCC) has become a critical driver for the idea that the international community has a responsibility to exercise leadership in defining and implementing a set of global policies that will address this challenge. The role of the Global Outbreak Alert and Response Network (GOARN) in providing the evidence base on which WHO could act in the SARS case is another example (Jones et al., 2009). The power of data was the engine behind the global appeal of the MDGs.

9.2. Leadership

If the generation of shared values lies at the core of advancing global public goods, then leadership in the UN becomes vital to success. Leadership is often posed as a choice between being an efficient secretary and an effective general (Traub, 2007). The efficient secretary serves the member states. The effective general seeks to embody within his person and office a concept of the international interest beyond that of individual member states. This choice is an unfortunate caricature. History would judge harshly an SG whose horizons never extended beyond the nation state. And the present would not tolerate for long an SG who had too ambitious a vision of the global interest. Boutros-Ghali was perceived to have crossed this line when he called for a standing UN army and global taxes.

Rather, the challenge for leaders of international institutions is the one identified by Mark Moore (1995) for public sector managers in general: they are explorers commissioned by society to search for public value. Leadership requires the strategic ability to align the proposed mission and its values with what is possible under the existing authorising environment as well as the capacity to deliver results. Obviously working with governments is central. But in today's age of porousness leadership also requires the ability to reach out and convene multiple stakeholders. Leveraging solutions requires a different kind of leadership from fixing problems.

Such leaders will not be found through a selection process based on political trade-offs. The contribution expected of the UN in the production of global public goods requires strong leadership and a selection process fit for purpose.

9.3. Governance

The UN system faces three critical governance challenges. The first is to embrace the newly emerging powers. Ensuring that these new powers are included as major stakeholders in the UN system is essential to the future credibility, legitimacy and effectiveness of the system. At the core of this challenge lies the issue of the reform of the Security Council. The challenge here is to make the UN a more legitimate expression of state power. The current distribution of power in the Security Council is a threat to the original Westphalian principles because it is no longer current.

The second governance challenge the UN faces is the need to find ways of engaging with a multitude of stakeholders in addition to governments. We have seen that in its initial construction phase, the UN was more inclusive in its approach to a variety of social actors. Markets in general, the private sector, civil society, policy networks – they will all play critical roles in the production of global public goods. Unless the UN can provide inclusive platforms that bring together all the relevant players, it is the UN itself which will see its relevance diminished.

Finally, the UN needs to revisit the character and the quality of the governance it provides. Convening power needs in many instances to replace controlling power as the primary indicator of relevance. A good example is provided in the current debate about the reform of United Nations Economic and Social Council (ECOSOC) and the need for that organ of the UN to have more authority over the development activities of the UN system. The focus is misguided. ECOSOC can provide a forum for convening critical actors, monitoring strategies and results, providing empirical data and sharing lessons learnt. The idea that ECOSOC can exercise significant authority over the development activities of the system is a holdover from a previous age.

9.4. Institutionalisation

International institutions have a critical role to play in the production of global public goods. An effective Department of Peace-keeping Operations has a major role to play in contributing to international peace, a strong International Monetary Fund (IMF) to the maintenance of financial stability, a credible World Trade Organization (WTO) to securing free trade, an effective International Criminal Court (ICC) to the enforcement of norms on crimes against humanity, and an effective Office of Human Rights for strong advocacy in this field. Institutionalisation is a necessary step in the creation of the capacity to pursue global missions and to produce global public goods. Critical analysis of performance should not detract from the importance of institutionalisation in the successful production of global public goods.

The UN system's 2010–11 estimated biennial budget is calculated at US$70 billion. There are some 77,000 staff in the UN secretariat, funds and programmes and specialised agencies combined (Jolly et al., 2009, 36). Currently, capacity is far too fragmented to be a strategic instrument. The process of institution-alisation needs to overcome historical legacies that have led to redundancies and duplication. The concept of critical mass can provide a new outward-oriented strategic framework to guide and align the UN's resources to priority global missions. The institutionalisation of the UN system's capacity to respond effectively to the challenge posed by climate change provides a historic opportunity for the UN to punch at the required weight on this critical issue.

9.5. Finance

The capacity of the UN system to contribute to the production of global public goods is heavily dependent on the character of its financing. Recent trends and reform proposals are potentially counterproductive and need to be revisited. Over the last 15 years, there has been a major shift to earmarked, non-core contributions. Today over 50 per cent of the UN Specialised Agencies' budget and over 75 per cent of the UN's Programmes and Funds are financed from non-core. This makes a long-term focus on global public goods agendas much more difficult to sustain.

Partly in response to this reality, recent reform proposals tried to resurrect the idea of a centralised funding system in the UN. A centralised treasury function would be established which would allocate resources throughout the system. In one variant, resources would be distributed to countries which would then allocate these resources according to their priorities. The current Delivering as One Initiative (United Nations Secretary-General, 2006), seen by many as the UN's current major reform initiative, builds on this principle.

This is counterproductive because it reinforces the concept of vertical state responsibility – resources get allocated to a single external black box with the label 'UN Fund'. On the contrary what is needed is the horizontal internalisation of the financing of the international dimensions of producing public goods. Innovative partnerships with the private sector will be key. The production of global public goods should create the opportunity for charging for services. The World Intellectual Property Organisation (WIPO) which is largely financed from fees in the granting of patents provides one example (May, 2007). Public/private partnerships in the area of insurance produce the public good of prevention by projecting the private cost of risk. The financing of global public goods and the cost of the UN's contribution to that effort cannot continue to rely exclusively on public resources, nor will the route of raising global taxes be very popular. Redesigning a financial architecture for the UN system which incorporates some market features is critical to the long-term sustainability of the UN's contribution to the production of global public goods.

9.6. Instruments

The variety of legal instruments which have been developed and are utilised within the UN system to implement collective action constitute one of its most important assets and one of its most significant contributions to the production of global public goods. Each instrument has its advantages and disadvantages. The unique authority vested in the Security Council to make commitments on behalf of the entire UN membership is balanced by the existence of the veto. The General Assembly can pass resolutions through majorities but these have only recommendatory authority. The UN system has generated an enormous number of treaties and conventions which are binding on those countries that sign up. Health regulations approved by the WHO's Assembly are binding on members of the conference unless a member specifically objects to the regulations within a certain time frame. Increasingly stringent provisions approved by a two-thirds majority and representing at least 50 per cent of total consumption of controlled substances under the Montreal Protocol are binding on all members who agreed to the original protocol (Barrett, 2007). Similar provisions have been enforced in technical areas of work, for example in conventions of the International Maritime Organisation (IMO) (Singh, 1993).

These instruments constitute a variable geometry of decision-making processes. This is a toolbox which needs to be preserved and strengthened. Much current commentary bemoans the inefficiency and inflexibility of decision-making in the UN system and often for good reason. But it is unfortunate that so little attention is given to this rich array of instruments as a fundamental contribution to strengthening international cooperation.

9.7. Focus

Focus is the Holy Grail of UN reform efforts. The assumption is that the key to reform lies in identifying a limited number of areas of comparative advantage, in order to set targets and monitor results. This chapter takes the view that the UN's core value creation proposition is to embed securely intergovernmental relations in a broader set of norms and values. That set of norms and values, whether they relate to concepts of security, human rights, development cooperation or climate, constitute in their totality a generic global public good to which the UN is positioned to contribute in a unique way. We need to reimagine focus in this context. Focus means the ability strategically to align mission and goals with what is possible in the authorising environment. Focus needs to be understood as strategic discipline in the service of alignment. Analyses of constraints and incentives in producing global public goods differentiate between situations in which single best efforts will be most effective because the free rider problem will not detract the single best effort from being made, situations in which global public goods depend on the participation of states that contribute to global public goods the least, and situations in which the production of global public goods depends on the combined efforts of all states. Focus requires the UN to possess high-level strategic capability and to exercise flexibility and imagination in the design and use of the most effective instruments.

9.8. Networks

The development of networks has deep consequences for a vision of international cooperation in the twenty-first century. It gives rise to a number of extraordinary challenges and opportunities. A quick look at the mission statements of Google, Facebook or Wikipedia illustrates this. Google's aim is to organise the world's information and make it universally accessible and useful (Auletta, 2009). Zuckerberg sees Facebook as a contribution to moving towards a form of 'universal connectivity that is truly new in human society' (Kirkpatrick, 2010). Wikipedia is based on the premise that knowledge can best be created by self-organising people. Creating knowledge, promoting universal connectivity, making knowledge accessible – these are all ambitious, transformative global missions.

They share a number of distinctive features. They operate at an extraordinary scale. Facebook has over 500 million active users. In over 30 countries, 30 per cent of citizens use Facebook. Self-organisation empowered by technology has proven to have tremendous leveraging capability. And they all operate at tremendous speed. Facebook's concept of the News Feed, by posting information of interest immediately, enabled very large groups to form almost instantaneously. It took 70 years for telephones to reach 50 per cent of US homes. It took

10 years for the internet to reach 50 per cent of the population of the US. It has taken five years for Facebook to reach 700 million people worldwide.

Scale, leverage and speed – these are the core characteristics of the power of these new technologies. Together they are having a transformative effect on the distribution of power between states, societies and individuals. These technologies have four other characteristics of direct relevance to the challenge of creating international public value. First, the creation of knowledge, universal connectivity and access to information – these represent quintessential public goods. Second, these public goods are being produced privately. Third, they are available to the public free, financed on a model that is a charge neither to the taxpayer nor to the consumer. Fourth, they are public goods that are created and consumed globally. The founders of the UN could only have dreamed of such a platform.

Global Pulse is an innovation initiative being led in the SG's office to support decision-makers in using real-time data to detect when populations are changing their collective behaviour in response to slow-onset crises. Pulse demonstrates the extraordinary potential of social media in transforming the content of international cooperation. The UN like many other large organisations still has a tendency to see social media as an instrument for advocacy and fundraising. It is still not seen as a truly strategic instrument for leverage. Disaster Relief 2.0 is an extraordinary account of the transformative impact of social networking on the humanitarian response in Haiti (United Nations Foundation, 2011). Leveraging networks must be central to any vision of the future of international cooperation and the achievement of global public goods. This is no doubt what Zoellick (2010) had in mind when he envisaged a new League of Networks. Networks of scientists and technical specialists need to become the face of a reinvigorated UN focused on critical global public goods.

10. Conclusion

There are two ways of producing global public goods: either through enlightened unilateral leadership or by means of an environment that nurtures the space and capacity to generate shared values (Stiglitz, 1995). Starting with the Charter itself, the UN's most important contribution to the generation of global public goods has been its role in creating that space and capacity. Each generation of UN leaders has had its opportunities to enlarge the space. It will be the UN's capacity to provide leadership in generating shared values which will determine its future relevance to the global public goods agenda. In today's globalised world, the successful production of global public goods requires the inclusion of a multitude of stakeholders. International consensus on a variety of global issues may in the end need to be reflected in intergovernmental agreements but the process and the path that will lead to that goal pass through a multiplicity of interests and stakeholders that will require exceptional leadership.

The founders of the UN created in the Charter a truly unique instrument. They also created a UN system based on communities of interest that embedded the intergovernmental system in broader values. This is a good place to start in reimagining the UN's future contribution to global public goods.

REFERENCES AND FURTHER READING

Auletta, K. (2009) *Googled: The End of the World as We Know it* (New York and London: Penguin).

Barrett, S. (2007) *Why Cooperate? The Incentive to Supply Global Public Goods* (Oxford: Oxford University Press).

Bobbitt, P. (2008) *Terror and Consent: The Wars for the Twenty-First Century* (New York: Knopf).

Boutros-Ghali, B. (1992) *An Agenda for Peace. Preventive Diplomacy, Peacemaking and Peace-Keeping: Report of the Secretary-General Pursuant to the Statement Adopted by the Summit Meeting of the Security Council on 31 January 1992,* A/47/277-S/24111 (New York: United Nations).

Boutros-Ghali, B. (1995) *Supplement to an Agenda for Peace: Position Paper of the Secretary-General on the Occasion of the Fiftieth Anniversary of the United Nations,* A/50/60-S/1995/1 (New York: United Nations).

Carnegie Commission on Preventing Deadly Conflict (1997) *Human Security Now* (New York: Carnegie Corporation).

Commission on Global Governance (1995) *Our Global Neighbourhood* (Oxford: Oxford University Press).

Commission on Human Security (2003) *Final Report* (New York: Human Security Commission).

DAC (Development Assistance Committee) (1996) *Shaping the 21st Century: The Contribution of Development Cooperation* (Paris: Organisation for Economic Cooperation and Development).

Doyle, M. and N. Sambanis (2007) 'Peacekeeping Operations', in Weiss, T.G. and S. Daws, *The Oxford Handbook on the United Nations* (Oxford: Oxford University Press).

Franck, T. and G. Nolte (1993) 'The Good Offices Function of the UN Secretary-General', in Roberts, A. and B. Kingsbury (eds) *United Nations, Divided World: The UN's Roles in International Relations* (Oxford: Clarendon Press, 2nd ed.).

Giddens, A. (2000) *Runaway World: How Globalisation is Reshaping Our Lives* (New York: Routledge).

Glemarec, Y. (2011) *Catalyzing Climate Finance: A Guidebook on Policy and Financing Options to Support Green, Low-Emission and Climate-Resilient Development* (New York: United Nations Development Programme).

Hammarskjöld, D. (1961) *The International Civil Servant in Law and in Fact: A Lecture Delivered to Congregation on 30 May 1961* (Oxford: Clarendon Press).

International Commission on Intervention and State Sovereignty (2001) *Responsibility to Protect* (Ottawa: International Development Research Centre).

International Task Force on Global Public Goods (2006) *Meeting Global Challenges: International Cooperation in the National Interest* (Stockholm: International Task Force on Global Public Goods).

Jolly, R., L. Emmerij and T.G. Weiss (2009) *UN Ideas that Changed the World* (Bloomington: Indiana University Press).

Jones, B., C. Pascual and S.J. Stedman (2009) *Power and Responsibility: Building International Order in an Era of Transnational Threats* (Washington, DC: Brookings Institutions Press).

Kennedy, P. (2006) *The Parliament of Man: The United Nations and the Quest for World Government* (London: Allen Lane).

Kirkpatrick, D. (2010) *The Facebook Effect: The Inside Story of the Company that is Connecting the World* (New York: Simon and Schuster).

MacFarlane, N. and Y. Khong (2006) *Human Security and the UN: A Critical History* (Bloomington and Indianapolis: Indiana University Press).

Martin, L. (1999) 'The Political Economy of Global Public Goods', in Kaul, I., I. Grunberg and M.A. Stern (eds) *Global Public Goods: International Cooperation in the 21st Century* (Oxford: Oxford University Press).

May, C. (2007) *The World Intellectual Property Organization: Resurgence and the Development Agenda* (London: Routledge).

Mitrany, D. (1943) *A Working Peace System* (London: Royal Institute of International Affairs).

Mitrany, D. (1975) *The Functional Theory of Politics* (London: M. Robertson on behalf of the London School of Economics and Political Science).

Moore, M. (1995) *Creating Public Value: Strategic Management in Government* (London: Harvard University Press).

Ramcharan, B.G. (2007) *Preventive Diplomacy at the UN* (Bloomington: Indiana University Press).

Shirky, C. (2008) *Here Comes Everybody: The Power of Organizing without Organizations* (New York: Penguin).

Singh, N. (1993) 'The UN and the Development of International Law', in Roberts, A. and B. Kingsbury (eds) *United Nations, Divided World: The UN's Roles in International Relations* (Oxford: Clarendon Press, 2nd ed.).

Slaughter, A-M. (2004) *A New World Order* (Princeton: Princeton University Press).

Stern, N. (2007) *The Economics of Climate Change: The Stern Review* (Cambridge: Cambridge University Press).

Stiglitz, J.E. (1995) *The Theory of International Public Goods and the Architecture of International Organisations,* Background Paper no. 7 (New York:

United Nations, Department for Economic and Social Information and Policy Analysis).

Traub, J. (2007) 'The Secretary-General's Political Space', in Chesterman, S. (ed.) *Secretary or General? The UN Secretary-General in World Politics* (Cambridge: Cambridge University Press).

United Nations Foundation (2011) *Disaster Relief 2.0: The Future of Information Sharing in Humanitarian Emergencies*, www.unfoundation.org/disaster-report (accessed on 30 August 2011).

United Nations General Assembly (2005) *2005 World Summit Outcome*, A/RES/60/1 (New York: United Nations).

United Nations Peacebuilding Commission (2010) *Review of the United Nations Peacebuilding Architecture, Final Report*, http://www.betterpeace.org/node/1564 (accessed on 30 August 2011).

United Nations Secretary-General (2001) *Prevention of Armed Conflict: Report of the Secretary-General*, A/55/985-S/2001/574 (New York: United Nations).

United Nations Secretary-General (2006) *Delivering as One: Report of High Level Panel on UN System-Wide Coherence in the Areas of Development,* *Humanitarian Assistance and the Environment*, A/61/583 (New York: United Nations).

United Nations Secretary-General (2009) *Implementing the Responsibility to Protect. Report of the Secretary-General*, A/63/677 (New York: United Nations).

Weiss, T.G. and R.C. Thakur (2010) *Global Governance and the UN: An Unfinished Journey* (Bloomington: Indiana University Press).

World Bank (2011) *World Development Report 2011: Conflict, Security, and Development* (Washington, DC: The World Bank).

Zoellick, R.B. (2010) *The End of the Third World? Modernizing Multilateralism for a Multipolar World*, speech at the Woodrow Wilson Centre for International Scholars, http://go.worldbank.org/BST6SVQC40 (accessed on 30 August 2011).

Websites

Global Pulse: http://www.unglobalpulse.org

World Economic Forum, Global Redesign Initiative: http://www.weforum.org/issues/global-redesign-initiative

4

THE TRANSFORMATION OF INTERNATIONAL NGOs AND THEIR IMPACT ON DEVELOPMENT AID

Thomas Richard Davies

Abstract

International non-governmental organisations (INGOs) are among the key actors in the transformation of development as a global public policy issue in the post-Cold War era. This chapter explores how in the past two decades INGOs concerned with development have transformed their structures and practices as well as development discourse. The author shows how development INGOs have globalised, in terms of both the formation of international confederations and the collaboration of multiple INGOs in global coalitions. A key development has been the erosion of the apparent North–South divide among development INGOs, with INGOs that originated in donor countries reforming their structures to give a greater voice to their affiliates in recipient countries, and organisations that originated in developing countries forming affiliates in developed countries. The reorientation of INGO advocacy from states toward intergovernmental and corporate actors is also explored, as is the creation of new forms of partnerships with both governmental and private actors. The chapter addresses how development INGOs have attempted to respond to critiques of their accountability and legitimacy through reforms such as the International NGO Charter on Accountability, while the conclusion explores the limitations of the transformations of development INGOs, and the challenges that these new configurations pose.

1. Introduction

Addressing representatives of international non-governmental organisations (INGOs) at the Millennium Forum in 2000, the then Secretary-General of the United Nations, Kofi Annan, praised their 'pioneering role' in development and claimed that they 'can work at the international level to lift billions out of poverty' (Annan, 2000, 2). It is now widely recognised that INGOs are crucial actors in international aid and development (Lewis and Kanji, 2009). The purpose of this chapter is to explore the different ways in which development INGOs have both transformed themselves and played a transformative role in international development in the post-Cold War era. In order to provide the context for the transformations analysed, the chapter begins by exploring the core characteristics of development INGOs and their evolution during the Cold War period. The main body proceeds to evaluate in turn the major aspects of the transformation of development INGOs in the post-Cold War era, including their structures and networking, their role in the developing world, their impact on development discourse and their development practices.

2. Development INGOs

There is no universally accepted definition of the characteristics of an INGO (Judge, 1978, 31). However, it has become common to follow the practice of the Union of International Associations (UIA), which collects data on organisations set up for non-profit-making purposes that were not established by governments and which operate in three or more countries. It is estimated that by 2009 there were more than 25,000 INGOs, of which more than 4000 were involved in development (UIA, 2010). Their diversity varies enormously and includes, but is not limited to, advocacy groups, grant-making foundations, research institutions and service-delivery organisations. As this piece will highlight, many INGOs concerned with development combine several of these roles. While some aim to promote development in general, others specialise in particular sectors such as education and health.

According to data of the Organisation for Economic Cooperation and Development (OECD) on 'net private grants', development aid originating from non-governmental sources amounted to more than US$22,000 million in 2009, the latest year for which data is available. Figure 4.1 indicates the dramatic increase in non-governmental development aid over the last two decades, with a slight dip following the economic downturn of 2008.

Figure 4.1 – Non-governmental development aid, 1990–2009 (in US$ million)

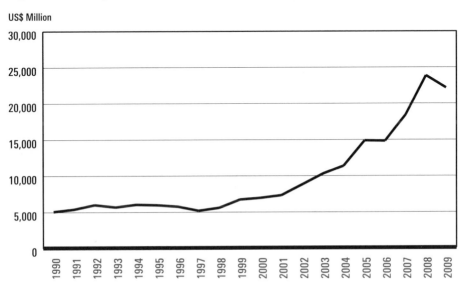

Source: OECD (2011).

These figures are almost certainly an underestimate of the total volume of development aid provided by non-governmental sources, with some estimates approaching double the figures of the OECD (Riddell, 2007, 418). With the aid budget of World Vision International in 2005 being greater than that of Italy, INGOs are now among the most economically significant actors in international development (Koch, 2008, 1).

The involvement of INGOs in development is far from a novel phenomenon: the activities of missionary groups and transnational humanitarian organisations predate the emergence of concepts such as 'international development' in the twentieth century (Chabbott, 1997, 227). A significant turning-point came with the decolonisation of European empires in the period following the Second World War, when organisations such as Oxfam and CARE turned their attention from post-war relief in Europe to assistance to newly independent countries in Africa and Asia (Walker and Maxwell, 2009, 43–4).

Many of the contemporary roles of INGOs in development were pioneered in the Cold War period. Advocacy was spearheaded by organisations such as War on Want, which is credited with having contributed towards the creation of the industrialised world's first separate government ministry dedicated to international development in the United Kingdom in 1964 (Willetts, 2011, 157). Six years earlier, the World Council of Churches is thought to have 'set the first target for official development assistance at one percent of gross national product for each high-income country', at a time when the overseas expenditure of the Ford Foundation exceeded that of many intergovernmental bodies dedicated to overseas development (Chabbott, 1997, 230–3). During the Cold War, the Society for International Development played an important role in the professionalisation of development work, in the reinterpretation of development from national economic growth to the well-being of the poor, and in pioneering the idea of a Human Development Report, later taken up by the United Nations Development Programme (UNDP) (SID, 2010). Government subsidies to development INGOs increased significantly from the 1960s onwards (Smith, 1990, 4–5). At the same time, there were a growing number of bodies created to coordinate the work of development INGOs, such as the International Council of Voluntary Agencies set up in 1962. Development INGOs were also established in an increasing variety of contexts, reflected in the creation in Japan, in 1961, of the International Organization for Cultivating Universal Human Spirit and the formation, in 1967, of the Aga Khan Foundation. In the 1970s and 1980s, novel networking forms were pioneered, most notably among those concerned with women and development and with providing a 'Southern' perspective on development, such as Development Alternatives with Women for a New Era and the Third World Network, respectively, both of which were established in 1984.

3. The transformation of development INGOs in the post-Cold War era

While much was pioneered during the Cold War, development INGOs have transformed in the two decades since its ending. One of the most significant changes is the increasingly global nature of the organisational structures adopted by development INGOs. One aspect of this transformation is the tendency for nationally-based organisations to unite in international confederal structures, evident in the experience of such groups as Oxfam, Save the Children and CARE. In 1995, for instance, nine Oxfams – in Australia, Belgium, Canada, Hong Kong, the Netherlands, New Zealand, Quebec, the UK and the US – united to form Oxfam International in order 'to further the Oxfams' common goals, promote, assist and co-ordinate collaboration among the Oxfams where this will result in a greater impact of the sum total of their joint efforts, [and] protect the Oxfam name and enhance its standing' (Oxfam International, 1996).

There is a spectrum of organisational forms adopted by INGOs, varying according to the degree of centralisation of their decision-making structures. Development INGOs have traditionally occupied the extremes of the spectrum: at the one end, loose groupings of nationally-based organisations that may share a common name but make decisions independently (such as the Oxfams in the early 1990s), and at the other end, unitary corporate bodies (such as early World Vision), which direct the actions of their offices in various countries from the centre. In the post-Cold War era, there has been an increasing tendency for development INGOs to move from these extremes to federal and confederal forms of organisation, which blend some centralised coordination with a degree of independence of member organisations (Lindenberg and Bryant, 2001, 139–45).

While nationally-based bodies have established international confederations and federations, these INGOs have in turn increasingly involved themselves in coordinated action with other INGOs. The organisation claiming to be 'the world's largest civil society movement calling for an end to poverty and inequality', the Global Call to Action against Poverty (GCAP), for instance, counts among its participating INGOs ActionAid International, *Agir Tous pour la Dignité Quart Monde*, CARE International, *Caritas Internationalis*, Oxfam International and Save the Children. GCAP is an example of a transnational coalition, which brings together national and international non-governmental organisations (NGOs) from a wide range of backgrounds to mobilise for a common cause. It is a more centralised form of organisation than the transnational network, and could even be described as a super-INGO, in that much of its membership consists of bodies that are themselves already INGOs. One of the most notable aspects of GCAP is the way in which it unites organisations with an exceptionally diverse range of backgrounds, from human rights groups such as Amnesty International, to peace associations such as the Women's International League for Peace and Freedom, to environmentalist organisations such as Friends of the Earth (GCAP, 2011a).

The participants in GCAP are indicative of the broad range of INGOs that are concerning themselves with development in the post-Cold War era. With the emergence of the 'sustainable development' agenda, many environmentalist INGOs are now among the most vocal actors in discourse concerning development. In addition, human rights organisations which have traditionally focused their attention on civil and political rights have increasingly turned to economic and social concerns, with Amnesty International expanding its mandate to include such issues following a contentious meeting of its International Council in Dakar in 2001 (Chong, 2009, 119–20). Amnesty International's change of direction was spearheaded by its Senegalese secretary-general Pierre Sané, reflecting the more diverse leadership of INGOs by the 1990s.

4. INGOs in the developing world

Among the most significant aspects of the transformation of development INGOs in the post-Cold War era is their relationship with countries in the developing world. In the case of development INGOs headquartered in OECD countries, efforts have been made to adjust decision-making procedures to provide a greater voice for affiliated bodies in recipient countries. A growing trend has been the adoption of 'global bumblebee' (as opposed to earlier donor-dominated) structures pioneered by organisations such as World Vision International, which adjusted its governing structures in 1995 to ensure that its international board was elected from seven regional forums (Foreman, 1999). The 'bumblebee' reference 'alludes to the intricate network of influence and interaction between member organizations and with the central organization' (Foreman, 1999, 181).

Global coalitions also feature a growing role for participant organisations based in developing countries. Such transformation is evident in the evolution of Publish What You Pay, which began as a coalition of predominantly British and other OECD country-based groups (Catholic Overseas Development Agency, Global Witness, the Open Society Institute, Oxfam Great Britain, Save the Children UK and Transparency International UK), but by 2011 featured a membership of over 600 organisations among which those based in developing countries outnumbered those in OECD countries by a ratio of approximately 4:1 (Publish What You Pay, 2011). Another transnational coalition, the Clean Clothes Campaign, comprises INGOs in 15 European countries that work with more than 200 national and local organisations in developing countries 'to identify local problems and objectives, and to [...] develop campaign strategies' (Clean Clothes Campaign, 2011). While older coalitions such as these have their origins in OECD countries, more recent coalitions such as GCAP have their origins in developing countries. GCAP, for instance, emerged in a series of meetings in Maputo in 2003, Johannesburg in 2004 and at the World Social Forum in 2005, and has a global secretariat based in Johannesburg, Mumbai, New York and Accra (GCAP, 2011b).

INGOs concerned with development that are headquartered in developing countries have multiplied in the post-Cold War period. Some of these operate within particular regions in the developing world, such as the Arab NGO Network for Development (ANND), established in 1997 and working in ten Arab countries 'for more sound and effective socio-economic reforms in the region, which integrate the concepts of sustainable development, gender justice, and the rights-based approach' (ANND, 2011). Others aim to represent the global 'South' more generally, such as Focus on the Global South, set up in 1995 and headquartered in Bangkok. For many of these INGOs the focus of their activities is upon research and advocacy rather than direct provision of development assistance.

With respect to service delivery, it has been common to note the dramatically increased role for local-level and national-level non-governmental bodies based in developing countries 'as neoliberal development policies have emphasized a decreasing role for governments as service-providers' (Lewis and Kanji, 2009, 92). It has less-commonly been observed that service-providing NGOs in developing countries are increasingly organising themselves internationally, and creating some of the most substantial INGOs operating in the present day. The Bangladesh Rural Advancement Committee (BRAC), for example, claims to be 'the largest development organisation in the world [...] employing more than 60,000 people, and organising and training an additional 60,000 self-employed health volunteers, agriculture and livestock extension agents and part-time teachers' (BRAC, 2011a). It now operates programmes not only in Bangladesh, but also in Afghanistan, Haiti, Liberia, Pakistan, Sierra Leone, Sri Lanka, Sudan, Tanzania and Uganda; and it has set up affiliate offices in the United Kingdom and the United States of America for 'resource mobilization' (BRAC, 2011b).

With development INGOs headquartered in donor countries reforming their governance structures to provide a greater voice for affiliates in recipient countries, and development INGOs headquartered in developing countries setting up 'resource mobilization' affiliates in developed countries, a convergence of organisational forms is emerging, which bridges the former divide between 'Northern' and 'Southern' INGOs.

5. INGOs, advocacy and the transformation of development discourse

While direct service delivery remains an important feature of the work of INGOs in international development, advocacy has acquired a greater significance in the post-Cold War era. This is in part the result of the growing number of INGOs headquartered in developing countries for which advocacy is their key focus. In addition, INGOs based in developed countries that formerly concentrated their attention upon service delivery are giving greater priority to advocacy. Among the most notable examples of the latter are the national Oxfams, which united to form an Advocacy Office in Washington in 1995, due to the perception that development issues had become 'global concerns calling for global analysis and action' (Anderson, 2007, 89). Another prominent example is CARE International, which has argued that advocacy better enables them to address the 'root causes of poverty and discrimination' and to 'reach a large segment of the population and broaden the scope of [their] impact' (Sprechmann and Pelton, 2001, 6).

Participation by INGOs in global coalitions is commonly primary for the purpose of advocacy. Some advocacy in global coalitions is perceived to have had considerable impact: the Jubilee 2000 coalition, for instance, has been especially lauded for having contributed to significant debt reduction for many developing countries (Birdsall and Williamson, 2002, 1). More recently, development INGOs have become involved in the broad movement for 'global justice', and have been among the most vocal participants in events such as the World Social Forums. GCAP, which was formally launched at the 2005 World Social Forum, has been credited with contributing towards promises at the Gleneagles G8 Summit of 2005 for substantial increases in official development assistance, although these largely failed to materialise (Willetts, 2011, 157). While less well known, INGO advocacy on a local scale has also been influential, with CARE International claiming to have made a difference by lobbying for change on issues as varied as pesticide use in Nicaragua and contraceptives in Cambodia (Sprechmann and Pelton, 2001, 3).

As the key relevant actors to international development have evolved, so have the targets of advocacy by INGOs. While advocacy traditionally focused on national institutions, intergovernmental actors have become increasingly important. The establishment of the World Bank Inspection Panel in 1994 was in part a response to non-governmental pressure (Clark et al., 2003), as was the creation of the Independent Evaluation Office of the International Monetary Fund in 2001 (Scholte, 2011, 93). Formal consultative mechanisms between the international financial institutions and INGOs remain limited, however.

Given the significance of transnational corporations in the contemporary era, these have been among the most common targets of INGO advocacy since the pioneering work of organisations such as War on Want in the 1970s and 1980s in developing the Nestlé boycott movement (Chetley, 1986). While confrontational strategies by INGOs with respect to corporations have become well known, some of the most effective initiatives have involved cooperation with corporations, including private certification schemes such as Fairtrade and international standards for social and environmental performance reporting such as those of the Global Reporting Initiative (GRI) that were used by more than a thousand organisations in 2009 (GRI, 2010, 16).

The most significant impact of INGOs' advocacy on international development has been in transforming understandings of the nature of international development. The role of INGOs in transforming development discourse towards human development during the Cold War has already been mentioned. In the post-Cold War era, INGOs have been important in bridging development discourse with numerous other discourses, from environmentalism to women's rights. A 'new rights advocacy' on development has emerged 'which makes explicit reference to internationally recognized human rights standards', due to a shift to 'rights-based' development methods by INGOs such as Oxfam and CARE, the turn to economic and social rights by INGOs originally primarily focusing on civil and political rights such as Human Rights Watch and Amnesty International, the creation of transnational coalitions such as GCAP that involve both development and human rights INGOs, and the emergence of INGOs explicitly focused on economic and social rights such as the International Network for Economic, Social and Cultural Rights (Nelson and Dorsey, 2008, 19–21).

INGOs have helped to transform development discourse in part because of their involvement with epistemic communities. Development INGOs and the 'development studies' academic community commonly collaborate, in organisations such as the Development Studies Association and in journals such as the *Journal of International Development*. This collaboration helps legitimise the perception of development INGOs as repositories of development 'expertise' on which governments and intergovernmental bodies may draw. While the use of non-governmental 'experts' in intergovernmental policy formulation is far from a novel phenomenon (it was used extensively by the League of Nations (Zimmern, 1930)), the practice is far more common in the post-Cold War era than it was during the previous four decades. At the World Summit on Sustainable Development in 2002, for instance, INGOs took part in the official proceedings by providing statements in the 'partnership plenary meetings' on specialist issues, the general debate, and a multi-stakeholder event, in addition to their numerous unofficial gatherings on the fringes of the conference (UN, 2002, 82–118; Willetts, 2011, 51–2). In environmental negotiations, governmental reliance on INGO expertise has extended as far as 'delegation capture', by which some governments such as that of Nauru have appointed as their entire delegations INGO 'experts' from foreign nations (Spiro, 1995). However, probably the most significant means by which INGOs have helped to transform discourse is not through their direct interactions with states, but by transforming wider public awareness and perceptions of development issues through their reports, propaganda, demonstrations and use of media.

6. The transformation of INGOs' development practices

Given the greater prominence of INGOs in development in the post-Cold War era, their activities have been subjected to increased scrutiny. By the mid-1990s a wide range of critiques of INGOs' roles in development had surfaced. Some critiques have focused on INGOs' effectiveness in service delivery, claiming that their impact can be 'highly localized and often transitory' (Edwards and Hulme, 2002, 53). Where their impact is more far-reaching, INGOs are vulnerable to the critique that they may weaken already often fragile state institutions in developing countries (Barber and Bowie, 2008). Others have critiqued INGOs' advocacy role, with apparent successes having counterproductive impacts, such as the promotion of a ban in 1993 on imports to the United States of textiles produced by child labour that is said to have 'forced young girls into much more abusive forms of work such as street trading, domestic work, and prostitution' (Harper, 2001, 253). While INGOs' roles in service delivery have been challenged with respect to their accountability, INGOs' roles in advocacy have been challenged with respect to their legitimacy.

Partly in response to such criticisms, INGOs involved in development have transformed many of their practices. In an effort to improve effectiveness and accountability, greater priority has been given to monitoring and evaluation procedures, reflected for instance in CARE's creation of a director of monitoring and evaluation in 1995 (Lindenberg and Bryant, 2001, 225). Like some transnational corporations, a number of INGOs now report to the global standards set by organisations such as the Global Reporting Initiative. Since 2007, for instance, Oxfam Great Britain has produced accountability reports to the standards of both the Global Reporting Initiative and the INGOs Accountability Charter (Oxfam Great Britain, 2007, 3). The INGOs Accountability Charter was launched in 2006 with the support of 11 INGOs and aims ultimately to become 'the authoritative voice and standard code of practice for all INGOs' (International NGO Charter of Accountability, 2011a). Previous efforts, whether international (such as AccountAbility, Humanitarian Accountability Partnership International, One World Trust and the Sphere Project) or national (such as Bond, InterAction and Zewo), are thought to have failed to address 'adequately…global cross-sectoral issues' (International NGO Charter of Accountability, 2011b).

Rather than challenging the authority of developing-country governments, INGOs in the post-Cold War era have commonly made greater efforts to work in partnership with them, and with local community structures. The combinations of partners can be extensive, and can include major corporations as well as governments. The World Economic Forum (WEF) has played a pioneering role in forging partnerships between transnational corporate actors, developing country governments and NGOs, such as in its Global Education Initiative, which claims to have 'helped over 1.8 million students and teachers and mobilized over US$100 million in resource support in Jordan, Rajasthan (India), Egypt, the Palestinian Territories and Rwanda' and to engage 'over 40 private sector partners, 14 governments, seven international organizations and 20 NGOs' (WEF, 2011).

The closeness between some INGOs and corporate and governmental actors has been criticised for being 'part of the same loose, political formation that oversees the neoliberal project' (Roy, 2004, 43). In some cases, INGOs are directly created by businesses, such as the World Business Council for Sustainable Development (WBCSD), which aims 'to provide business leadership as a catalyst for sustainable development and to support the business license to operate, innovate and grow in a world increasingly shaped by sustainable development issues' (WBCSD, 2011). However, the considerable diversity of INGOs should not be underestimated, since many INGOs have been among the most vocal critics of 'neoliberal' policies, such as Focus on the Global South. In addition, a number of INGOs are among the most central actors in advocating measures to address potential conflicts of interests between INGOs and business concerns. The Conflicts of Interest Coalition, for example, is leading calls for a code of conduct on managing conflicts of interests with respect to private sector involvement in global public policy, and calls for the United Nations to 'distinguish between industries, including business-interest not-for-profit organisations (BINGOs) and public interest non-governmental organisations (PINGOs), that are both currently under the "Civil Society" umbrella without distinction' (Conflicts of Interest Coalition, 2011).

By working together with organisations run from developing countries such as BRAC and Focus on the Global South in umbrella groups such as GCAP, INGOs headquartered in developed countries have endeavoured to enhance the legitimacy of their actions. Among the most significant steps towards enhancing the legitimacy of OECD-country-headquartered INGOs have been the reforms that have been taking place in their organisational structures outlined in section 4 of this chapter. Furthermore, however limited the organisational structures of INGOs run from OECD countries may be, they can often provide a greater voice to some sectors of society in developing countries than their own governments, such as the indigenous groups for the benefit of which Survival International aims to act. In addition, 'Northern' INGOs have been important in endeavours for capacity building of local and national NGOs in developing countries (James, 1998), and have played a crucial role in challenging failures to involve local civil society actors in poverty reduction strategies. Where local NGOs in developing countries operate in restrictive political environments, the assistance of some external INGOs has even extended to the dissemination of the techniques of non-violent resistance to authoritarian rule, with the Belgrade-based Centre for Applied Non-Violent Action and Strategies (CANVAS) training some of the activists that led the Egyptian revolution of 2011 (Davies, 2011a).

7. Conclusion

INGOs have been central to the transformation of development as a global public policy issue in the post-Cold War era. They have globalised their organisational structures and bridged former divisions between 'Northern' and 'Southern' organisations. The range of organisations with which INGOs cooperate on development issues has become much broader, including corporate as well as governmental and intergovernmental actors. INGOs have played a key role in transforming development discourse and advancing practices to promote the accountability and legitimacy of actors involved in development.

However, the changes that have taken place remain limited. The great majority of the governing structures of development INGOs headquartered in OECD countries are still dominated by their members in these countries. The volume of development INGOs headquartered in developing countries, although increasing, remains comparatively small, and they are greatly outnumbered in many transnational coalitions including GCAP. As of September 2011, only 24 INGOs are members of the INGOs Accountability Charter. Furthermore, local and national NGOs in developing countries still commonly operate in a dependent relationship with donor governments and INGOs in developed countries (Michael, 2004).

In addition to their limitations, aspects of the transformations that have taken place among development INGOs in the post-Cold War era may even be considered to be counterproductive. The increasing role of advocacy may have come at the expense of the operational capacity of INGOs in service delivery (Fioramonti et al., 2008, 364). Moreover, the increasingly close relationship between INGOs and corporate and governmental actors in multi-stakeholder initiatives and collaborative projects may reflect a growing corporatisation of international development, which is limiting the prospects for effective pluralism of approaches (Peña, 2011).

Historically, the formation of large coalitions of INGOs, such as the Central Office of International Associations in 1907 and the International Consultative Group in 1932, has preceded a precipitous collapse of transnational associational activity in subsequent years, in part because of the hubristic goals of their organisers (Davies, 2011b). Whether or not the global coalitions of the contemporary era will follow a similar path remains to be seen.

REFERENCES

Anderson, I. (2007) 'Global Action: International NGOs and Advocacy', in Rugendyke, B. (ed.) *NGOs as Advocates for Development in a Globalizing World* (London: Routledge).

Annan, K. (2000) *Secretary-General, Addressing Participants at Millennium Forum, Calls for*

Intensified 'NGO Revolution', United Nations Press Release SG/SM/7411 GA/9710 (New York: United Nations).

ANND (Arab NGO Network for Development) (2011) *About Us*, http://www.annd.org/about.php (accessed on 28 September 2011).

Barber, M. and C. Bowie (2008) 'How International NGOs Could Do Less Harm and More Good', *Development in Practice*, 18(6), pp. 748–54.

Birdsall, N. and J. Williamson (2002) *Delivering on Debt Relief: From IMF Gold to a New Aid Architecture* (Washington, DC: Center for Global Development).

BRAC (Bangladesh Rural Advancement Committee) (2011a) *Who We Are*, http://www.brac.net/content/who-we-are (accessed on 29 September 2011).

BRAC (2011b) *Where We Work*, http://www.brac.net/content/where-we-work (accessed on 29 September 2011).

Chabbott, C. (1997) 'Development INGOs', in Boli, J. and G. Thomas (eds) *Constructing World Culture: International Nongovernmental Organizations since 1875* (Stanford, CA: Stanford University Press).

Chetley, A. (1986) *The Politics of Baby Foods: Successful Challenges to an International Marketing Strategy* (London: Frances Pinter).

Chong, D. (2009) 'Economic Rights and Extreme Poverty: Moving towards Subsistence', in Bob, C. (ed.) *The International Struggle for New Human Rights* (Philadelphia, PA: University of Pennsylvania Press).

Clark, D., J. Fox and K. Treakle (2003) *Demanding Accountability: Civil-Society Claims and the World Bank Inspection Panel* (Lanham, MD: Rowman and Littlefield).

Clean Clothes Campaign (2011) *Who We Are*, http://www.cleanclothes.org/about-us (accessed on 19 October 2011).

Conflicts of Interest Coalition (2011) *Statement of Concern*, http://coicoalition.blogspot.com/search/label/statements (accessed on 20 October 2011).

Davies, T.R. (2011a) *The 2011 Uprisings and the Limits of 'People Power'*, http://www.city.ac.uk/social-sciences/international-politics/policy-briefs/the-2011-uprisings-and-the-limits-of-people-power (accessed on 20 October 2011).

Davies, T.R. (2011b) 'The Rise and Fall of Transnational Civil Society: The Evolution of International Non-Governmental Organizations since the Mid-Nineteenth Century', in Reydams, L. (ed.) *Global Activism Reader* (New York: Continuum).

Edwards, M. and D. Hulme (2002) 'Making a Difference: Scaling-Up the Developmental Impact of NGOs – Concepts and Experiences', in Edwards, M. and A. Fowler (eds) *The Earthscan Reader on NGO Management* (London: Earthscan).

Fioramonti, L., A. Fowler and V.F. Heinrich (2008) 'The Challenge of Socioeconomic and Democratic Development: Marrying Civil Society's Social and Political Roles?', in Heinrich, V.F. and L. Fioramonti (eds) *CIVICUS Global Survey of the State of Civil Society, Volume 2: Comparative Perspectives* (Bloomfield, CT: Kumarian Press).

Foreman, K. (1999) 'Evolving Global Structures and the Challenges Facing International Relief and Development Organisations', *Non-Profit and Voluntary Sector Quarterly*, 28(1), pp. 178–97, DOI: 10.1177/089976499773746519.

GCAP (Global Call to Action against Poverty) (2011a) *GCAP Supporting Organizations*, http://whiteband.org/en/about/supportingorgs (accessed on 27 September 2011).

GCAP (2011b) *Global Secretariat*, http://whiteband.org/en/content/globalsecretariat (accessed on 19 October 2011).

GRI (Global Reporting Initiative) (2010) *Year in Review 2009/10* (Amsterdam: GRI).

Harper, C. (2001) 'Do the Facts Matter? NGOs, Research, and International Advocacy', in Edwards, M. and J. Gaventa (eds.) *Global Citizen Action* (Boulder, CO: Lynne Rienner Publishers).

International NGO Charter of Accountability (2011a) *Charter Background*, http://www.ingoaccountabilitycharter.org/about-the-charter/background-of-the-charter/ (accessed on 29 September 2011).

International NGO Charter of Accountability (2011b) *The Five Years Strategy*, http://www.ingoaccountabilitycharter.org/wpcms/wp-content/uploads/INGO-Accountability-Charter-Five-Years-Strategy.pdf (accessed on 29 September 2011).

James, R. (1998) *Demystifying Organisation Development: Practical Capacity-Building Experiences of African NGOs* (Oxford: INTRAC).

Judge, A. (1978) 'International Institutions: Diversity, Borderline Cases, Functional Substitutes and Possible Alternatives', in Taylor, P. and A.J.R. Groom (eds) *International Organization: A Conceptual Approach* (London: Frances Pinter).

Koch, D.J. (2008) *A Paris Declaration for International NGOs?* (Paris: OECD Development Centre).

Lewis, D. and N. Kanji (2009) *Non-Governmental Organizations and Development* (London: Routledge).

Lindenberg, M. and C. Bryant (2001) *Going Global: Transforming Relief and Development NGOs* (Bloomfield, CT: Kumarian Press).

Michael, S. (2004) *Undermining Development: The Absence of Power among Local NGOs in Africa* (Bloomington, IN: Indiana University Press).

Nelson, P.J. and E. Dorsey (2008) *New Rights Advocacy: Changing Strategies of Development and Human Rights NGOs* (Washington, DC: Georgetown University Press).

OECD (Organisation for Economic Cooperation and Development) (2011) *OECD Stats Extracts*, http://stats.oecd.org/ (accessed on 13 September 2011).

Oxfam Great Britain (2007) *Accountability Report 06/07* (Oxford: Oxfam Great Britain).

Oxfam International (1996) *Oxfam International's Mission Statement*, http://www.oxfam.org/en/about/what/mission (accessed on 7 April 2010).

Peña, A.M. (2011) *ISO and Social Standardisation: Uncomfortable Compromises in Global Policy-Making*, Working Paper CUTP/009A (London: City University of London), http://www.city.ac.uk/__data/assets/pdf_file/0019/106822/CUWPTP009A_pena.pdf (accessed on 20 October 2011).

Publish What You Pay (2011) *Members of Publish What You Pay, 21/03/2011*, http://www.publish-whatyoupay.org/sites/pwypdev.gn.apc.org/files/Membership%20PDF.pdf (accessed on 19 October 2011).

Riddell, R.C. (2007) *Does Foreign Aid Really Work?* (Oxford: Oxford University Press).

Roy, A. (2004) *Public Power in the Age of Empire* (New York: Seven Stories).

Scholte, J.A. (2011) 'Civil Society and IMF Accountability', in Scholte, J.A. (ed.) *Building Global Democracy? Civil Society and Accountable Global Governance* (Cambridge: Cambridge University Press).

SID (Society for International Development) (2010) *History*, http://www.sidint.net/about-sid/history/ (accessed on 27 September 2011).

Smith, B. (1990) *More than Altruism: The Politics of Private Foreign Aid* (Princeton, NJ: Princeton University Press).

Spiro, P.J. (1995) 'New Global Communities: Nongovernmental Organizations in International Decision Making Institutions', *Washington Quarterly*, 18(1), pp. 45–56.

Sprechmann, S. and E. Pelton (2001) *Advocacy Tools and Guidelines: Promoting Policy Change* (Atlanta, GA: Cooperative for Assistance and Relief Everywhere).

UIA (Union of International Associations) (2010) *Yearbook of International Organizations, 2010–2011* (Berlin: de Gruyter).

UN (United Nations) (2002) *Report of the World Summit on Sustainable Development, Johannesburg, South Africa, 26 August–4 September 2002*, A/CONF.199/20 (New York: United Nations).

Walker, P. and D. Maxwell (2009) *Shaping the Humanitarian World* (London: Routledge).

WBCSD (World Business Council for Sustainable Development) (2011) *What Is the WBCSD's Mission?*, http://www.wbcsd.org/includes/getTarget.asp?type=p&id=Mjk0 (accessed on 20 October 2011).

WEF (World Economic Forum) (2011) *Global Education Initiative*, http://www.schwabfound.org/en/initiatives/gei/index.htm (accessed on 29 September 2011).

Willetts, P. (2011) *Non-Governmental Organizations in World Politics: The Construction of Global Governance* (London: Routledge).

Zimmern, A. (1930) 'Democracy and the Expert', *The Political Quarterly*, 1(1), pp. 7–25, DOI: 10.1111/j.1467-923X.1930.tb01466.x.

5
THE NEW REALITIES OF GLOBAL HEALTH: DYNAMICS AND OBSTACLES

Marine Buissonnière

Abstract

The past 15 years have seen the arrival of new actors in the field of global health and an increase in development aid in the healthcare sector. These actors have claimed a significant share of the additional public and private resources available becoming the driving force in this new paradigm, often at the expense of traditional institutions, which have gradually lost their policy hegemony. Making choices and formulating policies on the matter of healthcare have ceased to be the sole prerogative of the institutions that had hitherto held the mandate and the responsibility for doing so. Entire areas of the healthcare sector are now dominated by private funders, which have become the *de facto* decision-makers on public health policy. This new situation raises fundamental questions about governance and accountability. Who decides policy? How are decisions made? All too often, countries in receipt of aid continue to suffer from inadequate coordination between donors and from the lack of a common agenda. With this in mind, it is worth exploring a number of ways of ensuring that global healthcare policies best reflect the beneficiary countries' actual needs and aspirations.

Author's note
This text reflects the opinions of the author only and not those of the organisation.

1. Introduction

The past 15 years have seen a sea change in global health. Previously restricted by and large to national level, debates on healthcare policy have gradually forced their way onto international agendas and their scope now extends beyond the field of healthcare in the narrow sense (De Torrenté, 2009). The unique and devastating nature of the human immunodeficiency virus/acquired immune deficiency syndrome (HIV/AIDS) epidemic and the unprecedented mobilisation of civil society that it has brought about have played a part in this transformation. Other contributing factors include the fears associated with the socio-economic and political impact of epidemics and their potential consequences in terms of international destabilisation and security (UNIS, 2000), the transnational threats associated with pandemics and bioterrorism, and the liberalisation of international trade and its direct and indirect impact on healthcare (McDonald and Horton, 2009). These elements have come together to make health a key issue whose political importance has been confirmed by a series of commitments made in the early 2000s, such as the Global Fund to Fight AIDS, Tuberculosis and Malaria (GFATM) at the G8 summit in Okinawa in July 2000 or the adoption of the Millennium Development Goals[1] (MDGs) in September of the same year. This is also reflected in the increase in the funds allocated to this sector and the establishment of new bodies dedicated to healthcare issues. To grasp this new reality, it is not sufficient merely to consider how much in funding terms healthcare represents in today's aid environment; rather, one must strive for a better understanding of the new dynamics and the shift in the balance of power that this mobilisation has caused.

2. A sea change in the field of healthcare

2.1. Increase in the volume of aid

Between 1990 and 2010 international aid in the field of healthcare has markedly increased, both in terms of volume and as a percentage of total development aid (Figure 5.1).

This significant rise is due primarily to the increase in public funds made available by those governments that are the traditional providers of aid, particularly the US and UK (IHME, 2010). Public funding thus continues to make up the lion's share of aid provided in the field of healthcare. Although the increase in the contributions made by low- and middle-income countries also appears to be a factor in this growth, the data available at this stage are insufficient to determine their exact position (GHW, 2008). A second growth driver has been an increase in funding from businesses, individuals and foundations (Ravishankar et al., 2009; Murray et al., 2011). In 2008, private funding represented around one-fifth of the total aid for healthcare, two and a half times more than in 1990 (IHME, 2010). The Bill and Melinda Gates Foundation (BMGF) is largely responsible for the growing importance of private capital in this new paradigm. In the space of less than ten years, it has established itself as one of the most important actors on the global health stage, becoming the second largest source of funding behind the US and ahead of the British governments (Figure 5.2).

2.2. Matching resources to requirements?

The low level of development aid in the field of healthcare in the early 1990s left plenty of scope for improvement. Although the increase since then is genuinely pleasing, it cannot disguise the fact that the amounts given in aid continue to

---

1   Of the eight Millennium Development Goals (MDGs) three are devoted to health: reduce child mortality (no. 4); improve maternal health (no. 5); combat HIV/AIDS, malaria and other diseases (no. 6).

Figure 5.1 – Change in development aid in the healthcare sector, 1990–2010 (in US$ billion)

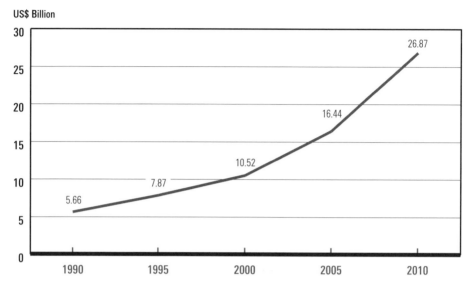

US$ Billion

Source: IHME (2010).

Figure 5.2 – Origin of development aid allocated to healthcare, 1990–2008 (in US$ million)

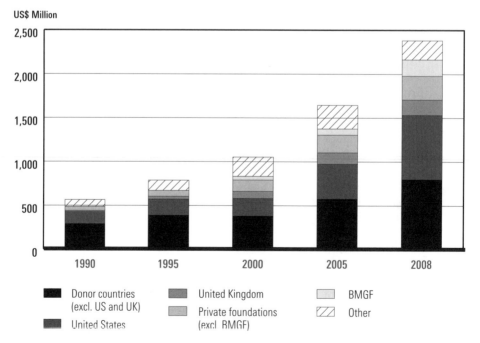

US$ Million

Source: IHME (2010).

fall far short of the generally quoted sums required to meet objectives such as the MDGs (GHW, 2008; HLTF, 2009). Against the background of a confirmed slowdown in growth following the 2008 financial crisis, this is a particularly timely wake-up call. The cuts already observed in the aid budgets of certain governments such as the Netherlands, Ireland and Italy (AidWatch, 2011) and the disappointing results of the efforts to top up the GFATM in October 2010 are giving rise to fears that the favourable development over the previous 15 years will be followed by a challenging period of austerity.

In a situation in which the resources available for healthcare – sizeable as they are – remain inadequate, the issue of matching aid to requirements remains the subject of debate. In 2009, Ravishankar et al. highlighted a growing correlation between aid and identified needs, observing that, on the whole, the hardest-hit countries receive the most aid. Yet significant exceptions remain: for instance, 11 of the 30 hardest-hit countries still receive less aid per capita than others with lower mortality rates and higher incomes (Murray et al., 2011). HIV/AIDS receives the lion's share of available resources (US$6.16 billion), followed by maternal and child health, which has recently become the focus of greater attention. Sector-specific support for healthcare and non-transmissible diseases continue to do badly out of this distribution (IHME, 2010). It has been argued that HIV/AIDS accounts for too large a share of available funds in view of the morbidity and mortality associated with other diseases (England, 2007). Nevertheless, even though 6.6 million patients currently receive antiretroviral drugs (ARVs), 16 million are still waiting for hypothetical treatment (The Economist, 2011). Generally speaking, such debates on the distribution of aid confirm – if confirmation were needed – that it is allocated based on various historical, political, economic, commercial, diplomatic and security criteria which go some way beyond a simple analysis of healthcare needs (Murray et al., 2011).

2.3. 'Unstructured pluralism'

The significant growth in funds set up to provide health aid has been inextricably linked to the increased number of actors in the field of healthcare, which have brought about a rapid and profound transformation of the sector. Foundations, alliances, fundraising vehicles, public–private partnerships, coordination mechanisms – over 90 new bodies had been set up by 2007 (DFID, 2007). In part, these actors have emerged in response to the difficulties that traditional organisations were experiencing in tackling alone the new challenges posed by global health. They brought new dynamics to the equation by using methods from the private sector (Buse and Harmer, 2007), by mobilising resources to focus on specific, quantifiable objectives, by concentrating on specific diseases or the development of particular drugs and equipment (e.g. diagnoses, vaccines), or by joining forces with new partners.

Of the actors emerging in the early 2000s, the GFATM and the Global Alliance for Vaccines and Immunisation (GAVI) were the first to benefit from the increase in available funding (Ravishankar et al., 2009), alongside the bilateral programmes which continued to grow. Although United Nations (UN) agencies have continued to receive public funds at a more or less constant rate, they have been largely excluded from the windfall triggered by the growth in funding, thus confirming the shift in power away from the traditional institutions. Non-governmental entities have become the key channels for aid (IHME, 2010). Gradually, an extremely complex, even tangled, network of organisations has developed without a natural hub, in which certain partnerships are themselves on the governing bodies of other institutions. In a context such as this, it can be difficult to pinpoint who makes the decisions and who is accountable to whom (Walt and Buse, 2000). It seems as though healthcare policy and related decisions have gradually ceased to be the sole prerogative of the public and international institutions that had hitherto held responsibility or the mandate for them. Within a decade, governance of global health issues has swung from a Westphalian to a post-Westphalian context, where not only state but also non-state actors contribute towards shaping the international response to health issues (Fidler, 2007).

3. New actors and questions of governance

3.1. The increased power of private donors

With public–private partnerships having become one of the dominant factors influencing global health, it is worth examining their governance in more detail, in particular the make-up of their executive boards. In 2006, with 23 per cent of seats, private enterprises were holding more seats than governments and international organisations together, a particularly significant presence in view of their meagre financial contributions (Figure 5.3) (Buse and Harmer, 2007; GHW, 2008). The confirmation of the partnership as the dominant model thus seems to have contributed to a weakening in public accountability while at the same time giving the private sector a chance to assert its influence.

Figure 5.3 – Makeup of the governing bodies of 23 public–private partnerships, 2006 (in percentage of seats)

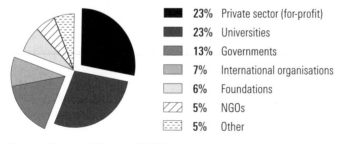

23%	Private sector (for-profit)
23%	Universities
13%	Governments
7%	International organisations
6%	Foundations
5%	NGOs
5%	Other

Source: Buse and Harmer (2007).

Although the involvement of the multinationals, including the major pharmaceutical laboratories, is by no means a new phenomenon, it has certainly evolved over the past ten years. As their commercial model has become less profitable (with research pipelines dried up and traditional markets saturated), the big pharmaceutical companies have turned their attention to low- and medium-income countries. They have gradually come to see partnerships as an attractive proposition, as they have been for generic producers for many years, offering as they do the opportunity for a company to establish itself in new markets at limited commercial risk yet with the promise of significant profits. Nobody would argue that the private sector cannot play a positive and central role in partnerships, as has been shown, for instance, by the development by the Drugs for Neglected Diseases Initiative (DNDI) and Sanofi-Aventis of ASAQ, an anti-malarial drug that is not patented, allowing southern hemisphere countries to market it at cost price. However, in terms of decision-making, industry's strong presence on partnerships' governing bodies is the subject of debate, with certain observers highlighting the inadequacy of the mechanisms in place to deal with conflicts of interest, the weakness of the selection process for private partners (Buse and Harmer, 2007), and the adoption of what have been criticised as pro-industry approaches that, in helping to tip the balance in favour of the private sector (GHW, 2008; Richter, 2004), are not making the best possible use of taxpayers' or donors' money (Kamal Yanni and Berman, 2011).

3.2. What should be the role for southern hemisphere countries?

Just as striking as the over-representation of for-profit actors from the private sector, the under-representation of southern hemisphere countries (barely 17 per cent of seats) raises questions about the extent to which the interests of the countries and populations directly affected are taken into consideration. Indeed, there is a risk that the decisions taken that will influence the situation beyond national borders will have very little or nothing at all to do with those that they will affect (Buse and Harmer, 2007). Nevertheless, this situation is changing. For instance, a number of seats on the executive board of UNITAID are reserved for representatives of southern hemisphere countries and of the populations affected. These efforts are both laudable and crucial, even if they often fail to do enough to counteract an imbalance of power that can be found on platforms such as these, which are frequently still dominated by the northern hemisphere (Martens, 2007).

In this context, it is worth noting the remarkable progress made by the GFATM, which, in the space of a decade, has demonstrated that it is possible to provide aid efficiently and transparently by devolving decision-making to the recipient countries and by allowing civil society to help further define the policies chosen via an apparatus of national coordination. Thus the GFATM finances programmes developed by the countries themselves and evaluated by an independent panel of experts. Representatives of civil society have proved to be essential for ensuring that the interests of the patients, including the most marginal, are taken into consideration when national response plans are formulated. This is important, as it shows that it is possible to turn an aid relationship into a true cooperation geared towards giving a voice to the people affected and enabling those responsible to implement a healthcare policy that they believe will be best suited to meeting their country's needs.

3.3. Private foundations and the special case of the Gates Foundation

It is also worth examining the increasing power of the private foundations, credited with having 'primed the pump' for global healthcare partnerships

(Buse and Harmer, 2007). Although the major family foundations have shaped the philanthropic and social landscape for many years, it is now the case that both the volume of their contributions and their funding policies are having a profound and transformative influence on global health (McCoy et al., 2009). This is particularly the case with the BMGF, which alone has contributed as much to the field of healthcare as all other US foundations put together. 'All the key contributors to global health have an association with the Gates foundation through some sort of funding arrangement', wrote McCoy et al. in 2009 (McCoy et al., 2009). And the picture is perhaps even more overwhelming than that: the foundation is the second largest contributor in the world to development aid for healthcare, the second most important donor to the World Health Organization (WHO) (2010b), and a founder of and donor to a number of product development partnerships. It supports major universities (Harvard, Columbia, Imperial College, etc.), research institutions and think-tanks, and provides major funding for journalists and media companies – such as PBS NewsHour, NPR, IPR and ABC – to cover healthcare issues (Doughton and Heim, 2011). The BMGF also has a seat on most public–private partnerships' executive boards and is a member of the self-constituted 'H8' group of world health leaders. The speeches by Bill Gates to the International AIDS Conference in Vienna in 2010 and the World Health Assembly in 2011, in which he outlined to the member states the path to follow and the priorities in terms of funding, only serve to remove any lingering doubts over the Microsoft founder's leading role in global health.

Nobody would dispute the fact that the BMGF has injected impetus and new and essential resources into the field of healthcare and has already achieved some major results in terms of the distribution of vaccines, maternal and child health, and research into neglected diseases (The Lancet, 2009). However, this dominance is not without its knock-on effects. Back in 2008, Dr Arata Kochi, former head of the WHO's Global Malaria Programme, alerted his superiors to research teams' growing dependence on the foundation's funding and the difficulty in obtaining critical independent reviews of research projects, also bemoaning the fact that the BMGF's dominance was stifling innovation and creativity in the scientific community (McNeil, 2008). Observers also challenged the suitability of the foundation's medical priorities, particularly in the field of poliomyelitis (McNeil, 2011), and cast doubt on approaches based essentially on technological and scientific solutions at the expense of a more global perspective that would, in particular, take account of socio-economic determinants of healthcare (Birn, 2005; McCoy et al., 2009).

Even if the BMGF has become a *de facto* decision-maker in terms of healthcare policy, it is under no obligation either to open up the decision-making process to those likely to be directly affected, or to put in place a system of accountability. Like any US foundation, it is entitled to spend its money as it sees fit within the bounds of the law. Not being answerable to an electorate as governments tend to be, private foundations operate outside traditional democratic boundaries and cannot therefore be influenced in the same way as elected representatives (Stuckler et al., 2011). As Bill Gates himself observed, 'Foundations are unusual because they don't have to worry about being voted out at the next election or board meeting' (Gates, 2009, 16). In this context, more inclusive and clearer decision-making processes would certainly help assuage the fears of those worried about the institution's lack of transparency and accountability. They would also allow the institution to respond to criticisms of the suitability and the legitimacy of a philanthropic system that supposes that 'private-sector managers are better than the government at managing public funds. [...] Is it really their place to decide on the key public health issues across the world?' wondered the Canadian tax expert Brigitte Alepin recently (Fay, 2011). Even if it is true that exempting private donations from tax results in the transfer of some of the tax revenue and social responsibility to the non-state sector, it must nevertheless be borne in mind that health aid given by non-profit private organisations often serves to make up for the shortcomings of the public authorities in the matter. For instance, it allows help to be given to marginalised or criminalised groups of people who often cannot access public services for fear of discrimination or harassment, or for reasons of confidentiality, as the example of drug users in Kyrgyzstan and Ukraine recently showed (Spicer et al., 2011).

4. Has global healthcare lost its way?

4.1. Erosion of the WHO's authority

In the new fragmented landscape of global health, the role of the WHO is coming under intense scrutiny. In accordance with its mandate, the organisation continues to establish the standards and directives that form the basis for healthcare policies at national and international level, and remains a vital platform for negotiating international agreements between its 193 member states. In certain areas, such as the control of epidemics, it has even been given greater powers. Nevertheless, the erosion of the organisation's authority and of its crisis management capabilities seems to have increased, as the recent cholera epidemic in Haiti demonstrated (Chow, 2010).

Some of the reasons behind this weakening are attributable to the agency's growing dependence on voluntary contributions (Figure 5.4),[2] which now make up 80 per cent of its total budget (compared with 20 per cent in 1970). Unlike regular contributions, voluntary contributions are primarily assigned to specific projects, the nature of which is determined by the donor.

Although these contributions have helped keep the WHO afloat, they do have problematic knock-on effects. They give rise to what can sometimes be a damaging level of competition between agency departments (GHW, 2008) and can fluctuate significantly from one budget period to the next – the fall of over 10 per cent in 2011 is a painful reminder of this (AFP, 2011). But, more worryingly still, they have also begun to deprive the WHO of the financial decision-making tools which are vital if it is to meet its strategic goals, allowing donors' short-term views and interests to take the place of the organisation's own shared vision, which it has negotiated and which is often more long-term in nature. Internal discussions at the WHO reflect these concerns: '[T]he current situation in which 80% of WHO's income relies on voluntary donor contributions [...] is not sustainable. In the absence of change, greater alignment

---

2   These can come from governments, United Nations (UN) agencies, foundations, non-governmental organisations or private companies.

Figure 5.4 – Change in regular and voluntary contributions to the WHO, 1990–2008 (US$ million constant 2008)

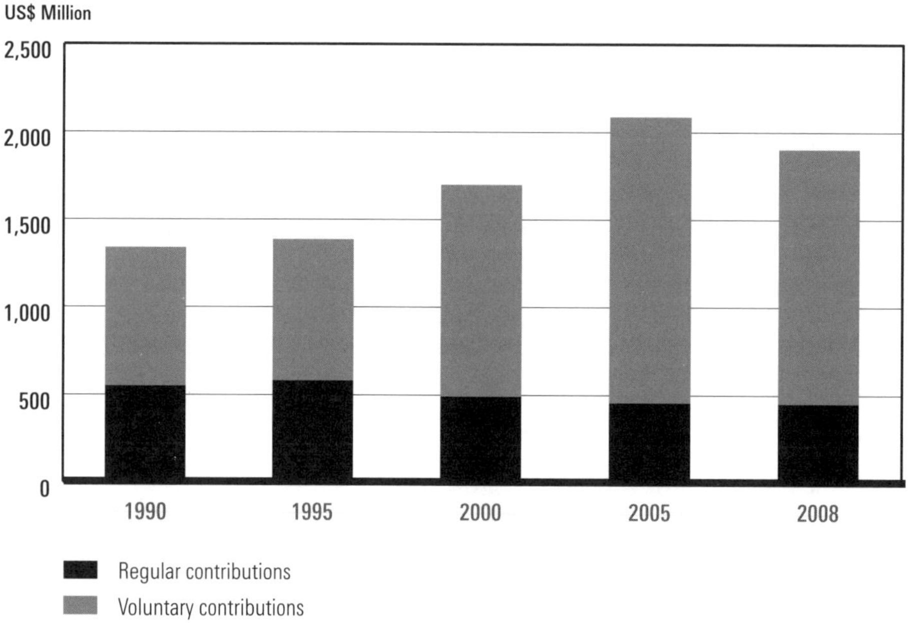

US$ Million

Regular contributions

Voluntary contributions

Source: IHME (2010).

with agreed priorities will be unattainable' (WHO, 2010a). Studies have already illustrated the distortions that this situation has created. For instance, 87 per cent of the agency's resources are allocated to infectious diseases, whether or not mortality in the regions receiving aid is primarily due to such illnesses (Stuckler et al., 2008). Even though discussions on funding are under way as part of WHO reform, there is as yet nothing to suggest that governments will be put to the test or that the suggestions made will bring about a fundamental change in the situation.

4.2. Is the WHO at risk of losing its independence?

The growing influence of the for-profit private sector on the WHO's decisions and policies is also fuelling regular debate. In particular, the organisation's groups of experts seem to present a fertile breeding ground for collusion. In December 2009, for instance, Wikileaks revealed that the International Federation of Pharmaceutical Manufacturers & Associations (IFPMA) had been able to comment on a confidential draft report by a working group on innovative methods of financing for research and development (KEI, 2009). At the 63rd World Health Assembly in May 2010, India and Latin America were highly critical of the experts' summary report, accusing them of having presented conclusions that were excessively favourable to the views of the major pharmaceutical companies (Benkimoun, 2011) and rejecting the majority of innovative measures that questioned certain aspects of the current intellectual property system. The establishment of a new group of experts including Paul Herrling, head of research at Novartis and author of one of the three proposals retained by the previous group of experts (Duparc, 2011a), only serves to heighten the concerns shared by civil society with regard to the problem of conflicts of interest within the WHO (HAI, 2011). With this in mind, the possibility of setting up a 'global health forum' which could 'help influence the WHO's decisions and plans of action' is pleasing some observers, who see it as an opportunity to inject a sense of coherence into a fragmented and unstructured landscape, but is perturbing others, who fear that it represents a significant expansion of industry's influence on the agency's healthcare policy (Duparc, 2011b). Even though Dr Margaret Chan, the WHO's Director-General, has given assurances that the reform currently under way will be conducted without 'compromising the WHO's independence', valid questions remain concerning the nature of the safeguards to be put in place to protect the public interest and prevent a *de facto* loss of the agency's precious independence, without which the impartiality of the organisation's judgments could reasonably be called into question.

5. Consequences of these transformations

5.1. What impact will they have on health aid?

Over the past 15 years, development aid for healthcare and the new actors have made a vital contribution to the expansion of activities and services in a wide range of fields. In September 2010, the United States President's Emergency Plan for AIDS Relief (PEPFAR) estimated that it had provided ARVs to over 3.2 million people across the world (PEPFAR, 2011). The GFATM (2011), for its part, reported that its actions had saved 6.5 million lives between 2002 and 2010. With courses of treatment, the distribution of treated mosquito nets and extensive vaccination campaigns, these actors have pushed the boundaries of what had generally been considered possible (Balabanova et al., 2010). At the same time, product development partnerships have given new impetus to research and development in fields hitherto neglected by industry due to the lack of viable markets. Similarly, the DNDI has managed within its barely eight years of existence to produce two new anti-malarials and the first improved treatment for trypanosomiasis in 25 years.

As impressive as they are, these results do not lead to any definitive conclusions regarding the impact of aid. There are many obstacles standing in the way of producing consolidated results, such as varying calculation methods, fragmentary data and the documented risk of the beneficiaries of aid being counted double by the providers (particularly in the field of AIDS). It must also not be forgotten that aid in the healthcare sector, sizeable as it may be, only represents a portion of spending on healthcare, alongside national contributions and household expenditure. Therefore, even though billions of dollars have been invested collectively, with the exception of certain vertical programmes it is difficult to precisely determine which part of the results is attributable to aid and which intervention measures in the field of healthcare or other areas (housing, sanitation, etc.) have contributed to these results. Furthermore, despite undoubtedly positive trends, the picture remains mixed. Although global average life expectancy continues to rise, it has fallen in sub-Saharan

Africa as a result of the devastating impact of the AIDS epidemic (GHW, 2008); and although there has been a general fall in infant mortality rates, over 7 million children will die before the age of five in 2011, with only a few countries on course to meet the MDGs in this area (IHME, 2010).

5.2. Access to drugs – time to rejoin the battle?

The expansion of the services mentioned above would not have been possible without the launch of cheap drugs onto the market. In 2000, the competition created by the introduction of generic drugs saw the price of ARVs plummet by 90 per cent in the space of a few months. This success is due to the sustained mobilisation of activists, the role played by the companies producing generic drugs and the leadership shown by a number of southern hemisphere countries, particularly Brazil, Thailand and South Africa. Today, however, the situation is quite different. Countries that produce generic drugs are now subject to the obligations arising from their membership of the World Trade Organization (WTO), which include in particular the requirement to obtain patents for drugs (India was thus forced to amend its law on intellectual property in 2005). Whereas in the past they had been able to produce copies of brand-name drugs, generic producers are now required to wait 20 years before being able to copy new medicines. With the lack of competition, there is a high risk that innovative treatments which are less toxic and more effective – but patented – will remain beyond the reach of patients in the southern hemisphere. Although the exceptions provided for in the agreements on the protection of intellectual property allow countries to use certain tools to improve access (mandatory licence, parallel import, etc.), the pressure applied by the countries of the northern hemisphere to restrict the use of these options and the threats of commercial repercussions are huge, as Thailand witnessed in 2007. Furthermore, the countries of the northern hemisphere are relentless in their attempts to impose ever stricter regulations (particularly via bilateral and multilateral treaties), which is threatening the ability of the southern hemisphere countries to produce or import the generic drugs that they need. Thus what we are witnessing today is nothing less than a challenge to the balance fiercely negotiated at Doha between the interests of patent holders on the one hand and those of patients on the other.

5.3. Health systems: still room for improvement

The fragmentation of the health landscape has not been without its problems for the recipient countries. Various studies have illustrated the problems associated with the explosion in the number of parties involved, including increased transaction costs (Balabanova et al., 2010) and the increased pressure on national institutions which, by definition, have limited capacity. The example of Tanzania, for instance, would raise a smile if it were not true: when the number of donors shot up in the late 1990s, the government found itself having to produce 2400 reports every quarter, and this with virtually no change in the amount of aid it received (Birdsall and Deese, 2004). In addition to the sheer number of parties involved, which is a problem in itself, the vertical approaches adopted by some within the sphere of influence of the new actors and certain bilateral donors, and their systemic impact, have sparked one of the fiercest debates of the past ten years. Although these programmes have demonstrated their effectiveness in improving access to healthcare for certain diseases, they have also encountered several obstacles, which have become more significant as the response has developed: not enough health workers, shortcomings in information systems, weaknesses in supply chains, etc. Various studies have concluded that, overall, vertical programmes have had 'primarily positive, [but also] certain negative' effects on health systems (World Health Organization Maiximizing Positive Synergies Collaborative Group, 2009). For instance, HIV/AIDS programmes have helped broaden access to peri-natal services in Haiti and improve the expertise of health workers in Rwanda (Walton et al., 2004; Price et al., 2009). Other observers, on the other hand, have highlighted the distortion of national healthcare budgets caused by vertical programmes (Sridhar and Batniji, 2008); the fact that funded activities and the actors charged with setting them up have swallowed human resources (Shiffman, 2008; Hanefeld and Musheke, 2009); the partial displacement of domestic spending on healthcare (IHME, 2010); and the ploys used to get quick results at the expense of trying to address more systemic problems. Aware of these changing realities, the actors have gradually evolved. For instance, the GFATM estimated in 2009 that 35 per cent of its funds made a direct contribution towards bolstering systems. It is now generally acknowledged that the vertical/horizontal distinction is outdated and that both approaches have a role to play, provided that they are utilised in a way that enables synergies to be exploited to the full and capabilities to be strengthened.

In addition to the obstacles mentioned above, there are the problems associated with how development aid operates in general: commitment of donor countries to annual appropriation cycles which impair countries' ability to draw up long-term plans; the unpredictable nature of the funding available; the small sums allocated to sector-specific support; and the fact that a large part of the funding is fed back into the northern hemisphere in the form of orders, consultants or staff costs (Delaunay, 2011).

Differences of opinion and clashes of ideology between donor countries are also causing tensions for the recipients (Balabanova et al., 2010), with the donors influenced by their own national tradition, which often dictates their preferences in terms of healthcare policy. They can have different, even contradictory ideas about the role of the markets, private actors and public institutions or the significance of intellectual property (CHW, 2008), as has been demonstrated by the heated discussions on insurance schemes or the issue of mandatory licences. It should also be borne in mind that governments frequently find their autonomy to formulate healthcare policies restricted as a result of macro-economic parameters (e.g. the International Monetary Fund (IMF)) and of commercial agreements, which are often negotiated with no consideration for their potential impact on healthcare. From Paris to Accra, donor countries have repeatedly made commitments to try to rectify the deficiencies in the aid system. Although noticeable progress may have been made, observers have nevertheless expressed regret that alignment, coordination and harmonisation efforts have been too slow and that the implementation of reforms has been far from ideal at a national level (ROA, 2010).

6. Conclusion

Over the past few years, the issue of health has succeeded in mobilising new resources and new energies. The requirements have been huge and a response has not just been due but has been vital for millions of patients. This global awareness of health issues and the mobilisation that it has triggered can only be applauded, even if it still remains inadequate in view of the great need. The explosion in the number of actors involved has not just served to increase the critical mass of the organisations involved in the healthcare sector, it has also brought about a sea change in the architecture of global health. The new actors on the healthcare stage have claimed a significant share of the additional public and private resources available and have become the driving force in this new paradigm at the expense of the traditional institutions, which have gradually lost their hegemony and have seen their position of power weaken.

The private for-profit sector has been given a seat at the negotiating tables, gradually establishing itself as one of the key players in this new reality alongside the foundations, whose contributions are continuing to influence the agenda to an ever greater extent. This transformation in the field of healthcare has not been without its problems or tensions for the beneficiary countries. Although substantial efforts have been made, decisions are still taken with insufficient consideration for those that they are likely to affect and their representatives.

With this in mind, it is worth exploring a number of ways in which the benefits of this rich diversity can be maximised. First, the countries of the southern hemisphere and the representatives of civil society urgently need to be involved more closely in the decisions that affect them. This does not mean simply giving them token representation on decision-making bodies, but genuinely transforming the aid relationship so that it enables those responsible to implement a health policy that they believe will be best suited to meeting their country's needs.

As part of the coordination programmes for the GFATM in Ukraine or in the public forums of Umgungundlovu in South Africa, civil society is playing an increasingly important role in demanding more robust mechanisms in terms of consultation and accountability. We can only call for this form of commitment to be strengthened in order to help ensure that the policies of the actors involved best reflect the needs and aspirations of the people affected. Against an increasingly fragmentary background, it also seems more important than ever to bolster the guiding and normative role of the WHO, an institution uniquely placed to offer independent technical advice and safeguard the public interest. This can only be achieved through a concerted effort by member states to ensure that the organisation's operating budget is sufficient to allow it to perform this role.

Furthermore, in a situation where health issues cannot be tackled in an isolated manner, greater coordination between sectors is desirable, especially to ensure that the efforts made in the field of healthcare are not thwarted by approaches adopted in other areas (such as commerce). Finally, it is worth taking the time to investigate in more detail the risks and benefits associated with the public–private partnership model currently dominating the field of healthcare. Although the position now occupied by the private for-profit sector cannot be ignored, it is necessary to better understand the interests that it represents, to explore in greater detail the formal and informal influence that it exerts on the various actors, and to establish sound mechanisms for managing conflicts and safeguarding the public interest and that of patients.

REFERENCES

AFP (Agence France Presse) (2011) *L'OMS ouvre sa 64ᵉ Assemblée sur fond d'austérité budgétaire et de réforme*, 5 May.

AidWatch (2011) *Between Austerity and Political Will: EU MS ODA Budgets in 2011*, February.

Balabanova, D., M. McKee, A. Mills, G. Walt and A. Haines (2010) 'What Can Global Health Institutions Do to Help Strengthen Health Systems in Low Income Countries?', *Health Research Policy and Systems*, 8(22), DOI 10.1186/1478-4505-8-22.

Benkimoun, P. (2011) 'La complaisance à l'égard d'un laboratoire peut miner une institution', *Le Monde*, 23–24 January.

Birdsall, N. and B. Deese (2004) 'Hard Currency: Unilateralism Doesn't Work for Foreign Aid Either', *Washington Monthly*, March, http://www.washingtonmonthly.com/features/2004/0403.birdsall.html (accessed on 22 April 2011).

Birn, A.E. (2005) 'Gates's Grandest Challenge: Transcending Technology as Public Health Ideology', *The Lancet*, 366(9484), pp. 514–19, DOI 10.1016/S0140-6736(05)66479-3.

Buse, K. and A.M. Harmer (2007) 'Seven Habits of Highly Effective Global Public-Private Health Partnerships: Practice and Potential', *Social Science and Medicine*, 64, pp. 259–71.

Chow, J.C. (2010) 'Is the WHO Becoming Irrelevant?', *Foreign Policy*, 8 December.

Delaunay, S. (2011) *Etats des lieux de l'infection VIH en république de Centrafrique et piste de réflexion pour MSF*, MSF internal report, April.

De Torrenté, N. (2009) *The Global Health Landscape: Mapping Trends and Developments of Relevance to MSF*, MSF internal report, June.

DFID (Department for International Development) (2007) *The International Health Partnership Launched Today*, 5 September, http://webarchive.nationalarchives.gov.uk/+/http://www.dfid.gov.uk/Media-Room/ News-Stories/2007/The-International-Health-Partnership-Launched-Today/ (accessed on 15 April 2011).

Doughton, S. and K. Heim (2011) 'Does Gates Funding of Media Taint Objectivity?', *The Seattle Times*, 19 February, http://seattletimes.nwsource.com/html/localnews/2014280379_gatesmedia.html (accessed on 5 May 2011).

Duparc, A. (2011a) 'L'OMS face à un nouveau conflit d'intérêts', *Le Monde*, 23–24 January.

Duparc, A. (2011b) 'L'Organisation mondiale de la santé, une agence de plus en plus privée', *Le Monde*, 19 May.

England, R. (2007) 'Head to Head: Are We Spending too much on HIV?', *British Medical Journal*, 334(7589), DOI 10.1136/bmj.39113.402361.94.

Fay, S. (2011) 'Les "philanthropes" confisquent l'action publique', *Le Nouvel Observateur*, 31 March–6 April.

Fidler, D.P. (2007) 'Architecture amidst Anarchy: Global Health's Quest for Governance', *Global Health Governance*, 1(1), http://www.ghgj.org/Fidler_Architecture.pdf (accessed on 4 October 2011).

Gates, B. (2009) *2009 Annual Letter from Bill Gates: The Role of Foundations* (Seattle: Bill&Melinda Gates Foundation), http://www.gatesfoundation.org/annual-letter/2009/Pages/2009-role-of-foundations.aspx (accessed on 4 October 2011).

GFATM (Global Fund to Fight AIDS, Tuberculosis and Malaria) (2011) *Making a Difference. Global Fund Results Report 2011* (Geneva: GFATM).

GHW (Global Health Watch) (2008) *Global Health Watch 2: An Alternative World Health Report* (London and New York: Zed Books).

HAI (Health Action International) (2011) *Statement on Conflicts of Interest Delivered at WHA on behalf of HAI, Berne Declaration, KEI, TWN, PHM, IBFAN*, 20 May, http://haieuropestaffblog.blogspot.com/2011/05/statement-on-conflicts-if-interest.html (accessed on 23 May 2011).

Hanefeld, J. and M. Musheke (2009) 'What Impact Do Global Health Initiatives Have on Human Resources for Antiretroviral Roll-Out? A Qualitative Policy Analysis of Implementation Processes in Zambia', *Human Resources for Health*, 7(8), DOI 10.1186/1478-4491-7-8.

HLTF (High Level Task Force on Innovative Financing for Heath Systems) (2009) *Working Group 1: Constraints to Scaling Up and Costs*, final draft, 5 June.

IHME (Institute for Health Metrics and Evaluation) (2010) *Financing Global Health 2010: Development Assistance and Country Spending in Economic Uncertainty* (Seattle, WA: IHME).

Kamal-Yanni, M. and D. Berman (2011) *Erring on the Side of the Poor and not Profits*, http://www.msfaccess.org/main/vaccines/erring-on-the-side-of-the-poor-and-not-profits, 6 July (accessed on 12 July 2011).

KEI (Knowledge Ecology International) (2009) *Wikileaks Documents Related to the WHO EWG*, 9 December, http://keionline.org/node/ (accessed on 5 May 2011).

Martens, J. (2007) *Multistakeholder Partnerships: Future Model of Multilateralism?* Dialogue on Globalization no. 29, occasional paper (Berlin: Friedrich-Ebert-Stiftung).

McCoy, D., G. Kembhavi, J. Patel and A. Luintel (2009) 'The Bill and Melinda Gates Foundation's Grant-Making Programme for Global Health', *The Lancet*, 373(9675), pp. 1645–53, DOI 10.1016/S0140-6736(09)60571-7.

McDonald, R. and R. Horton (2009) 'Trade and Health: Time for the Health Sector to Get Involved', *The Lancet*, 373(9660), pp. 273–4, DOI 10.1016/S0140-6736(08)61773-0.

McNeil, D. (2008) 'Gates Foundation's Influence Criticized', *The New York Times*, 16 February.

McNeil, D. (2011) 'Gates Calls for a Final Push to Eradicate Polio', *The New York Times*, 31 January.

Murray, C., B. Anderson, R. Burstein, K. Leach-Kemon, M. Schneider, A. Tardif and R. Zhang (2011) 'Development Assistance for Health: Trends and Prospects', *The Lancet*, 378(9785), pp. 8–10, DOI 10.1016/S0140-6736(10)62356-2.

PEPFAR (United States President's Emergency Plan for AIDS Relief) (2011) *PEPFAR Funding: Investments That Save Lives and Promote Security*, http://www.pepfar.gov/press/80064.htm (accessed on 22 April 2011).

Price, J.E., J.A. Leslie, M. Welsh and A. Binagwaho (2009) 'Integrating HIV Clinical Services into Primary Healthcare in Rwanda: A Measure of Quantitative Effects', *AIDS Care*, 21(5), pp. 608–14.

Ravishankar, N., P. Gubbins, R.J. Cooley, K. Leach-Kemon, C.M. Michaud, D.T. Jamison and C.J.L. Murray (2009) 'Financing of Global Health: Tracking Development Assistance for Health from 1990 to 2007', *The Lancet*, 373(9681), pp. 2113–24, DOI 10.1016/S0140-6736(09)60881-3.

Richter, J. (2004) *Public-Private Partnerships and International Health Policy-Making: How Can Public Interests Be Safeguarded?* (Helsinki: Ministry for Foreign Affairs of Finland, Development Policy Information Unit).

ROA (Reality of Aid) (2010) *Aid and Development Effectiveness: Towards Human Rights, Social Justice and Democracy* (Quezon City: IBON Books), http://www.realityofaid.org/roa-reports/index/secid/375/part/1 (accessed on 22 April 2011).

Shiffman, J. (2008) 'Has Donor Prioritization of HIV/AIDS Displaced Aid for Other Health Issues?', *Health Policy and Planning*, 23(2), pp. 95–100, DOI 10.1093/heapol/czm045.

Spicer, N., D. Bogdan, R. Brugha, A. Harmer, G. Murzalieva and T. Semigina (2011) '"It's Risky to Walk in the City with Syringes": Understanding Access to HIV/AIDS Services for Injecting Drug Users in the Former Soviet Union Countries of Ukraine and Kyrgyzstan', *Globalization and Health*, 7(22), DOI 10.1186/1744-8603-7-22.

Sridhar, D. and R. Batniji (2008) 'Misfinancing Global Health: A Case for Transparency in Disbursements and Decision-Making', *The Lancet*, 372(9644), pp. 1185–91, DOI 10.1016/S0140-6736(08)61485-3.

Stuckler, D., S. Basu and M. McKee (2011) 'Global Health Philanthropy and Institutional Relationships: How Should Conflicts of Interest Be Addressed?', *PLoS Med*, 8(4), DOI 10.1371/journal.pmed.1001020.

Stuckler, D., L. King, H. Robinson and M. McKee (2008) 'WHO's Budgetary Allocations and Burden of Disease: A Comparative Analysis', *The Lancet*, 372(9649), pp. 1563–9, DOI 10.1016/S0140-6736(08)61656-6.

The Economist (2011) 'The End of AIDS? Fighting Transmission', *The Economist*, video, 3 June, http://www.economist.com/blogs/multimedia/2011/06/end-aids (accessed on 10 June 2011).

The Lancet (2009) 'What Has the Gates Foundation Done for Global Health?', *The Lancet*, 373(9675), p. 1577, DOI 10.1016/S0140-6736(09)60885-0.

UNIS (United Nations Information Service) (2000) *Security Council Holds Debate on Impact of AIDS on Peace and Security in Africa*, press release, 11 January, UNIS/SC/1173 (New York: United Nations).

Walt, G. and K. Buse (2000) 'Partnership and Fragmentation in International Health: Threat or Opportunity?', *Tropical Medicine and International Health*, 5(7), pp. 467–71, DOI 10.1046/j.1365-3156.2000.00596.x.

Walton, D.A., P.E. Farmer, W. Lambert, F. Léandre, S.P. Koenig and J.S. Mukherjee (2004) 'Integrated HIV Prevention and Care Strengthens Primary Health Care: Lessons from Rural Haiti', *Journal of Public Health Policy*, 25(2), pp. 137–58.

WHO (World Health Organization) (2010a) *The Future of Financing for WHO*, report of an informal consultation convened by the Director-General, WHO/DGO/2010.1 (Geneva: WHO).

WHO (2010b) *Voluntary Contributions by Fund and by Donor for the Financial Period 2008–2009*, A63/INF.DOC./4 (Geneva: WHO).

World Health Organization Maximizing Positive Synergies Collaborative Group (2009) 'An Assessment of Interactions between Global Health Initiatives and Country Health Systems', *The Lancet*, 373(9681), pp. 2137–69, DOI 10.1016/S0140-6736(09)60919-3.

6

CHINA'S FOREIGN AID AND ITS ROLE IN THE INTERNATIONAL AID ARCHITECTURE

Meibo Huang, Peiqiang Ren

Abstract

China has long been an aid provider, although the recent and remarkable surge in China's foreign aid has important implications for the global aid architecture. It relies on aid principles that diverge in many ways from those of traditional Development Assistance Committee (DAC) donor countries, particularly in relation to non-interference, mutual benefit and non-conditionality. China's foreign aid also relies on a mixing of economic cooperation, trade and investment deals. While several Western scholars have examined the Chinese development cooperation system, few voices from China have been heard in European and North American journals and media. This chapter aims to offer a Chinese perspective on the evolution of China's foreign aid. It focuses on the aid principles that have thus far informed Chinese development assistance, highlighting the successful outcomes achieved so far in Africa and South-East Asia. The chapter also addresses the main shortcomings of the Chinese approach, by recommending the improvement of institutional transparency, and strengthening of dialogue with DAC donors, all with a view towards learning from past experiences and exchanging best practices.

1. Introduction

In recent years, China's foreign aid has rapidly developed, and correspondingly had an important impact on the international aid architecture. However, as practical needs govern China's aid – and its development finance generally diverges from Organisation for Economic Cooperation and Development (OECD) standards in terms of norms, definitions, principles, etc. – people outside the country have few tools to understand China's foreign aid. This chapter aims to fill this gap by explaining and analysing the Chinese system of development cooperation from a Chinese perspective. The chapter begins by introducing the history of China's foreign aid, and then proceeds to provide data about its volume and channels of distribution. It goes on to present the main rationales behind China's development cooperation, describing the principles informing it, with the aim of evaluating the extent to which they differ from those of the traditional Development Assistance Committee (DAC) donors. Finally, it discusses recent trends in the management of China's foreign aid.

2. History of China's foreign aid and its evolution

China's foreign aid can be traced back to the early 1950s. Roughly, it can be divided into the following two phases: the period between the founding of the People's Republic of China (PRC) and the age of economic reform (1949–78), and the period after China's 'opening' to the world (since 1978).

From the 1950s to the 1970s, ideology was the most important factor influencing China's foreign aid policy. After the founding of the PRC, the country was under threat of military and economic blockade from the United States and, subsequently, the former Soviet Union. During this same period, the countries of the Third World were fighting for national independence. Following a sense of common historic destiny, China regarded the Third World as an important ally in an 'International United Front' against imperialism and colonialism (Burke et al., 2007). For this reason, it began to provide aid to other Third World countries and engaged in the ideological exportation of China's experience in construction of socialist society, regarding it as an important part of its commitment to proletarian internationalism (Li, 2008). The influence of this ideology was strongly felt in the 1960s and reached its peak between 1970 and 1975 (Zhu, 2001).

'The Eight Principles of China's Foreign Aid',[1] which were first put forward by Zhou Enlai during his visit to 14 Asian and African countries in 1964, are founded upon the core principles of equality, mutual benefit and non-conditionality. Since that time, they served as the basic framework governing China's foreign aid to other developing countries.

Most of China's development assistance during this period was granted in the form of cash, goods and personnel. The balance was made up of low- or non-interest loans with long-term repayment conditions. Before 1979, grants made up 70 to 80 per cent of China's total aid. By 1976, in terms of the sheer number of contracts, construction projects accounted for 67 per cent of China's economic aid programmes. In 1972, a time when China's total gross national product (GNP) was only 28 per cent of that of the Soviet Union, China overtook the Soviet Union as an economic aid donor in total volume (Zhu, 2001). Aid in terms of overall financial expenditure and as a percentage of total GNP was very high, constituting a large burden on China's economy (see Table 6.1).

---

1   The Eight Principles are as follows: 1. China always bases itself on the principle of equality and mutual benefit in providing foreign aid; 2. China never attaches any conditions or asks for any privileges when providing aid; 3. China helps lighten the burden of recipient countries as much as possible; 4. China aims at helping recipient countries to gradually achieve self-reliance and independent development; 5. China strives to develop aid projects that require low levels of investment but yield rapid results; 6. China provides the best-quality equipments and materials of its own manufacture; 7. In providing technical assistance, China shall see to it that the personnel of the recipient country fully master such techniques; 8. The Chinese experts are not allowed to make any special demands or enjoy any special amenities.

Table 6.1 – Total amount of China's foreign aid, 1950–73 (in US$ million*)

Year	Total amount of foreign aid	Total GNP	Foreign aid's percentage of GNP
1950–73	16,175	1,627,844	0.99

* CNY converted into US$ at the 1973 exchange rate (CNY2.0202 to US$1)
Source: Li (2009).

After the adoption of the policies of 'Economic Reform and Opening-up' in 1978, China's focus shifted towards domestic economic growth, with corresponding adjustments regarding its foreign aid away from an ideologically-based policy towards one that prioritised economic restructuring (Kjollesdal and Welle-Strand, 2010). In the 1980s, China amended its basic principles of foreign aid to become: 'Equality and Mutual Benefit, Effect Orientation, Diversity in Forms, and Common Development' (Beijing Review, 1983). On the one hand, the Chinese government realised that aid should be provided in accordance with China's economic capacity (Brautigam, 2009a, 41). As such, from 1983 on, the volume of Chinese foreign aid began to decrease – though in the 1990s, aid was expanded once again. On the other hand, China's foreign aid policies began to emphasise a 'win-win' cooperation principle focusing especially on economic collaboration with other developing countries. A large proportion of aid was linked to promoting exports and market access (Brautigam, 2009a, 52–3, 62–3). Trade between China and recipient countries developed quickly, and an increasing number of Chinese enterprises became involved in economic cooperation with developing countries.

From the 1980s on, particularly following the 1995 reform of foreign aid, China has decreased the share of its aid grants, and provided fewer interest-free loans, with an increase in concessional loans. China has been successful in applying a combination of official aid, as well as trade and investment, using government funds to leverage financing for, and investment in, developing countries from the Chinese private sector. This has expanded the scale of China's foreign aid and played an important role in promoting growth in recipient countries, thus raising their citizens' standard of living.

Capacity building in recipient countries has been an additional emphasis of aid policy since the 1990s. In order to build up self-development capacity, the Chinese government has paid great attention to training local technical personnel and other professionals in developing countries, a process furthered by the transfer of applicable technologies. By way of larger-scale training and government scholarship programmes, between 2007 and 2009 the Chinese government trained 16,000 technical African personnel in China (Editorial Board of the China Commerce Yearbook, 2010). Huawei, China's telecom giant, has established regional institutes in Angola, South Africa, Nigeria, Egypt, Tunisia and Kenya to teach local staff the skills needed to operate and maintain the company's wireless and broadband systems. These capacity-building efforts may perhaps be motivated by profit, rather than altruism, but they may ultimately provide a more sustainable form of support (Brautigam, 2010b).

3. Volumes and channels of distributions of China's foreign aid

After the 1990s, especially in the twenty-first century, following rapid economic growth and enhanced overall national strength, aid has become increasingly important within China's foreign policy. It should be particularly noted that since 2004, China's central government aid expenditure has grown at a yearly average rate of 18 per cent (see Table 6.2).

Table 6.2 – China's central government expenditure for external assistance, 2002–09 (in CNY and US$ million)

Year	Expenditure for foreign aid	
	CNY* million	US$ million
2002	5,003	603
2003	5,223	630
2004	6,069	731
2005	7,470	903
2006	8,237	1,033
2007	11,154	1,460
2008	12,559	1,769
2009	13,296	1,945

* Exchange rates are based on the rate at the end of each year from 2002 to 2009 recorded by the State Administration of Foreign Exchange, Statistics and Reports. The data only refers to China's central government aid expenditure, not including local government's.
Sources: derived from entries in 'Main items of budgetary expenditure of central government' table (State Statistical Bureau of the People's Republic of China, 2003–10).

China's aid is primarily conducted through bilateral channels. In order to most effectively meet the needs of developing countries, China conducts rigorous economic assessments to assess the feasibility of aid projects proposed by recipient countries before funding is granted (IOSC-PRC, 2011). In addition to its bilateral relationships, China also gives aid through multilateral institutions, though on a much smaller scale. The PRC is a member of the World Bank, the International Monetary Fund (IMF), the Asian Development Bank and the African Development Bank. It is also a long-standing member of United Nations (UN) organisations such as the United Nations Development Program (UNDP), the Food and Agriculture Organization (FAO), the United Nations World Food Program (WFP) and the World Health Organization (WHO).

With regard to the geographical distribution of the recipient countries, Asia and Africa – homes of the largest poverty-stricken populations in the world – have thus far received approximately 80 per cent of China's foreign aid. Correspondingly, in terms of income level, about two-thirds of Chinese aid goes to the least developed and low-income countries (see Figures 6.1 and 6.2) (IOSC-PRC, 2011).

Figure 6.1 – Geographical distributions of China's foreign aid, 1950–2009 (in percentage of total aid)

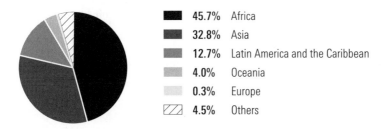

■ **45.7%**	Africa
■ **32.8%**	Asia
■ **12.7%**	Latin America and the Caribbean
■ **4.0%**	Oceania
■ **0.3%**	Europe
▨ **4.5%**	Others

Source: IOSC-PRC (2011).

Figure 6.2 – Distribution of China's foreign aid by income of recipient countries, 1950–2009 (in percentage of total aid)

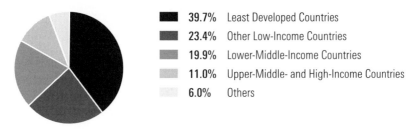

■ **39.7%**	Least Developed Countries
■ **23.4%**	Other Low-Income Countries
■ **19.9%**	Lower-Middle-Income Countries
■ **11.0%**	Upper-Middle- and High-Income Countries
■ **6.0%**	Others

Source: IOSC-PRC (2011).

Aid projects are oriented towards agriculture, industry, economic infrastructure, public facilities, education and medical healthcare. These projects are selected with a focus on improving recipient countries' industrial and agricultural productivity, laying a solid foundation for economic and social development, and improving basic education and healthcare. In recent years, coping with climate change has become a new area of China's aid (IOSC-PRC, 2011).

By the end of 2009, China had provided aid to 161 countries and more than 30 international and regional organisations, for a total volume of US$39 billion in the form of grants (16 billions), interest-free loans (12 billions) and concessional loans (11 billions) (Figure 6.3).

Grants are primarily used to help recipient countries to build hospitals, schools and low-cost houses; to support well digging or water supply facilities; and fund other medium and small-sized projects aimed at improving social welfare. In addition, grants finance human resource development cooperation, technical cooperation, the delivery of goods and materials, and emergency humanitarian aid. Interest-free loans chiefly target the construction of public facilities and launch projects to improve people's livelihood. They are generally granted to developing countries on relatively favourable terms. Concessional loans are targeted for large and medium-sized infrastructure projects (61 per cent are used to build transportation, communication and electricity infrastructure), or for delivering manufacturing plant, mechanical, electrical and other material and technical services. By the end of 2009, China had provided concessional loans to 76 foreign countries, supporting 325 projects, of which 142 have since been completed (IOSC-PRC, 2011).

Figure 6.3 – Chinese aid by type, 1950–2009 (in percentage and US$ billion*)

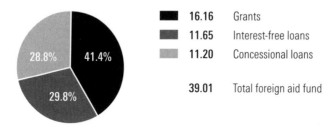

■ 16.16	Grants
■ 11.65	Interest-free loans
■ 11.20	Concessional loans
39.01	Total foreign aid fund

* Converted into US$ at the following rate: CNY6.5717 to US$1.
Source: IOSC-PRC (2011).

Figure 6.4 – Sectoral distribution of concessional loans from China, 1950–2009 (in percentage of total aid)

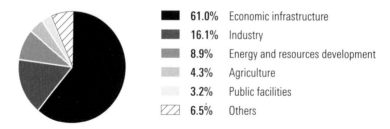

■ 61.0%	Economic infrastructure
■ 16.1%	Industry
■ 8.9%	Energy and resources development
4.3%	Agriculture
3.2%	Public facilities
▨ 6.5%	Others

Source: IOSC-PRC (2011).

4. Motivations structuring China's foreign aid policy

Foreign aid motivations fall into four categories, encompassing diplomatic (including political), economic, developmental and humanitarian rationales. Like many traditional DAC donors, China's foreign aid objectives are influenced by political considerations, strategic interest and the promotion of bilateral trade and investment (Lancaster, 2007; Johnson et al., 2008; Brautigam, 2009b).

Some analysts have stressed that China's rationales for giving aid to Africa were largely diplomatic: to forge friendship among 'non-aligned' nations and to compete with Taiwan for recognition. Similarly, it is argued, aid to Latin America aimed to isolate Taiwan and bolster China's diplomatic presence in the region, while China's aid activities in South-East Asia were meant to provide greater long-term diplomatic gains in comparison with relatively fewer short-term economic benefits (Lum et al., 2009). There is an extent to which these points make sense. Particularly prior to 1978, diplomacy and politics were important concerns of China's foreign aid. In a somewhat symbiotic relationship, China helped developing countries to win national independence and develop their economies, which in turn generated support throughout the developing world for the improvement of China's international status and maintenance of its territorial integrity. With the support of other developing countries, the PRC achieved its legal seat at the UN. It also gained substantial support from most developing countries on the issues of Taiwan, Tibet and, more recently, the accession to the World Trade Organization (WTO). Therefore, diplomatic concerns are indeed an important component of China's foreign aid.

Since the 1980s, to say nothing of the 1990s, however, economic motivations have become increasingly important in Chinese development cooperation for two primary reasons: resources and markets. Asian, African and Latin American countries have abundant natural resources and their domestic markets hold great potentials, access to each of which is an overriding concern influencing China's development (Huang and Lang, 2010). First, in order to maintain its rapid economic growth, China will need more resources in the future than its domestic stock can supply (Bosshard, 2007). In other words, demand exceeds supply. China regards the natural resources of South-East Asian, African and Latin American countries as a reliable guarantee for its sustainable development (Lum et al., 2009). Second, many developing countries show a high demand for textile, mechanical and electrical products. As a developing country, China can provide machinery and experience that are better suited for African societies than those from industrialised countries (Bosshard, 2007). Developing countries have thus become an important target of China's 'going out' strategy (Huang and Lang, 2010).

As declared in the recent White Paper on Foreign Aid, China's development cooperation policy places an overall emphasis on improving infrastructure, domestic resource exploration and training of local personnel in the recipient countries (IOSC-PRC, 2011).

Humanitarian aid has also been an area of greater emphasis since the late 1990s. As its overall national wealth has increased, China has provided substantial humanitarian assistance to countries suffering from war and natural disasters. From 2006 to 2010, the Chinese government supported foreign countries in coping with nearly 200 emergencies, including: emergency technical aid to South-East Asia for the prevention and treatment of bird flu; emergency aid in materials and financial assistance provided to Guinea-Bissau following a period of a locust infestation and cholera; aid to Ecuador to fight dengue fever; and additional assistance to Mexico to fight influenza A (H1N1). It also assisted Iran, Pakistan, Haiti, Chile and Japan following severe earthquakes. In 2009, China delivered CNY96 million in kind and US$17 million in cash to 27 countries around the globe (MOFCOM, 2010). In 2010, the total amount of emergency aid hit CNY480 million (MOFCOM, 2011). All this shows that China, while remaining committed to its own development, has also provided aid to the best of its ability to other developing countries experiencing economic difficulties, in fulfilment of its international obligations (IOSC-PRC, 2011).

5. Principles of China's foreign aid

As a developing country, China has a peculiar international political status, economic development challenges and unique diplomatic principles that distinguish the state from traditional DAC donors. China is the world's most populous country, with very low per capita income, uneven economic development and very limited access to basic public services. As domestic development remains an arduous and persistent task, China's foreign aid falls into the category of South–South Cooperation.

5.1. Western versus Chinese aid conditionality

The foundation of China's foreign aid is found in the 'Five Principles for Peaceful Coexistence',[2] presented by then-Premier Zhou Enlai at the Bandung Conference in 1955. These principles emphasise the centrality of mutual non-interference, equality, mutual benefit and South–South solidarity to Chinese foreign policy. These principles were then directly reflected in 'The Eight Principles of China's Foreign Aid'.[3]

Some Western scholars question the non-conditionality of China's foreign aid, on the assumption that recognition of Taiwan as an integral part of China is a political precondition for receiving Chinese aid (Weston et al., 2011). It is further argued that China imposes economic conditions on recipients by tying its aid to both market access for Chinese exports and the extraction of local natural resources (Chin and Frolic, 2007). The argument concerning Taiwan, however, is not confirmed by evidence. Every country in Africa, with the exception of Swaziland, has been a recipient of China's aid despite the fact that several countries, such as Chad, Burkina Faso and Gambia, have been inconsistent in their political attitudes towards Beijing and Taiwan (Brautigam, 2010a).

In terms of tied aid, according to the DAC country peer reviews, a majority of DAC members, to a greater or lesser extent, also tie their aid. Western donors always impose various conditions on recipient countries when providing aid (Cabello et al., 2008). For instance, DAC members generally believe that liberal economic reforms are the key to economic growth, and that good governance, human rights and democracy are the cornerstones of long-term sustainable development. Hence, to eradicate poverty, DAC states require developing countries to reform their economic and political systems according to these principles. However, in the 1980s, this practice came under fire, as the aid from most traditional donors clung to discredited conditionalities hampering the promotion of coordination and alignment (Woods, 2008). Since the 1990s, DAC members have emphasised the protection of human rights and democratic governance as important characteristics of recipient states, and worked to ensure their aid would bring about both political and socio-economic progress. Yet conditioned aid can never play a key role in stimulating the economy. In fact,

---

2   The 'Five Principles for Peaceful Coexistence' are as follows: mutual respect for territorial integrity and sovereignty; mutual non-aggression; non-interference in each other's internal affair; equality and mutual benefit; and peaceful coexistence.
3   See *Common Development Through Selfless Foreign Aid* (author's translation), http://yuanwaizhan.mofcom.gov.cn/syjsarticle/syjs/201009/1061_1.html (accessed on 19 September 2011).

it can be a great burden on the recipients, as expert estimates indicate that conditioned aid costs Africa about US$1.6 billion per year (Ssenyange, 2010).

In contrast, aid from China does not entail conditionalities that affect recipients' domestic economic policy. In fact, it is usually based on requests from beneficiaries, and is aligned with their urgent public infrastructure and investment needs (Naidu and Herman, 2008). From the recipient countries' standpoint, China provides technical assistance, especially for agriculture, which is often preferable to Western forms of aid (Shinn, 2006). Crucially, China also provides more predictability in terms of overall financial resources than Northern donors, because Chinese disbursement is carried out as scheduled within the financial year. This not only enables more accurate fiscal planning on the part of recipient countries, but also means that aid projects are more likely to be completed as planned (Johnson et al., 2008).

5.2. Development effectiveness rather than aid effectiveness

In providing foreign aid, China generally tries to achieve 'development effectiveness' instead of the 'aid effectiveness' stressed by DAC members. China's aid focuses on whether its assistance can meet the primary need of recipient states – the promotion of employment and economic growth. The Chinese government tries to do this through two main strategies: combining aid with trade, investment and economic cooperation; and sharing experience and best practices in poverty alleviation.

Guided by the precept that it is better to 'teach a man to fish than to give him a fish', China aims at helping recipient countries to increase their development capacity. Chinese aid therefore focuses on infrastructure, public facilities and productive sector investment, with a view toward fostering local technical capacity. At the same time, China takes positive measures to expand two-way import and export exchanges, to encourage Chinese companies to make equal and mutually beneficial investments in developing countries, and to engage in economic and technological cooperation. All such efforts are intended to lay a solid foundation for the eventual self-reliance and independent development of the recipients. Evidence suggests countries that have intensified aid, trade and investment links with China have improved their rates of growth and terms of trade, and have increased their export volumes and public revenues (Goldstein et al., 2006; OECD and ADB, 2007; Zafar, 2007; Woods, 2008).

Since 1978, China has achieved remarkable progress in domestic poverty alleviation, becoming the first developing country to achieve the relative target(s) set by the Millennium Development Goals (MDGs) prior to the 2015 deadline. According to World Bank statistics, China accounts for 70 per cent of the total global population lifted out of poverty over the last 25 years. By China's official standard of poverty, its poor population in rural areas dropped from 250 million people in 1978 to 36 million in 2009. Further, poverty rates are expected to fall to around 5 per cent of its total population by 2015 (MOFA, 2010). Aid from developed countries has also contributed to the enormous success of poverty alleviation in China, although the government has proved remarkably adept at leveraging these limited resources to eliminate poverty. Its successful experience in the adroit use of foreign aid, and sense of common historic destiny, enables China to understand the pressing aid requirements of developing countries better than industrialised countries. Therefore, China believes that the exchange of information regarding best practices among developing countries is a fundamental tool for poverty eradication. For this reason, in 2006, in cooperation with the UNDP, China founded the International Poverty Reduction Center.

6. The evolution of China's foreign aid management

Throughout its history, the scale and scope of China's foreign aid have gradually improved and expanded. Still, China's development assistance differs greatly from that of the OECD/DAC countries, and many aspects of aid require improvement.

6.1. Within the system of Chinese aid

The architecture of the Chinese aid system is composed of decision-making, management and coordination mechanisms. Decision-making is carried out by organs such as: the Central Political Bureau and its Standing Committee, the Central Foreign Affairs Leading Group of the Party and the government's State Council. The State Council,[4] at the pinnacle of the government hierarchy, undoubtedly wields the most important decision-making influence over foreign aid policy (Lancaster, 2007).

Unlike most DAC countries, in China, the Ministry of Commerce (MOFCOM) plays the central role in coordinating foreign aid policy and administration among the various relevant ministries.[5] One of the MOFCOM's responsibilities is to implement China's foreign aid policies and plans through its Department of Aid to Foreign Countries (DAFC), the primary agency responsible for foreign aid policy design, management and coordination. As such, the MOFCOM and its overseas officers (economic and commercial counsellors), along with the relevant provincial commerce departments, are in charge of aid management.

That said, however, the Ministry of Foreign Affairs (MOFA) is responsible for defining the overall foreign policy. Hence, the MOFA usually plays an advisory role to the MOFCOM in setting the tone and the general direction of foreign aid, especially when diplomatic objectives are particularly relevant. In order to achieve coordination and effective dialogue on foreign aid across the various ministries and departments involved, therefore, the MOFCOM communicates regularly with the MOFA, the Ministry of Finance (MOF), and the Export–Import Bank of China (CEXIM) to seek their suggestions. Also along these lines, in 2008, the MOFCOM, the MOFA and the MOF established the country's foreign aid inter-agency liaison mechanism, which, in February 2011, was upgraded to an inter-agency coordination mechanism (IOSC-PRC, 2011).

---

4   The State Council is composed of the premier, four vice-premiers, five state councillors, ministers, the auditor-general and the secretary-general.
5   Apart from the Ministry of Commerce (MOFCOM), 20 other ministries take part to varying degrees in foreign aid activities, including the Ministries of Finance (MOF), Education, Health, Science and Technology, and Agriculture, among others.

6.2. Foreign aid management and transparency

Institutions matter a great deal in implementing foreign aid. Effective and efficient institutions, with a good record regarding the quality of governance and rule of law, are the primary determinant of success in development assistance. There is a significant gap between China and traditional DAC donors in terms of the effectiveness and efficiency of their aid institutions. To address this disparity, the MOFCOM has recently begun to stress personnel management, rules and regulation construction, and project management as important aspects of its operations. In order to make aid agencies more effective, China should emphasise communication with the OECD/DAC countries, and strive to learn from their experience. Finally, greater administrative attention should also be paid to the design of aid evaluation mechanisms (Huang, 2007).

Furthermore, the transparency of China's assistance is relatively low. There are currently, strictly speaking, no general laws or regulations governing China's foreign aid. China's development cooperation legislation however is composed mainly of ministerial regulations, documents, and bylaws. It is even difficult to confidently estimate the total volume of China's aid, as aid is the responsibility of a wide range of ministries (King, 2007), and, as such, the official figures are not transparent (Brautigam, 2008).

After being urged by the international community to improve its transparency, China recently publicly published some of its foreign aid data. Examples of this practice include: the White Paper on China's Foreign Aid issued by the Information Office of the State Council (IOSC) of the PRC in April 2011; the news regarding China's foreign aid projects constantly released by the MOFCOM of the PRC on its website; and the publication of the 'Foreign Aid Communication' journal within the MOFCOM. In order to strengthen the theoretical development of aid-related research, and share the outcomes of these efforts with the international community, the Chinese Academy of Sciences (CAS) sponsors international academic conferences and enables Chinese scientists to participate in multilateral activities organised by international organisations. The CAS also cooperates with international organisations such as the Academy of Sciences for the Developing World, the InterAcademy Council (IAC) and the InterAcademy Panel (IAP) (Chin and Frolic, 2007). Through the timely release of such information, China has allayed, to some extent, the concerns of Western countries, and has constructed an international environment that is more receptive of China's foreign aid practices. Nevertheless, much remains to be done in this field.

6.3. Communication with the international community

China also needs to strengthen communication with the international community. In order to reach consensus and avoid misunderstandings about its foreign aid, since 2005, China has collaborated on development assistance with many international multilateral organisations. It has sent delegations to participate in conferences and dialogues regarding international development and cooperation, such as the UN High-Level Meeting on Financing for Development, the UN High-Level Meeting on the MDGs, and the High-Level Forum on Aid Effectiveness. Similarly, China has also begun to strengthen its communication and exchanges with DAC countries on a bi-lateral basis

(IOSC-PRC, 2011). Fu Ziying, Vice Minister of the MOFCOM, led several study groups to the US in 2009 aimed at strengthening communication and share experiences. China often expresses its willingness to enhance its aid-related relationship with the US in two main areas: the exchange of information, and collaboration upon infrastructure projects and trilateral development cooperation (MOFCOM, 2009).

The MOFCOM and the Ministry of Science and Technology provide funding to Chinese scholars and research institute managerial staff to travel to developing countries to provide technical assistance, engage in the exchange of research outcomes, or attend scientific seminars and conferences (Chin and Frolic, 2007). In this same spirit, China also needs to enhance its communication with other emerging countries, to exchange experiences and to actively promote South–South cooperation.

6.4. Cooperation with multilateral aid agencies

As previously discussed, China's foreign aid is generally conducted through bilateral channels, while the scale of its aid channelled through multilateral organisations is small. Recently, the efficiency of China's bilateral foreign aid has significantly improved. Like many Southern contributors, China has generated successful models and practices that compare favourably with those of the Northern donors in terms of meeting the needs of recipient countries (Johnson et al., 2008). A study of China's construction and infrastructure projects in four African countries – Angola, Sierra Leone, Tanzania and Zambia – shows that China's aid provided better value for money[6] than assistance by Northern donors (Burke et al., 2007). China's foreign aid in Africa and Cambodia has demonstrated similar effects (Brautigam, 2008; Sato et. al., 2010). However, bilateral aid is likely to overlap with multilateral aid agencies' projects, thus wasting resources and slowing the long-term development coordination of the international aid system.

China has increasingly engaged in trilateral and regional cooperation, involving multilateral organisations and other countries in capacity building, training and infrastructure construction. China should keep strengthening its cooperation with multilateral agencies, respect the interests of all participants and jointly promote the realisation of MDGs as soon as possible.

7. Conclusion

The scale and scope of China's foreign aid have gradually expanded since the 1970s, attracting international attention and recasting the role of China in development aid. But does China want to be a critical player in the international aid architecture?

If one considers solely the volume of Chinese aid and its evolution, China remains a small-scale international donor. Although China's gross domestic product ranks second in the world, GDP per capita ranks about 100th. As a

---

6 Better value for money, in particular, can be achieved through access to less expensive financing, lower labour costs, higher productivity, cheaper procurement of materials and the transfer of more appropriate technology.

poor country, China is neither prepared nor willing, at the present time, to be a critical player in the global architecture of development assistance.

China's aid represents a case of mutual help among developing countries, and, as such, falls into the category of South–South Cooperation. The Chinese government will continue to promote South–South Cooperation, as it has always done, and will gradually increase its foreign aid output in accordance with the continuous development of its economy. It will join hands with other aid providers to promote the process of global poverty alleviation. Within the framework of South–South Cooperation, China will work with all relevant parties in complementary and fruitful trilateral and regional cooperation that both respects the needs of recipient countries and promotes the realisation of the MDGs.

When providing foreign aid, China maintains that foreign aid is a 'win-win' interaction between developing countries and, correspondingly, will focus more on economic projects with other non-industrialised countries. That is one of the main reasons why the MOFCOM administers China's foreign aid. This 'win-win' mentality also accounts for the fact that a large proportion of foreign aid is linked to promoting exports and investment between China and the recipient countries within the government's overall economic cooperation development policy.

It is time for China's foreign aid policymakers to initiate a dialogue with DAC countries, and to learn from their experience and practices. China must keep pace with reform and innovation in the field of development assistance by continually adjusting its aid management mechanisms to improve their effectivity, and by promptly adapting to contextual changes both globally and domestically.

REFERENCES

Beijing Review (1983) 'Zhao Ziyang's Four Principles of Economic and Technological Cooperation', *Beijing Review*, January 24, p. 19.

Bosshard, P. (2007) *China's Role in Financing African Infrastructure* (Berkeley: International River Network).

Brautigam, D. (2008) *China's African Aid: Transatlantic Challenges* (Washington, DC: The German Marshall Fund of the United States).

Brautigam, D. (2009a) *The Dragon's Gift: The Real Story of China in Africa* (Oxford: Oxford University Press).

Brautigam, D. (2009b) 'China's Challenge to the International Aid Architecture', *World Politics Review*, 1(4), pp. 1–10.

Brautigam, D. (2010a) *China, Africa, and the International Aid Architecture*, Working Paper no. 107 (Tunis: African Development Bank).

Brautigam, D. (2010b) 'China Overseas: "Export Hordes of Experts" or "Teaching How to Fish"?', *Norrag News*, 44, pp. 53–6.

Burke, C., L. Corkin and N. Tay (2007) *China's Engagement of Africa: Preliminary Scoping of African Case Studies. Angola, Ethiopia, Gabon, Uganda, South Africa, Zambia* (Stellenbosch: University of Stellenbosch, Centre for Chinese Studies).

Cabello, D., F. Sekulova and D. Schmidt (2008) *World Bank Conditionalities: Poor Deal for Poor Countries* (Amsterdam: A SEED Europe).

Chin, G.T. and B.M. Frolic (2007) *Emerging Donors in International Development Assistance: The China Case* (Ottawa: International Development Research Centre, Partnership & Business Development Division).

Editorial Board of the China Commerce Yearbook (2010) *China Commerce Yearbook* (Beijing: China Commerce and Trade Press).

Goldstein, A.N., N. Pinaud, H. Reisen and X. Chen (2006) *The Rise of China and India: What's in it for Africa?* (Paris: OECD Development Centre).

Huang, M. (2007) 'Chinese Foreign Aid System and Its Trends' (Zhong Guo Dui Wai Yuan Zhu Ji Zhi: Xian Zhuang He Qu Shi), *International Economic Cooperation* (Guo Ji Jing Ji He Zuo), author's translation.

Huang, M. and J. Lang (2010) 'China's Foreign Aid to Africa and Its Challenges' (Zhong Guo De Dui Fei Yuan Zhu Ji Qi Mian Lin De Tiao Zhan), *International Economic Cooperation* (Guo Ji Jing Ji He Zuo), author's translation.

IOSC-PRC (Information Office of the State Council of the People's Republic of China) (2011), *China's Foreign Aid* (Beijing; IOSC-PRC) http://www.scio.gov.cn/zxbd/wz/201104/t896900.htm (accessed on 10 November 2011).

Johnson, A., B. Versailles and M. Martin (2008) *Trends in South-South and Triangular Development Cooperation* (New York: United Nations Economic and Social Council).

King, K. (2007) *China's Aid to Africa: A View from China and Japan*, lead paper to the seminar on 'China's aid to Africa' organised by the Japan International Cooperation Agency, Tokyo.

Kjollesdal, K. and A. Welle-Strand (2010) 'Foreign Aid Strategies: China Taking Over?', *Asian Social Science*, 6(10), pp. 3–13.

Lancaster, C. (2007) *The Chinese Aid System* (Washington, DC: Center for Global Development).

Li, X. (2009) *China's Foreign Aid to Africa*, www.iprcc.org.cn/ppt/2008-05-13/1210662570.pdf (accessed on 1 December 2011).

Lum, T., H. Fischer, J. Gomez-Granger and A. Leland (2009) *China's Foreign Aid Activities in Africa, Latin America, and Southeast Asia* (Washington, DC: Congressional Research Service).

MOFA (Ministry of Foreign Affairs of the People's Republic of China) (2010) *China's Progress Towards the Millennium Development Goals* (Beijing: Ministry of Foreign Affairs of the People's Republic of China, United Nations System in China).

MOFCOM (Ministry of Commerce of the People's Republic of China) (2009) *The High-level Dialogue of Foreign Aid Between China and the United States*, Foreign Aid Communication, no. 11.

MOFCOM (2010) *The Great Achievements of China's Foreign Aid in 2009*, Foreign Aid Communication, no. 1.

MOFCOM (2011) *The New Development Stage of China's Foreign Aid in 2010*, Foreign Aid Communication, no. 1.

Naidu, S. and H. Herman (2008) 'China and India in Africa: Challenging the Status Quo?', *Pambazuka News*, no. 394, http://pambazuka.org/en/category/comment/50252 (accessed on 10 November 2011).

OECD (Organisation for Economic Cooperation and Development)/African Development Bank (2007) *African Economic Outlook* (Paris: OECD Development Centre).

Sato, J., H. Shiga, T. Kobayashi, H. Kondoh (2010) *How do 'Emerging Donors' Differ from 'Traditional' Donors? An Institutional Analysis of Foreign Aid in Cambodia*, Japan International Cooperation Agency Research Institute (JICA-RI) Working Paper n° 2 (Tokyo: JICA-RI).

Shinn, H. (2006) *Africa and China's Global Activism*, paper presented at the National Defense University Pacific Symposium 'China's Global Activism: Implications for U.S. Security Interests'.

Ssenyange, E. (2010) *South-South Development Cooperation: A Challenge to Traditional Aid Relations?* (Quezon City: The Reality of Aid/Ibon Books).

State Statistical Bureau of the People's Republic of China (2003–10) *China Statistical Yearbook* (Beijing; China Statistics Press).

Weston J., C. Cambell and K. Koleski (2011) *China's Foreign Assistance in Review: Implications for the United States* (Washington: US-China Economic and Security Review Commission).

Woods, N. (2008) 'Whose Aid? Whose Influence? China, Emerging Donors, and the Silent Revolution in Development Assistance', *International Affairs*, 84(6), pp. 1205–21.

Zafar, A. (2007) 'The Growing Relationship between China and Sub-Saharan Africa: Macroeconomic, Trade, Investment, and Aid Links', *The World Bank Research Observer*, 22(1), pp. 103–30.

Zhu, T. (2001) 'Nationalism and Chinese Foreign Policy', *The China Review*, 1(1), pp. 1–27.

7

EMERGING 'DONOR', GEOPOLITICAL ACTOR: SOUTH AFRICA IN THE GLOBAL TERRAIN

Elizabeth Sidiropoulos

Abstract

An active participant in the various global debates and motivated by a desire to address global inequalities and power imbalances in rule-making, South Africa seeks to balance its domestic imperatives with an enlightened developmentally-minded foreign policy where Africa is the priority. Since 1994 South Africa has initiated many activities that may be described as development cooperation. However, with the exception of the African Renaissance Fund (ARF), it has lacked an overarching architecture for its assistance, which has been fragmented among various departments and agencies with very little coherence, bar their focus on Africa. The establishment of the South African Development Partnership Agency (SADPA) within the Department of International Relations and Cooperation (DIRCO) by the first half of 2012 is poised to address many of these shortcomings, ensuring greater intra-governmental coordination and evaluation. In embarking on this path, South Africa will engage more in the future structure of international development, arguing for a broader definition of development cooperation and a framework that has evolved with input from the South. The fluidity in global development provides an opportunity for South Africa to help bridge the divide between North and South, and encourage policy innovation in the aid debate.[1]

'South Africa will continue to focus its foreign policy on (…) working with other countries for a global system of governance that is democratic and responsive to the interests and aspirations of developing countries. […]

As changes sweep across the globe and touch the lives of people in even the most remote of habitats, we cannot be mere spectators.

Our people, our history and our diplomacy demand more of us. We will continue to engage in the international community with a sense of purpose, to effect change rather than to just be affected by it.'

Minister of International Relations and Cooperation, Maite Nkoana-Mashabane, Budget vote, National Assembly, Cape Town, 31 May 2011

---

1 A longer version of this article is appearing in Chaturvedi, Fues and Sidiropoulos (forthcoming).

1. Introduction

By far the biggest economy on the African continent, and a recent entrant to the political version of the Goldman Sachs construct 'BRIC',[2] South Africa has not been absent from the global stage since its re-entry into the international arena in 1994. While South Africa's demographic and economic size preclude it from ever competing for first-tier power status with a China or an India, this has not detracted it from carving a vocal space for itself in the global governance terrain. More recently, especially in the wake of the financial crisis, South Africa accelerated its intentions to deepen relations with other key emerging Southern players. The invitation to South Africa by China, in December 2010, to join the BRICs was not an accident but the result of a single-minded pursuit of this objective by the Zuma administration.

Acutely sensitive to the imperative of identifying itself as a member of the South and of Africa when it returned to the international fold, South Africa has become more convinced that its economic prosperity lies in linking itself more closely to the rising South, of which the BRIC now seems to be the pre-eminent grouping and a potential counterbalance to the G7, although an effective, coherent agenda still has to evolve.

This dimension which has become all the more apparent is important to appreciate in understanding the trajectory of South Africa's international engagement in the medium term. It can still and will probably play a consensus-building role in certain global engagements, with climate change potentially being one such example. However, it is likely to increasingly assert its independent foreign policy in multilateral forums such as the United Nations (UN) Security Council, where it feels strongly that the US, France and the UK use it to advance narrow political interests – the most notable recent case being the Security Council vote on a no-fly zone over Libya, which South Africa supported, but which very soon thereafter became dominated by the 'Western' narrative of 'regime change', an objective which SA believed clearly contravened Resolution 1973.[3]

Within the ruling African National Congress (ANC), the discourse of anti-imperialism and anti-colonialism is still extremely strong, and forms a thread in its articulation of international relations.[4] The rise of China, followed by India and others, highlights for the ANC the opportunity to end Western-dominated global rule-making, which it perceives as still espousing a neo-imperialist mindset.

This chapter will focus on the evolution of South Africa's development cooperation activities and policies. The terminology of the Organisation for Economic Cooperation and Development (OECD) characterises South Africa as an 'emerging donor', while South Africa and other similarly defined Southern states prefer to consider themselves 'partners', helping other developing

2   The BRIC acronym refers to Brazil, Russia, India and China. It was introduced in 2003 by Jim O'Neill of Goldman Sachs, who predicted that these four countries will become leading economies by 2050 and have the potential to form a powerful economic bloc.

3   Much was made in the South African press about the fact that South Africa did not vote with the other BRICS on the United Nations Security Council Resolution 1973.

4   See, for example, the resolutions of the ANC national conference in Polokwane in December 2007, http://www.anc.org.za/show.php?id=2536 (accessed on 2 October 2011).

countries where they can and sharing developmental experiences. I first discuss the role that global governance plays in South Africa's international engagement. Then, development cooperation since 1994 is discussed against that background. This section will also explore South Africa's initiatives in triangular cooperation and its plans to establish a Development Partnership Agency. Finally, I will briefly discuss emerging trends in South–South Cooperation (SSC) as well as the need for a new discourse on development aid and cooperation that transcends the OECD-DAC perspectives, to include the new developments represented by the rise of new donors over the last two decades which has now reached a critical mass.

2. Global governance in South Africa's foreign policy

Democratic South Africa's point of departure in the debates around the strengthening of a rules-based multilateral system is twofold. First, the aptness of the apartheid narrative in characterising the current world order – one where a few wealthy states determine the rules of the global game, and the vast majority of poor states have very little choice but to operate within it.[5] Thus, much like domestic apartheid was defeated (runs the South African narrative), this unfair global order also needs to be overturned. Second, in breaking with its apartheid past, South Africa is a responsible global citizen, by 'assuming good conduct at home and abroad' (Landsberg, 2010). Such responsibility means engaging in the evolution and review of global rules such as those on nuclear non-proliferation and the land mines ban to committing to an Africa-oriented foreign policy that aimed to help bring peace and security to the continent and build institutions that responded more ably to the challenges facing Africa.

Although a goal such as overturning global apartheid may imply a revolutionary fervour, South Africa's post-1994 approach to multilateralism has focused in the main on seeking reforms, building bridges and consensus among different parties. Post-apartheid South Africa has had an immensely valuable tool of soft power at its disposal. That tool is its reputation for occupying the moral high ground as a result of the peaceful manner of its own negotiated transformation, its decision to abandon its nuclear weapons stockpile, and its focus early on on a values-based foreign policy derived from the principles the national liberation movement fought for. This has given it the platform to punch above its weight and to be listened to – and to become an international norm entrepreneur (Geldenhuys, 2006) – even though it has discovered the difficulty of adopting a consistently ethical foreign policy across the board.

However, its global governance agenda also displays inherent tensions that although they will not disappear, need to be managed carefully. The foremost tension is that between being an African state and being legitimised in global forums as 'representing' Africa versus its global and economic interests that are often more closely aligned with some of the emerging Southern powers such

---

5   At the 2002 World Summit on Sustainable Development, President Thabo Mbeki spoke of the need for the 'peoples of the world […] to achieve a decisive victory against global apartheid' (Mbeki, 2002).

as India and Brazil. The tension lies in pursuing both without undermining either objective. They are both necessary for South Africa's international relations. South Africa's aspiration to sit at various global tables, including at the UN Security Council, requires it to work assiduously at cultivating its African neighbours, while deepening alliances with emerging markets from other geographies.

In truth South Africa emphasises that it has no formal mandate to represent Africa in any of the forums it participates in; however, it does seek to bring broader African concerns to such forums, with perhaps the recent and notable example being its chairmanship of the Committee of 10 finance ministers and central bank governors that feeds into the deliberations of the G20, of which it is the only African member. This does not eliminate the inevitable rivalries (direct or indirect) with other aspiring leaders of Africa, or the tensions between its interests and the positions espoused by the continent. For example, the India-Brazil-South Africa Forum (IBSA) established in 2003 is considered a key alliance of three developing democracies sharing a similar perspective on the current global system. With all three aspiring to become members of the UN Security Council, there were clear synergies among them in advocating reforms; however, although South Africa had sympathy with the G4 grouping (Brazil, India, Germany and Japan) on the issue of permanent membership of the Security Council when it was being discussed in 2005, it chose in the end to support the African Union (AU) position, rather than break ranks with Africa.

Its global prominence is reinforced in many African countries by its economic weight as one of the largest investors on the continent. Together with this goes the concern of being perceived as 'big brother', all too reminiscent of the way in which apartheid South Africa conducted itself in the rest of Africa.

These tensions and constraints create an engagement that has both helped to put African issues on the global agenda as well as set the country apart from its nearest neighbours.

3. Development cooperation as a tool of foreign policy

In the first decade of the twenty-first century South Africa is the pre-eminent African economic (and sometimes political) regional power and is likely to continue for some years to come. Its companies broadened their footprint across Africa, the government invested in continental institutions such as the AU (contributing some 15 per cent to its annual budget), while also working in the early 2000s with other key states in crafting a continental vision for Africa.

Partly a recognition of Africa's support for the anti-apartheid struggle, partly pragmatic motivation that South Africa cannot exist as an island of prosperity in a continent racked by insecurity and poverty, the continent has been the central plank in South Africa's foreign policy since 1994. The concept of an 'African Renaissance', of which former President Mbeki became the architect and which culminated in the New Partnership for African Development (NEPAD), came to represent the essence of this thinking. The African Renaissance was nothing less than a vision aimed at the holistic reinvigoration of Africa in all aspects of human affairs – economic, cultural, political and social.

Against that background South Africa early on in its constitutional democracy began providing various types of support to African countries. This often originated from interactions between the South African president or his ministers and their counterparts in other African countries, especially those emerging from conflict or political instability. The projects were then carried out by the relevant line ministries and funded from existing budgets. There was no overarching agency coordinating or monitoring the varied interventions.

Thus, an overall determination of the funds South Africa makes available to African countries for various initiatives is extremely difficult to discern, as such assistance is fragmented and is not separated from ordinary budget line items within each departmental vote. The only exception is the Department of International Relations and Cooperation's African Renaissance and International Cooperation Fund (ARF).

Such assistance has not been regarded as aid in the traditional sense but is considered in the mould of SSC which, some argue, differs from the traditional development cooperation model. South Africa has also espoused the view of 'African solutions for African problems', and its support for elections or post-conflict reconstruction is regarded as embodying this principle. The country has been an arch proponent of this type of cooperation, considering its Africa agenda and SSC as foreign policy priorities.

For the purposes of this chapter, South Africa's 'development cooperation' is regarded as including support for regional integration and projects related to the NEPAD; South Africa's conflict resolution initiatives, including peacekeeping and support for the continent's institutional architecture; and technical assistance in state capacity-building.

A coherent and streamlined development cooperation policy must be a vital component of South Africa's desire to play a more central and leading role in Africa and the world. This recognition of the strategic function that development cooperation can play galvanised the ANC government more recently to establish a development partnership agency. It will, however, require adroit diplomatic navigation around some of Africa's stereotypical perceptions of South Africa as a hegemon on the continent.

3.1. The ARF

The ARF that was established in 2001 became one of the tools used, albeit initially in an *ad hoc* fashion,[6] to advance what the Department of International Relations and Cooperation (DIRCO) calls the government's 'Africa agenda'.

The ARF, established by an Act of Parliament in 2000, is the most visibly structured component of South Africa's development cooperation, although not the only one. Its aim is to enhance cooperation between South Africa and other countries, particularly in Africa, through the promotion of democracy and good governance, socio-economic development and integration, humanitarian assistance and human resource development, and the prevention and resolution of conflict. Start-up funding was about US$30 million in 2001. The ARF forms part of DIRCO and falls under its NEPAD Directorate, a reporting line reflecting

---

6   In recognition of the need to monitor more effectively what is disbursed and its impact, the Treasury undertook a survey in 2006 to inform a White Paper on development cooperation.

Table 7.1 – ARF approved funding,* 2007–12

Indicator	Programme/ activity	Past			Current	Projection
		2007–08	2008–09	2009–10	2010–11	2011–12
Number of projects approved (per year)	Bilateral** and other projects	6	9	9	10	15
				ZAR million		
Total value of projects approved	Bilateral and other projects	352	476	631	401	450
Funds approved for promoting democracy and good governance (per year)	South Africa's participation in the observer missions in the continent	96	4	394	141	110
Funds approved for the prevention and resolution of conflict (per year)	Bilateral projects related to post-conflict, reconstruction and development in particular the Great Lakes Region	8	10	100	90	80
Funds approved for humanitarian assistance and disaster relief (per year)	Funding, humanitarian and technical assistance to countries in need of disaster relief	22	300	10	10	15
Funds approved for cooperation between South Africa and other countries in particular African (per year)	Bilateral projects related to socio-economic development in Africa	35	42	72	70	130
Funds approved for human resources development (per year)	Technical assistance to identified countries; and training Congolese public service officials	176	20	25	80	55
Funds approved for socio-economic development and integration (per year)	Bilateral projects	15	100	30	10	60

* The ARF has been replaced by the South African Development Partnership Agency (SADPA), established in 2012.
** Bilateral projects include support in areas such as agriculture and health services.
Source: National Treasury (2011b, 82).

the Fund's alignment with the implementation of NEPAD projects. The Fund utilises both concessionary loans and grants, although the latter make up the bulk of its operations.

The Fund is managed by an Advisory Committee that also makes recommendations to the Ministers of International Relations and Cooperation and of Finance on the disbursement of funds through loans or other financial assistance. The Advisory Committee consists of the Director-General of International Relations and Cooperation or his delegate; three officers of DIRCO appointed by the Minister; and two officers of the National Treasury appointed by the Minister of Finance.

Some examples of the support the ARF has provided to African countries include cooperative projects and direct assistance to specific sectoral initiatives, such as funding for infrastructural projects in Lesotho; training of Comorian armed personnel to provide security during the presidential elections; a water supply scheme in Katanga province in the Democratic Republic of Congo; and trilateral cooperation with Vietnam on efficient rice production in Guinea (National Treasury, 2009, 2010). While the ARF's engagement is largely in Africa, in December 2010 the government announced that it was writing off Cuba's debt of US$143 million (about ZAR1 billion) for diesel engines it had bought from South Africa in the 1990s (Sapa, 2010). Ranging from ZAR330 to ZAR630 million (US$47–90 million), total annual expenditure of the ARF has been relatively small. A survey conducted by the National Treasury in 2006 calculated that the ARF's contribution as a proportion of South Africa's overall assistance was only 3.8 per cent in 2002 and 3.3 per cent in 2004.[7]

3.2. Other agencies

As noted earlier, it is very difficult to present an overall picture of South Africa's development cooperation funding because the activities of other departments and agencies in Africa are not individually captured, nor have they been recorded as 'development cooperation'. According to the 2006 Treasury survey, the bulk of the government's development cooperation since 2000 has been conducted by various government departments, parastatal bodies, government agencies and other statutory bodies. Some of the government departments involved include defence, education, public service and administration, science and technology and agriculture. The Independent Electoral Commission has helped conduct or provide support for elections in various African countries, while PALAMA, the Public Administration Leadership and Management Academy, is training public servants from Burundi, Rwanda and South Sudan.

Furthermore, two of South Africa's key development finance institutions, the Development Bank of Southern Africa (DBSA) and the Industrial Development Corporation, have units charged with support for NEPAD. These institutions are capable of playing a significant part in Africa, especially in infrastructure development. More recently, the DBSA was appointed by the government to represent South Africa and the region on capacity-building and financing within the BRICS in the context of South Africa's operating as a gateway into Africa in communications, information technology and financial services, key elements in advancing regional integration and development.[8] The South African Development Partnership Agency (SADPA) envisages a role for both institutions.

Apart from these activities, South Africa's membership of the Southern African Customs Union (SACU), comprising also Botswana, Lesotho, Namibia and Swaziland, is in fact a vehicle for a type of budget support to these countries via the common revenue pool. Lesotho and Swaziland in particular rely substantially on these transfers to manage their fiscus. The South African government's *Budget Review 2011* reported that SACU revenues make up

7   The Treasury has not conducted a further study of development assistance, the discussion having shifted to the establishment of the South African Development Partnership Agency (SADPA). There are therefore no more recent figures on the sum of South Africa development cooperation.
8   Presentation by the CEO of the DBSA, Mr Paul Baloyi, SAIIA, Johannesburg, 9 June 2011.

between 20 per cent and 70 per cent of total government income for South Africa's SACU partners (National Treasury, 2011a).

3.3. Triangular cooperation

Triangular cooperation has received much prominence as a new way of cooperation between Northern and Southern partners in other developing countries. It is not without its detractors in the South, some of whom argue that its *raison d'être* emerged from Northern countries' concerns about losing influence in developing countries to the 'new donors'. It is important to stress that for triangular cooperation to work, three key elements are required:

- trust between the Northern and Southern partners and beneficiaries;
- the specific comparative advantages that each party may bring to the cooperation; and
- the degree to which there is a confluence of interests among all three parties.

South Africa's approach to triangular cooperation has been far more pragmatic, motivated in part by the recognition that it could provide much-needed resources to carry out projects it had identified but had only limited means to execute. Triangular cooperation is included in the draft SADPA Bill, which sees the Agency also operating as a bridge between North and South in this regard (DIRCO, 2011).

South Africa has been involved in triangular cooperation together with traditional donors. The roles and responsibilities of South Africa and the second donor vary from case to case. Since the first projects of this kind in 2000, triangular cooperation has grown. South Africa now has partnerships with the Netherlands, Switzerland, Sweden, Norway, Belgium, Germany, France and the UK. These partnerships are almost entirely in Africa.

Since 2008 South Africa and the Nordic countries have had a declaration of intent on triangular cooperation opportunities. South Africa has already almost completed a project with Sweden for training police in Rwanda. Another area of possible cooperation with Sweden is in South Sudan on tax administration, which would include the South African and Swedish revenue services. Since 2007 Norway and South Africa support Burundi in conflict resolution, reconciliation and prevention through the African Centre for the Constructive Resolution of Disputes ('ACCORD'), a South African non-governmental organisation.

The South African Treasury and the German development agency *Deutsche Gesellschaft für Internationale Zusammenarbeit* (GIZ) are joined in a Trilateral Cooperation Fund (TRICO) aimed at supporting the establishment and implementation of development programmes of African countries and regional initiatives. Using funding from the Canadian International Development Agency, South Africa's PALAMA runs a five-year (2008–13) programme on building public sector capacities in post-conflict countries. Partners include Rwanda's Institute for Administration and Management (RIAM), Burundi's *École Nationale d'Administration* and South Sudan's Capacity Building Unit.

Apart from these North–South triangular cooperation initiatives, South Africa is part of the India, Brazil and South Africa Facility for Poverty and Hunger

Alleviation (IBSA Trust Fund), which was created out of the IBSA Dialogue Forum held in New Delhi in March 2004. Its purpose is to identify small projects in the fight against poverty and hunger that can be implemented quickly.[9] The fund is managed by the UN Development Programme's Special Unit for SSC and managed by a board of directors against a set of project guidelines.[10] Each IBSA member contributes US$1 million a year to the fund. Individual grants may not exceed US$50,000.[11] The IBSA Fund could become the springboard for increased development cooperation activities using a pure South–South model. Another South–South triangular initiative, funded by the ARF, involves South Africa, Cuba and Sierra Leone to provide Cuban medical doctors to Sierra Leone.

The draft SADPA bill, as elaborated by DIRCO during a briefing to the Select Committee on Trade and International Relations of the National Council of Provinces in August 2011, made explicit mention of triangular cooperation, and the future SADPA Fund will be able to receive third party funding for this purpose.

The enunciation of a standard *modus operandi* and framework of principles reflecting South Africa's perspectives on development cooperation in a post-'exclusively DAC' global landscape might make a significant contribution to the evolving triangular cooperation modalities.

As South Africa scales up its overall development cooperation, it will have to consider how to avoid the sometimes unavoidable criticisms of other African states of its actions as a 'donor'. Much as it may shun the moniker, its economic dominance, its presence at some of the global high tables (often as the only African representative) may spur latent resentment especially if it is not assiduous in cultivating key bilateral relations on the continent and managing its SADPA programmes in a participatory manner to ensure they are owned by the beneficiaries.

In addition, while recognising that development cooperation will have elements that are interest driven, it will be important for the agency to champion the development elements of assistance, while DIRCO focuses on the political aspects of development cooperation (PMG, 2011). Only in this way can one be assured of a healthy balance among these policy elements. Lastly, South Africa should be modest in what it undertakes and clear about where its particular niche and competitive advantage lies.

3.4. SADPA: a foreign policy tool?

The announcement by the Minister of International Relations and Cooperation in April 2010 (Nkoana-Mashabane, 2010) that South Africa would establish the SADPA as a channel for its international cooperation efforts was both the outcome of a realisation of the operational necessity of streamlining the

9   In September 2010 the three governments were recognised by the Millennium Development Goal Awards, in partnership with the UN Development Programme's Millennium Campaign and the Office for Partnerships, for 'their leadership and support of the IBSA Facility for Poverty and Hunger Alleviation (IBSA Fund) as a break-through model of South–South Technical Cooperation'.
10   The directors are the accredited representatives of the three countries to the UN.
11   In Guinea-Bissau, it funded the introduction of new seeds and capacity-building in improved agricultural techniques. In Cape Verde, it financed the refurbishment of two local and isolated health units to support the elderly and the disabled, while in Burundi it supported capacity-building workshops to improve the national Human Immunodeficiency Virus/Acquired Immune Deficiency Syndrome (HIV/AIDS) plan. The fund has also been active in Haiti and in Palestine.

government's activities in this domain as well as the need to be more strategic in its partnerships and the instruments it utilises. In one of these paradoxes that dogs South Africa's diplomacy, it must deepen its strategic relations with BRIC states because it sees many economic and diplomatic benefits deriving from them, but these countries are also its competitors for contracts, investments and political influence in its 'backyard'. After all, one can argue that Africa is South Africa's 'hemisphere'. Inasmuch as the continent is now perceived as the next economic frontier and receives the approaches of both new and old friends, South Africa must step up its engagement, presence and influence.

An up-scaled and revamped development cooperation diplomacy, thoughtfully deployed, can be a useful tool. A policy of development cooperation or partnership is an overtly political act as much as it may also be driven by some of the altruism of helping fellow African and developing countries advance economically.

While South Africa is often at pains to argue that its cooperation activities are not motivated by narrow self-interest, a number of senior officials consider that its numerous conflict resolution efforts from the Democratic Republic of Congo to Burundi are not sufficiently appreciated by other Africans; nor have they brought direct rewards to South Africa; they have, rather, benefited other countries which have received contracts, or access to resources, after hostilities ended. On the other hand, some Africans see South Africa's involvement as driven by selfish economic interests (Grobbelaar, 2008). Thus, while South Africa's current development cooperation originated in normative drivers of promoting peace and security on the African continent, the debate within government circles has gradually shifted to identifying the correct mix of self-interest and normative imperatives.

In the briefing by DIRCO to the Select Committee on Trade and International Relations of the National Council of Provinces, one of the first public discussions on the Bill, the following elements emerged (PMG, 2011):

- development cooperation via SADPA is a tool that would advance South Africa's foreign policy goals of addressing poverty, underdevelopment and the marginalisation of Africa and the global South. Specifically, the Agency would focus on Africa, regional integration, SSC and the achievement of the Millennium Development Goals;
- DIRCO noted in its briefing that international agencies that had been used effectively had supported foreign policy goals and contributed to the achievement of domestic objectives;
- the span of sectors would include humanitarian aid and disaster management, peace missions, preventive diplomacy, peace-building, election support, multilateral commitments made via international financial institutions and infrastructure;
- SADPA could be a tool for creating opportunities for the South African business sector, where it engaged in infrastructure development: 'The Fund was not meant to be an egalitarian instrument that churned out development assistance without necessarily creating opportunities for South Africa's investments';

- SADPA would be responsible for government-wide coordination of South Africa's outgoing international development cooperation (including bilateral, trilateral and multilateral partnerships with states, development institutions, civil society and the private sector). It would coordinate policy formulation on development cooperation and ensure coherence throughout government;
- the SADPA Fund that would be created would be able to receive funds from foreign donors directly for joint projects of a triangular nature;
- SADPA would be created as an entity within DIRCO, with its own head reporting to the Minister.

It is clear that the establishment of SADPA aims to address the shortcomings of South Africa's development cooperation initiatives to date. Since 2009 a number of study visits were undertaken to both Northern and Southern countries to look at various models in preparation for the establishment of a development cooperation agency. The SADPA bill mentioned the necessity of monitoring and evaluation, the use of a results-based management approach and a rigorous project methodology (DIRCO, 2011).

4. SSC: ideologies and realities

The global financial crisis had a significant impact on the way the Western economic model is viewed by developing countries. It also compelled developed states to re-examine the volume of their aid and its purposes in the context of contracting economies and pressures to cut costs across the board. For some years to come, the OECD-DAC will continue to be the major provider of development assistance. Yet the development discourse is no longer perceived to be the exclusive competence of the West. It is also widely acknowledged now that aid is only one aspect of development that needs to be considered. The way in which many 'new donors' engage with developing countries, in the context of what they emphasise is SSC, includes trade and investment, technology exchanges and/or transfers – with the emphasis being on mutual benefit, at least at the rhetorical level. The term 'aid' is associated in many emerging countries with the G7 and the OECD. This view certainly holds among South African officials too, who believe that a re-thinking of global discourse on the aid–development nexus and the instruments required to achieve development in poor countries is now necessary.

There is a strong argument to be made for a shift from equity- to growth-oriented development policies (Hallet, 2011), a debate accelerated by the 2008–09 financial crisis. Given that these emerging 'donors' or partners are themselves grappling with the challenges of realising development in their own countries, their engagement may potentially take on a different (and more relevant) dimension from that of traditional partners.

A noteworthy development was South Korea's initiative in the G20 group of major economies, in November 2010, to establish a development working group, of which South Africa is the co-chair. The Seoul Development Consensus for Shared Growth, adopted at the G20 summit, emphasises the need for 'strong, sustainable, inclusive and resilient growth' because 'consistently high levels of inclusive growth in developing countries and [low income countries] in particular, are critically necessary, if not sufficient for the eradication of extreme poverty' (G20, 2010).

In Southern eyes, SSC is cooperation among equals driven by mutual benefit, and for that reason falls outside the donor–recipient mould. Clearly, while this is the rationale and perhaps the aspiration, reality may be quite different. SSC may come without some of the historical baggage of the North but it is also driven by specific interests and political aims – as indeed are the actions of traditional development aid partners. The current debate within South Africa's foreign policy establishment in the run-up to the publication of the White Paper on foreign policy in August 2011, about the balance between self-interest and broader developmental objectives, illustrates this, and dilutes the rhetoric there and elsewhere in the developing world of South–South solidarity.[12]

Like other countries of the South, and in pursuing an end to global power inequality as reflected in the multilateral rules that apply to various international frameworks, South Africa is also unwilling to accept 'as is' the aid effectiveness principles developed by the OECD-DAC for its own development cooperation. The OECD's drive to persuade 'new donors' to comply with Paris principles is regarded by many countries of the South as a means of locking them into a specific framework, not determined by them, which in turn may constrain their relations with other developing countries. While advocating a rules-based international system that is fair and equitable, South Africa increasingly emphasises that these rules must be developed with inputs from the developing world.

The Paris Declaration was not developed by Southern states, it is limited to aid only; and distinguishes in effect between donors and recipients, a nomenclature avoided by South Africa and other Southern states because it reflects an inherently unequal 'partnership'. However, South Africa is not oblivious to the value of elements of the Paris Declaration. In the presentation to the National Council of Provinces in August 2011, DIRCO noted that it would use both Paris declaration principles and South–South principles in SADPA (PMG, 2011).

5. Conclusion

South Africa stands before two great opportunities in the development cooperation terrain. The first is in the crafting of its development cooperation policies in a way that underscores both its domestic socio-economic imperatives, which require it to be an alert geopolitical player, and its commitment to peace, security and economic development in the region. The second opportunity lies in the fluidity that characterises the global development cooperation landscape. This fluidity, and South Africa's relative 'smallness', mean that it can seek to be a global policy innovator in these spaces, without being considered as a threat to either one or the other side. After all, SSC itself is evolving; large emerging

---

12   South Africa's apartheid legacy has generated an aversion since 1994 to adopting a vigorous, exclusively self-interested engagement with the rest of Africa. The White Paper consultations debated the definition of national interest and how one should pursue it without alienating important partners on the continent and elsewhere.

economies are now much bigger global economic players and have strategic interests that may supersede the ideas of *mutual benefit* of SSC that ostensibly differentiate it from traditional aid.

South Africa could be bold and initiate a new set of discussions around development that incorporate new Southern actors and move beyond the Paris paradigm. What might that entail?

- A new forum and a clean slate so that new development cooperation players feel they can contribute to rule-making.
- A new set of rules that nevertheless do not ignore the body of knowledge accumulated by traditional donors and Southern partners.
- A legitimating framework that is shorn of perceptions of being an unequal one with first and second tier countries. This may be the UN, but its inherent weaknesses of efficacy, execution and monitoring would have to be addressed.

If the intention is to develop a new development architecture, then some of the questions that should be addressed include integrating other aspects of the development agenda, marrying growth with inclusivity, and tackling policy coherence across all sectors from trade and investment to development cooperation projects.

For South Africa such an exercise forms part of the rationale for working towards a 'rules-based system [...] which limits the possibility of unilateral action by major powers' (Fransman, 2011). Nevertheless, it is also a great opportunity to position itself as both an effective development partner and a creative and geopolitically savvy norm entrepreneur.

REFERENCES AND FURTHER READING

AFDB (African Development Bank) and OECD (Organisation for Economic Cooperation and Development) (2010) *African Economic Outlook 2010*, Special Theme on Public Resource Mobilisation and Aid (Paris: OECD).

ARF (African Renaissance and International Cooperation Fund) (2004–10) *Annual Financial Statement* (Pretoria: Department of International Relations and Cooperation).

Berger, A. and S. Grimm (2010) 'SSC and Western Aid: Learning from and with Each Other?', *The Current Column*, 6 September (Bonn: German Development Institute).

Chaturvedi, S., T. Fues and E. Sidiropoulos (eds) (forthcoming) *Development Cooperation and Emerging Powers: New Partners or Old Patterns* (London: Zed Books).

Cilliers, J., B. Hughes and J. Moyer (2011) *African Futures 2050. The Next Forty Years*, monograph no. 175 (Pretoria: Institute for Security Studies and Pardee Center for International Futures).

DIRCO (Department of International Relations and Cooperation) (2011) Powerpoint presentation on 'Establishment of SADPA' to the NCOP Select Committee on Trade and International Relations, August 3, http://www.pmg.org.za/files/docs/110803sadpa-edit.pdf (accessed on 2 October 2011).

DBSA (Development Bank of Southern Africa) (2011) *DBSA and Zambian RDFA Sign a Historic Road Development Loan*, media release, 26 January (Johannesburg: DBSA), http://www.dbsa.org/(S(fndr1a3dsfvwe545s10axdu3))/Mediaroom/Pages/DBSAandZambianRDFASignaHistoricRoad-DevelopmentLoan.aspx (accessed on 2 October 2011).

Fransman, M. (2011) *Budget Vote Speech*, budget speech to the National Assembly by the Deputy Minister of International Relations and Cooperation, 31 May, http://www.dfa.gov.za/docs/speeches/2011/frans0531.html (accessed on 2 October 2011).

G20, *Seoul Development Consensus for Shared Growth*, G20 Seoul Summit 2010, http://media.seoulsummit.kr/contents/dlobo/E3._ANNEX1.pdf (accessed on 2 October 2011).

Games, D. (2010) *Renaissance Fund's Random Spending Should Be More Strategically Focused*, post on Africa@Work, December 13, http://www.africaatwork.co.za/?p=342 (accessed on 2 October 2011).

Geldenhuys, D. (2006) 'South Africa's Role as International Norm Entrepreneur', in Carlsnaes, W. and P. Nel (eds) *In Full Flight: South African Foreign Policy after Apartheid* (Midrand: Institute for Global Dialogue).

Grimm, S. (2011) *South Africa as a Development Partner in Africa*, ECD 2020 Policy Brief, no. 11, March (Bonn: EADI).

Grobbelaar, N. (2008) 'Experiences, Lessons and Policy Recommendations', in Grobbelaar, N. and H. Besada (eds) *Unlocking Africa's Potential: The Role of Corporate South Africa in Strengthening Africa's Private Sector* (Johannesburg: South African Institute of International Affairs – SAIIA), pp. 94–104.

Grobbelaar, N. and H. Besada (eds) (2008) *Unlocking Africa's Potential: The Role of Corporate South Africa in Strengthening Africa's Private Sector* (Johannesburg: SAIIA).

GTZ (German Technical Cooperation) (2010) *Trilateral Cooperation Fund: German/South African Partnership to Support Development of African Countries and Organisations*, document provided by German Embassy in South Africa.

Hallet, M. (2011) 'The Economic Foundations of Growth-Oriented Development Policies', keynote speech presented at the Institut für Wirtschaftsforschung Halle – International Network for Economic Research Workshop on Applied Economics and Economic Policy on 'The Empirics of Imbalances and Disequilibria', 14 February 2011.

IRIN (2011) 'South Africa: Aid Agency to Be Launched', *Irinnews.org*, 17 January, http://www.irinnews.org/report.aspx?reportid=91651 (accessed on 2 October 2011).

Landsberg, C. (2010) *The Diplomacy of Transformation: South African Foreign Policy and Statecraft* (Johannesburg: Macmillan).

Langeni, L. (2011) 'Southern Sudan Referendum in Spotlight', *Business Day*, 5 January, http://www.businessday.co.za/articles/Content.aspx?id=130783 (accessed on 2 October 2011).

Mbeki, T. (2002) *Address at the Welcome Ceremony of the World Summit on Sustainable Development*, 25 August, http://www.dfa.gov.za/docs/ speeches/2002/mbek0825.htm (accessed on 2 October 2011).

Monyae, D. (2011) *The Role of South African DFIs in Regional Infrastructure Development in Africa*, Policy Brief no. 2 (Midrand: Development Bank of Southern Africa), http://www.dbsa.org/Research/Policy%20Briefs/Policy%20Brief%20No.%202.pdf (accessed on 2 October 2011).

Muthayan, S. and J. Pangech (2009) *Regional Capacity Building Project: Innovations through South-South Partnerships*, PowerPoint presentation (unpublished), 30 September.

National Treasury (2006) *South Africa as a Partner in Africa: A Review of South Africa's Development Assistance to Africa*, presentation to the SAIIA workshop held in Johannesburg in December 2006.

National Treasury (2009) *Estimates of National Expenditure 2009* (Pretoria: National Treasury, Republic of South Africa).

National Treasury (2010) *Estimates of National Expenditure 2010* (Pretoria: National Treasury, Republic of South Africa).

National Treasury (2011a) *Budget Review 2011* (Pretoria: National Treasury, Republic of South Africa).

National Treasury (2011b) *Estimates of National Expenditure 2011* (Pretoria: National Treasury, Republic of South Africa).

Nkoana-Mashabane, M. (2010) *Budget Vote Speech*, budget speech to the National Assembly by the Minister of International Relations and Cooperation, 22 April, http://www.dfa.gov.za/docs/speeches/2010/mash0422.html (accessed on 2 October 2011).

Nye, J.S. (2004) *Soft Power: The Means to Success in World Politics* (New York: Public Affairs).

PMG (Parliamentary Monitoring Group) (2011) *Minutes of the Briefing by Department of International Relations & Co-operation on Legislation for Establishment of SADPA, Select Committee on Trade and International Relations*, 3 August, http://www.pmg.org.za/report/20110803-department-international-relations-co-operation-legislation-establish (accessed on 2 October 2011).

SAIIA (2008) *Emerging Donors in International Development Assistance: The South African Case* (Ottawa: IDRC).

Sapa (2010) 'South Africa Cancels R1.1bn Cuba Debt, Unveils Credit Package', *Engineering News*, 8 December, http://www.engineeringnews.co.za/article/cubas-r11bn-debt-cancelled-2010-12-08-1 (accessed on 2 October 2011).

Sidiropoulos, E. (2011) *India and South Africa as Partners for Development in Africa?*, Chatham

House Briefing Paper (London: Chatman House), http://www.chathamhouse.org/publications/papers/view/109646 (accessed on 2 October 2011).

Sidiropoulos, E. and T. Hughes (2004) 'Between Democratic Governance and Sovereignty: The Challenge of South Africa's Africa Policy', in Sidiropoulos, E. (ed.) *Apartheid Past, Renaissance Future: South Africa's Foreign Policy 1994–2004* (Johannesburg: SAIIA).

Sidiropoulos, E. (2006) 'A New International Order? Multilateralism and its Discontents: A View from South Africa', in SAIIA, *South African Yearbook of International Affairs 2005* (Johannesburg: SAIIA).

UNCTAD (United Nations Conference on Trade and Development) (2010) *Economic Development in Africa Report 2010. South-South Cooperation: Africa and the New Forms of Development Partnership*, UNCTAD/ALDC/AFRICA/2010 (Geneva: UNCTAD).

Vivek, A. and A. Vamvakidis (2005) *The Implications of South African Economic Growth for the Rest of Africa*, WP/05/58, International Monetary Fund Working Paper (Washington, DC: IMF).

World Bank (2008) *Global Development Finance 2008: The Role of International Banking* (Washington, DC: World Bank).

8

BRAZIL'S GENEROUS DIPLOMACY: FRIENDLY DRAGON OR PAPER TIGER?

Robert Muggah, Eduarda Passarelli Hamann

Abstract

Featuring a stable democracy and dizzying economic growth, Brazil is fast on the way to acquiring global power status. The country is investing in enhanced multilateral and bilateral relationships as a means of leveraging trade and reducing vulnerability abroad and on the domestic front. This chapter demonstrates how Brazil has increasingly aligned its foreign policy with a South–South Cooperation (SSC) agenda as a means of achieving these parallel objectives. But while Brazil's trade activities have received attention, there has been comparatively less focus on the country's aid policy and practice. Moreover, there is surprisingly little discussion of how the country's foreign policy pillars – trade and aid – are explicitly linked.

The chapter demonstrates how Brazil's emerging aid agenda is fundamentally informed by trade considerations. Over the past decade Brazil has positioned its foreign policy agenda in such a way as to re-shape the global terms of trade in its favour and decrease its dependency both domestically and internationally. Brazil's relatively modest development aid allocations are amplified by a wider effort to advance trade, foreign direct investment and technology transfer. As Brazil seeks to expand to new markets for its products, services and investment, it anticipates that its South–South Development Cooperation (SSDC) stance will facilitate the extension of its influence in bilateral and multilateral arrangements, including the World Trade Organization (WTO) and the United Nations (UN) Security Council.

1. Introduction

Brazil's development agenda is fundamentally conditioned by wider South–South foreign policy considerations. Since at least 2003, Brazil has situated its aid agenda within a broader commitment to improving the terms of trade and decreasing vulnerability at home and abroad. These political and economic considerations profoundly shape the form and function of official development assistance (ODA) and so-called technical assistance. Moreover, the diversification of trade and aid arrangements – including coverage, sectors and modalities – is occurring at a rapid pace. Such trends are raising pressing questions about the future trajectories of Brazilian development cooperation. On the one hand, key institutions – from the Brazilian Agency for Cooperation (ABC) to other public and private entities – are being forced to rapidly adjust. Likewise, domestic factors ranging from rigid legislation, constraints on ABC's autonomy and limited knowledge management/impact assessments to political ambivalence may well thwart Brazil's diplomacy of generosity. Nevertheless, Brazil has made and will continue making a major contribution to a wider South–South Cooperation (SSC) agenda – indeed many of its current and planned aid investments are framed to do precisely this.

2. Trade determines aid

Brazil's engagement with SSC can be traced back to the mid-twentieth century. Its earliest incarnation emerged in the wake of the formation of the Non-Aligned Movement (NAM) established in 1961[1] and the Group of 77 in 1964. But the strategic use of SSC to secure both economic and political interests and advance the country's 'soft-power' genuinely surfaced as a result of former President Lula's so-called 'new world' foreign policy agenda, from 2003 to 2010. Put succinctly, Brazilian foreign policy was expected to promote economic development while simultaneously reducing vulnerabilities to external shocks. Then-President Lula's stated ambition was to achieve a more equitable international order through better positioning in key institutions such as the United Nations (UN) Security Council together with enhanced bilateral, regional and global 'partnerships'. However, Brazil's push for trade liberalization placed a greater weight on ensuring social justice: trade was to be made freer and fairer.

Brazil's foreign policy establishment swiftly turned to strengthening multilateral relationships and new alliances and coalitions in order to support the realignment of the international order. Geopolitically, Brazil's efforts to promote SSC were designed to counterbalance North–South postures that dominated conventional fora. In Latin America, Brazil has sought to establish what Burges (2009) describes as a 'consensual hegemony' in order to gain regional support for international initiatives. This re-positioning played out prominently in the World Trade Organization (WTO) and its Doha Development Agenda. Brazil was also a key contributor to the formation of the G-20 (2003) which had (and continues to have) a direct link with the WTO.[2] Brazil has also been an active contributor to the Global System of Trade Preferences (GSTP) and of course, closer to home, Mercosur.[3] These and other new coalitions were regarded as a way of enhancing the negotiating potential and clout of emerging

---

1 Brazil had 'observer' status to the Non-Aligned Movement (NAM) since its inception.
2 Indeed, while the agenda of the G-20 has grown over the past decade, its primary objective remains the positive outcome in agricultural negotiations in order to preserve the interests of developing countries.
3 Mercosur is an economic and political agreement between Argentina, Brazil, Paraguay and Uruguay. It was founded in 1991 by the Treaty of Asunción (later amended as the 1994 Treaty of Ouro Preto) with the stated goal of promoting free trade and the fluid movement of goods, people and currency (http://www.mercosur.int/).

powers, not least Brazil. And their effects on the multilateral trading system were swift and visible.

The most visible outcome of the SSC agenda and these new coalitions was the collapse of the 5th WTO Ministerial Conference in 2005. The failure to complete the trade round set off a rash of bilateral trade agreements (BTAs). There were fears that these BTAs, many of which promised to set less favourable terms of trade, could undermine certain established non-discrimination principles of the WTO, including the most-favoured nation clause (MFN) (Peterson, 2005). The collapse of the trade talks also catalysed a sudden increase in regional trade agreements (RTAs). These highly diverse forms of cooperation arrangements reconfigured the world trade landscape and are not the subject of this chapter.[4]

The explicit positioning of Brazilian foreign policy along a South–South axis has generated some challenges. The country's wide-ranging approach amounts to forum shopping and potentially dilutes its stated objectives of creating a fairer trading system benefiting both Brazilian and developing country exports but also reducing poverty. As one of the most active participants in the WTO – seeking to push the agricultural agenda and preserve integrity of the more pro-poor Doha mandate – Brazil is a member of a bewildering array of regional groupings including the Free Trade Area of the Americas (FTAA) and the Mercosur. In addition it has signed trade agreements with the European Union and other countries.[5] Some analysts are concerned that the diffuse membership in BTAs and RTAs may undermine the country's bargaining potential.[6] Indeed, Lula opened more than 37 embassies during his term alone, a source of considerable pride to the country's diplomatic establishment.[7]

As noted above, a defining objective of Brazil's positioning at the centre of the SSC agenda was to champion hunger and poverty reduction globally and domestically. On the domestic and foreign policy front, Brazil's programme Fome Zero was premised on promoting social rights such as access to food, education, social welfare and employment protection. Trade policy was at least partially regarded as a means of fostering sustainable economic growth but also reducing the country's vulnerability to global financial market volatility. Brazil has long sought to promote enhanced access for agricultural products through multilateral and bilateral negotiations. This is not surprising: the country is a biotechnology and agribusiness colossus.[8]

It is worth noting that as part of its wider SSC agenda, Brazil also purposefully sought to diversify its export partners. Of course, the country's major partners continue to be the traditional ones – the US and Europe. But since 2009 China has assumed its place as the country's largest trade partner, a feat that, in 2004, Presidents Lula and Hu Jintao described as contributing to a 'new geography of world trade'.[9] There are also significant increases in Brazilian trade with Africa

---

4   There are considerable concerns that bilateral trade agreements (BTAs) and regional trade agreements (RTAs) are inferior to multilateral liberalization since gains for developing countries are marginal by comparison.
5   Brazil is not alone – the average Latin American country belongs to no less than eight BTA/RTAs.
6   See, for example, Americas Quarterly Special Edition (2011).
7   See Amorim (2011).
8   See The Economist Intelligence Unit (2010).
9   Sakia Sassen describes the process of 'glocalization' – how Chinese businesses are now also dealing directly with major cities such as São Paulo and Rio de Janeiro. See Sassen (2011).

(which rose over 110 per cent in the past five years), the Middle East (equally rapid increases), Eastern Europe and Asia. All of these activities have similarly enhanced opportunities for more foreign direct investment. Furthermore, Brazil's rapid market integration into the global economy has reinforced its priorities in agricultural and manufactured goods and increasing investments through the Brazilian Development Bank (BNDES).[10]

Put succinctly, SSC is both a product of and a contributor to a transforming global trading infrastructure.[11] The SSC framework is also giving rise to new transnational alliances. For example, the Brazil-Russia-India-China-South Africa (BRICS) and India-Brazil-South Africa (IBSA) alliances are widely discussed. The latter has formed a trilateral business council to encourage mutual investments and even a small 'development fund' of roughly US$3 million to sell the package. Meanwhile, Brazil has also initiated a rash of trade agreements including through Mercosur. The result of all this cooperation and the fact that emerging economies are substituting imports from rich industrialised economies with cheaper Southern products is that South–South trade is moving at a much more rapid pace than the global average. This realignment has been met with considerable criticism from the Brazilian private sector that complains of foreign policy considerations trumping lucrative North–South trading arrangements. While fears of a 'radical new foreign policy' have not been borne out,[12] there is recognition of the need to invest in both North–South and South–South arrangements.

3. Brazil's 'Southern' aid agenda

It is worth recalling that the wider SSC agenda predates Brazilian and others' more contemporary manifestations. During the 1950s the concept of 'technical cooperation among developing countries' – later described as SSC – emerged in the context of anti-colonial struggles. The so-called Bandung Conference in 1955 assembled 29 countries from across Asia and Africa to promote economic and cultural collaboration.[13] While Brazil was not part of the Indonesian event, it later joined the G77 in the 1960s as a means of ensuring its voice was heard. The goals were to promote more solidarity and self-reliance in order to reduce dependent relations on Northern countries. During the military regime (1964–85) Brazil played a comparatively low-key role in these wider debates concentrating on modest technical cooperation agreements with African countries to secure raw materials and expand its trade linkages.

Notwithstanding its more radical roots, the potential dividends of South–South Development Cooperation (SSDC) were not lost on the multilateral aid system. In 1978 the UN established a special unit for technical cooperation – named SSC – hosted and administered by its Development Programme (UNDP). Overseen by the UN General Assembly, the entity was expected to facilitate and

---

10 It is still useful to put these developments in perspective. As of 2009, the country still accounts for just 1.3 per cent of world trade.
11 See Beattie (2010).
12 See Lafer (2001).
13 See Mulyana (2011).

encourage the sharing of economic and technological knowledge and skills. Predictably, lacking supporting resources, the initiative had comparatively little impact. But as trade and incomes steadily grew in emerging countries during the late 1990s and 2000s, SSDC acquired a new resonance and influence.[14]

Both the Brazilian government and some in the multilateral development sector have skilfully updated the concept for the twenty-first century. As noted above, Lula crafted a wider South–South agenda in which development was situated. Likewise, more traditional donors – particularly the members of the Organisation for Economic Cooperation and Development (OECD) – also played up the idea. For example, the OECD's Development Assistance Committee (DAC) listed SSDC as a major component of realising the so-called Paris Declaration and Accra Agenda for Action's commitment for inclusive partnerships.[15] During negotiations in both Bogota and later New York, in 2010, the OECD attempted to explicitly address the relationships between aid effectiveness and SSDC. There, 'wealthy' donor countries sought to provide lessons on their aid experience and called for more evidence of the outcomes of SSDC and, predictably, more global dialogue.

To some extent, the OECD-DAC-led SSDC agenda has failed to lift off, since major Southern voices – from Brazil and China to India and Saudi Arabia – are missing. Despite contributing more than half of Southern ODA, they are not present on the OECD-DAC's steering committee. For its part, Brazil appears to be reluctant to engage in debates it sees as fundamentally unbalanced and dominated by views and standards set by the North.[16] Notwithstanding repeated attempts at wooing them into the fold and the recent launch of the International Network on Conflict and Fragility (INCAF), just a small number of emerging economies (such as South Korea) have participated in ostensibly Northern forums. Of course the reasons for their absence are part strategic and part ideological.

Indeed, BRICS countries and others often reject the donor–recipient dichotomy and the lexicon of 'new' and 'old' donors embedded in the Paris Declaration and the Accra Agenda for Action. Since the mid-1950s Southern countries have been reluctant to reproduce traditional donor–client hierarchies and repeatedly emphasise the importance of non-conditionality. Brazil considers itself neither a donor nor a recipient, much less new, established or old.[17] In fact, at some point between 2005 and 2010, Brazil passed the threshold where it actually disbursed more ODA than it received. Eschewing the language of the OECD it prefers instead the concepts of 'solidarity', 'respect for sovereignty and autonomy', 'diversity of circumstances and solutions'. The language of SSC reflects the priorities of these countries and OECD countries risk ignoring this at their peril.

---

14 See ECOSOC (2008). See also ECOSOC (2009).
15 The 2008 Accra Agenda for Action of the Third High Level Forum on Aid Effectiveness notes that 'South–South Cooperation (SSC) on development aims to observe the principle of non-interference in internal affairs, equality among developing partners and respect for their independence, national sovereignty, cultural diversity and identity and local content. It plays an important role in international development cooperation and is a valuable complement to North–South cooperation'.
16 See Cabral and Weinstock (2010). See also Burges (2005).
17 For a discussion of the 'emergent' and 'established' labels among new donors consult Woods (2008).

The fact is that Southern aid is not inconsequential. Moreover, it is growing much faster than more traditional OECD donors.[18] In 2009 the total volume of South–South ODA was estimated at US$17.5 billion (10–12 per cent of global ODA), though there is considerable disagreement over the figures owing to the way that Southern countries count their aid dollars.[19] This compares to roughly US$121 billion spent by OECD countries in the same year. A widely cited UN Economic and Social Council (ECOSOC) assessment has grappled with the definition, providing an imperfect definition of South–South ODA.[20]

While still dwarfed by China[21] and India,[22] as noted by Cabral and Weinstock (2010), Brazil has quietly become one of the world's more significant aid providers. Official figures appear to unintentionally conceal the extent of support. Indeed, the ABC – originally established in 1987 to 'coordinate' ODA and cooperation[23] – reportedly spent just US$30 million in 2009. Yet Britain's Overseas Development Institute and Canada's International Development Research Centre suggest that spending by the Brazilian government and associated institutions was between 10 and 15 times higher.[24] Brazil also provides between US$25 and 100 million to the UNDP, US$300 million to the World Food Programme (WFP), US$350 million to Haiti and US$3.3 billion in commercial loans since 2008 from the state development bank – up to US$4 billion a year.[25] While potentially less than medium-sized donors such as Canada and Sweden, the spread and extent of cooperation is rapidly increasing.[26]

In practice, the current Brazilian model reflects a genuine commitment to the early ethos and spirit of SSDC. Brazil draws extensively on internal capacity and innovation and exporting social policy success stories abroad. The examples are now widely known and include the wildly successful Bolsa Familia programme (itself a social technology imported from Mexico), which was exported to post-earthquake Haiti offering multiple incentives (targeting mothers) to encourage school attendance and enhanced nutrition. Other areas of social innovation include tropical agricultural research, including high-yield cotton projects in Mali, Benin, Burkina Faso and Chad. Brazil's vocational training programmes – including support for centres of education excellence in Angola, Mozambique and Paraguay – are other prime examples.[27] Other investments range from new developments in human immunodeficiency virus/

---

18   See The Reality of Aid (2010).
19   See Harmer and Cotterrel (2005).
20   This includes 'grants and concessional loans (including export credits) provided by one Southern country to another to finance projects, programmes, technical cooperation, debt relief and humanitarian assistance and its contributions to multilateral institutions and regional development banks'. The definition continues to be subject to debate and is not consistently applied by Southern governments. See ECOSOC (2009).
21   China is allegedly the largest Southern donor totalling about US$2 billion in 2009 (State Statistical Bureau of the People's Republic of China, 2010).
22   India established the Indian Technical and Economic Cooperation (ITEC) programme in 1964 and has reportedly transferred more than US$2 billion since then. It does not report figures to the Organisation for Economic Cooperation and Development (OECD) and the Development Assistance Committee (DAC). See The Reality of Aid (2010).
23   Brazil first created the National Commission for Technical Assistance (CNAT) in 1950. It was composed of a wide range of Ministries and was located under the Office of the President. See Costa Vaz and Yumie Aoki Inoue (2007).
24   See The Economist (2010).
25   See IPEA (2011).
26   The distribution of aid relative to other donors such as Canada and Sweden is discussed by Baker (2010).
27   Brazil set up a centre for training and enterprise development in Luanda in 1999 and in Paraguay it created a centre of excellence for professional training. Other innovations include the Bolsa Escola in Mozambique.

acquired immune deficiency syndrome (HIV/AIDS) treatment for the poor in Mozambique to the building of police training institutes in Guinea-Bissau. In fact, Brazil currently has technical cooperation agreements with more than 50 countries from across the Global South.

While still early days, Brazil's approach to SSDC has repeated political and commercial dividends. On the one hand, it has extended the country's soft power in Africa and across Latin America and the Caribbean so that it can enhance its profile in multilateral fora while competing with India and China. Brazil had until recently focused primarily on Portuguese-speaking countries,[28] but by 2010 had brokered more than 400 SSDC projects across African, Latin American, Asian and Middle Eastern countries. It has also served to bolster the country's claim to a UN Security Council seat, as it assumes more burden and responsibility attendant with its economic status. On the other hand, it serves Brazil's growing commercial interests. As noted in *The Economist*, Brazil currently is the world's most efficient ethanol producer and seeks to promote markets in green fuel: spreading technology to poorer countries creates new suppliers and bolsters global market demand. These successes are not without some *hubris*. The former Minister for Strategic Affairs has noted how 'since rising powers like Brazil will one day run the world...they can save trouble later by reducing poverty in developing countries now'.[29]

Brazil exhibits certain comparative advantages when it comes to promoting SSDC. On the one hand, the country has purposefully sought to break down the traditional 'donor–recipient' model and these efforts are born of a domestic belief, albeit still untested, that cultural, linguistic and historical affinities ostensibly matter in shaping development outcomes.[30] Likewise, while broadly playing by the international rules of development cooperation, Brazil has charted out an approach that still deviates somewhat from certain OECD principles. It is also fair to say that Western donors are less preoccupied about Brazilian aid than China, which they see as a rival power, fostering corruption and fundamentally 'bad' development policy. Since Brazil is widely regarded as having a stable democratic foundation and good neighbourly relations, the country is increasingly solicited by OECD countries for trilateral cooperation agreements. Moreover, as the Brazilian aid agency is focused on social policy, health and agriculture it is not regarded as a competitor.[31] China, meanwhile, is more focused on financing roads, railways and docks for expedient resource extraction.[32]

4. Challenges for Brazil

While rapidly evolving, it is important to stress that Brazil's SSDC model is still nascent. There are still a great many challenges confronting the country,

---

28   See Federative Republic of Brazil (2008).
29   See *The Economist* (2010).
30   See Muggah and Szabó de Carvalho (2010).
31   Meanwhile, Brazilian 'private' firms are focusing on activities ranging from roads and railways to mining and dam projects. Companies such as Andrade Gutierrez, Odebrecht, Queiroz Galvão, Petrobras and Vale are all extremely active abroad.
32   It is worth stressing that Brazilian firms and business leaders, most notably Eike Batista, are picking-up commodities and extraction firms. See, for example, Burges (2007).

including the future mandate and organisation of the development cooperation agency. What is clear is that Brazil's relationship with more traditional donors is adapting as it shifts from receiving to providing assistance.[33] It has spurred on more trilateral – or three-party – modalities with the traditional donor providing financial support, Brazil offering technical assistance, and the receiving country also engaged. There are an abundance of examples ranging from Canada, Japan and the US to the International Labour Organization (ILO), UNDP and others. According to Cabral (2010, 3) 'ABC currently manages 88 such initiatives across 27 countries...[which] represent one fifth of Brazil's technical cooperation projects'.

And while Brazil exhibits a host of comparative advantages with respect to SSDC, it also faces a number of critical deficits. For example, partly owing to the novelty of many activities, Brazil has yet to demonstrate the outcomes and impacts of its major investments.[34] This will require a greater awareness of the existing portfolio, knowledge management, and monitoring and evaluation capabilities. As noted by Cabral (2010, 3) 'the lack of reliable and accurate data on aid volumes and their impact is a common problem amongst emerging donors'. This is especially true for projects that started before 2004–05. And while some discussion is emerging about how to link aid effectiveness agendas to the wider SSDC approach, questions remain about the extent to which Southern partners are ready to engage.

Related to this, Brazil confronts the challenges of an apathetic and potentially hostile domestic constituency to a more proactive SSDC mandate. For example, systemic (but gradually improving) social and economic challenges and far-reaching inequality in Brazil's major cities and rural areas highlight the very real 'development' challenges on the home front. Some constituents have demonstrated a level of ambivalence to ODA, including to Haiti where the country is most visibly invested in the UN Stabilization Mission (MINUSTAH) and beyond. Without the vigorous backing of the executive and effective lobbying, there is a real possibility of the trade agenda becoming the dominant vehicle for multilateralism and development slipping off the radar.

Most assessments of the future of Brazil's SSDC agenda have centred on the administrative and bureaucratic modalities of assistance. On the one hand, there are well-known legal conditionalities that limit monetary transfers from the public sector to other governments. As such, Brazil focuses primarily on technical assistance and provides financial assistance only through existing multilateral modalities. Similar rules abound relating to constraints on procurement and contracting non-public servants. Likewise, ABC itself is institutionally locked into a subordinate position in Brazil's Ministry of Foreign Affairs (known as *Itamaraty*) and will need to carve out more autonomy and political support if it is to genuinely transform into a full-fledged development agency.[35] Similarly,

---

33 See Cabral (2010, 3).
34 For example, the so-called Cotton 4 project established in 2008 between Brazil and Mali, Burkina Faso, Benin and Chad seeks to enhance the region's cotton value chain. While anecdotal evidence suggests that it is generating positive returns, no comprehensive evaluation has been undertaken.
35 The Brazilian Agency for Cooperation (ABC) is located in one of seven divisions of the Ministry of Foreign Affairs under the General Sub-Secretariat for Cooperation and Commercial Promotion.

as Brazil's trade and aid agenda expands, civil servants are overwhelmed.[36] While the current President Dilma Rousseff mulls over the creation of a new aid agency, there is a danger of inertia taking hold.

A commonly cited challenge for Brazil relates to the way SSDC is currently coordinated and managed. Indeed, the regulatory framework is currently designed for 'receiving' rather than 'providing' assistance. Notwithstanding its critical central role, however, ABC is just one of many agencies engaged in promoting international development. Examples of other agencies include *Embrapa* (agricultural research), the Ministry of Health, the Ministry of Social Development (social protection), the National Service for Industrial Apprenticeship (SENAI) and many others.[37] As the number of Brazilian institutions engaged continues to expand, the decision-making authority of *Itamaraty* has arguably weakened (Cabral and Weinstock, 2010). And while some improvements are being registered, the development cooperation architecture has thus been described as 'fragmented' and characterised by uneven coordination in terms of strategic vision, standards and procedures.

REFERENCES

ABC (Agência Brasileira de Cooperação-Brazilian Agency for Cooperation) (2005) 'O que é a Agência Brasileira de Cooperação?', *Via ABC*, July (Brasilia: Agência Brasileira de Cooperação, Ministério das Relações Exteriores), http://www.abc.gov.br/lerNoticia.asp?id_Noticia=65 (accessed on 30 August 2011).

Americas Quarterly Special Edition (2011) *The New Brazil and the Changing Hemisphere*, 5(2), http://www.americasquarterly-digital.org/americasquarterly/spring2011#pg1 (accessed on 30 August 2011).

Amorim, C. (2011) 'Reflections on Brazil's Global Rise', *Americas Quarterly*, 5(2), http://www.americasquarterly.org/node/2420 (accessed on 30 August 2011).

Baker, E. (2010) 'Brazil gives as much aid as Canada and Sweden? Maybe not...', http://blog.aiddata.org/2010/07/brazil-gives-as-much-aid-as-canada-and.html (accessed on 30 August 2011).

Beattie, A. (2010) 'BRICS: The Changing Faces of Global Power', *Financial Times*, January 17, www.ft.com/cms/s/0/95cea8b6-0399-11df-a601-00144feabdc0.html (accessed on 30 August 2011).

Burges, S. (2005) 'Auto-Estima in Brazil: The Logic of Lula's South-South Foreign Policy', *International Journal*, 60(4), pp. 1133–51.

Burges, S. (2007) 'Building a Global Southern Coalition: The Competing Approaches of Brazil's Lula and Venezuela's Chavez', *Third World Quarterly*, 28(7), pp. 1343–58.

Burges, S. (2009) *Brazilian Foreign Policy after the Cold War* (Miami: University Press of Florida).

Cabral, L. (2010) *Brazil: An Emerging Aid Player. Lessons on Emerging Donors, and South-South and Trilateral Cooperation* (London: Overseas Development Institute), www.odi.org.uk/resources/download/6295.pdf (accessed on 5 December 2011).

Cabral, L. and J. Weinstock (2010) *Brazilian Technical Cooperation for Development: Drivers, Mechanics and Future Prospects* (London: Overseas Development Institute), www.odi.org.uk/resources/download/6137.pdf (accessed on 5 December 2011).

Costa Vas, A. and C. Yumie Aoki Inoue (2007) *Emerging Donors in International Development Assistance: The Brazil Case* (Ottawa: International Development Research Centre, Partnership and Business Development Division).

ECOSOC (United Nations Economic and Social Council) (2008) *Background Study for the Development Cooperation Forum. Trends in South-South and Triangular Development Cooperation* (New York: United Nations), http://www.un.org/en/ecosoc/

---

36 There are roughly 160 employees in ABC, including both diplomats and technical experts seconded from the United Nations Development Programme (UNDP).
37 In principle, and most often in practice, all Brazilian ministries and agencies are expected to 'partner' with ABC in order to sign and implement technical cooperation projects.

docs/pdfs/south-south_cooperation.pdf (accessed on 30 August 2011).

ECOSOC (2009) *Support to UN Development Cooperation Forum 2010. South-South and Triangular Cooperation: Improving Information and Data* (New York: United Nations), http://www.un.org/en/ecosoc/newfunct/pdf/analytical%20study%20(ssc)%20-%20november%202009.pdf (accessed on 30 August 2011).

Federative Republic of Brazil (2008) *Trends in Development Cooperation: South-South and Triangular Cooperation and Aid Effectiveness. The Brazilian Experience*, Cairo High-Level Symposium, http://www.un.org/en/ecosoc/newfunct/pdf/brazil_ssc_cairo.pdf (accessed on 30 August 2011).

Harmer, A. and L. Cotterrel (2005) *Diversity in Donorship: The Changing Landscape of Official Humanitarian Aid* (London: Overseas Development Institute, Humanitarian Policy Group), http://www.odi.org.uk/resources/download/234.pdf. (accessed on 30 August 2011).

IPEA (Instituto de Pesquisa Econômica Aplicada – Institute of Applied Economic Research) (2011) *Cooperação Brasileira para o Desenvolvimento Internacional: 2005–2009* (Brasilia: IPEA).

Lafer, C. (2001) *A Identidade Internacional do Brasil e a Política Externa Brasileira: Passado e Presente* (São Paulo: Perspectiva).

Muggah, R. and I. Szabó de Carvalho (2010) *The Southern Effect: Critical Reflections on Brazil's Engagement with Fragile States* (Paris: OECD).

Mulyana, Y.G.H. (2011) 'The 1955 Bandung Conference and its Present Significance', *Jakarta Post*, 29 April, http://www.thejakartapost.com/news/2011/04/29/the-1955-bandung-conference-and-its-present-significance.html (accessed on 30 August 2011).

Peterson, L.E. (2005) *The Global Governance of Foreign Direct Investment: Madly Off in All Directions*, Dialogue on Globalisation Occasional Paper no. 19 (Geneva: Friedrich Ebert Stiftung) http://www.nuso.org/upload/fes_pub/Peterson.pdf (accessed on 6 December 2011).

Sassen, S. (2011) 'The Americas go Glocal', *Americas Quarterly*, 5(2), http://www.americasquarterly.org/node/2430 (accessed on 30 August 2011).

State Statistical Bureau of the People's Republic of China (2010) *China Statistical Yearbook* (Beijing; China Statistics Press).

The Economist (2010) 'Brazil's Foreign-Aid Programme. Speak Softly and Carry a Blank Check', *The Economist*, July, http://www.economist.com/node/16592455. (accessed on 30 August 2011).

The Economist Intelligence Unit (2010) *Brazil Industry: Global Farmer – Latin America*, News Release, The Economist Intelligence Unit, November, http://latinamerica.economist.com/news/brazil-industry-global-farmer/186 (accessed on 30 August 2011).

The Reality of Aid (2010) *South-South Development Cooperation: A Challenge to the Aid System? Special Report on South-South Cooperation* (Quezon City: IBON Books), http://www.realityofaid.org/roa-reports/index/secid/373/South-South-Development-Cooperation-A-challenge-to-the-aid-system (accessed on 30 August 2011).

Woods, N. (2008) 'Whose Aid? Whose Influence? China, Emerging Donors and the Silent Revolution in Development Assistance', *International Affairs*, 84(6), pp. 1205–21.

PART 2: REVIEW

MAJOR DEVELOPMENT POLICY TRENDS

9
THE CHALLENGES FACING THE MULTILATERAL TRADING SYSTEM IN ADDRESSING GLOBAL PUBLIC POLICY OBJECTIVES

Christophe Bellmann, Jonathan Hepburn, Marie Wilke

Abstract

Despite a record-breaking 14.5 per cent increase in world merchandise exports, the effects of the financial crisis and global recession are still hampering faster economic recovery. Relatively high oil prices combined with persistent unemployment and measures designed to reduce budget deficits have undermined short-term growth prospects. While South–South trade continues to explode, trade imbalances – i.e. the gap between exports and imports – widened in 2010 compared to 2009 (although smaller than pre-crisis levels). Meanwhile, trade negotiations under the Doha Round have reached an impasse, generating uncertainties about the future of the World Trade Organization (WTO) as a negotiating forum. Under these circumstances, should the system rethink its decision-making process founded upon the predominance of member states, the principle of consensus and the notion of single undertaking, as some critics have suggested? And, if so, how could such a reform agenda be initiated at the WTO? Moreover, beyond the negotiating function of the WTO, the paralysis of the system also raises urgent questions about the ability of the system to respond to pressing challenges of our times, such as trade and climate change, or food security and price volatility.

'*What we are seeing today is the paralysis in the negotiating function of the WTO, whether it is on market access or on the rule-making. What we are facing is the inability of the WTO to adapt and adjust to emerging global trade priorities, those you cannot solve through bilateral deals.*'

Pascal Lamy, at an informal heads of delegation meeting of the
Trade Negotiating Committee, 26 July 2011

1. Introduction

The 2008–09 financial crisis and the current sovereign debt crisis in Europe have not only highlighted the high level of economic interdependencies existing worldwide, but also the growing challenges in pursuing international collaborative actions to address urgent sustainable development challenges. In a rapidly changing multi-polar world in which economic wealth is progressively shifting towards the East and the South, and in which resource constraints have become increasingly pressing, international cooperation remains in crisis. The rise of emerging countries like China, India or Brazil and the relative decline of traditional economic powers have created new opportunities, as reflected by the unprecedented growth in South–South trade observed over the last decade or so. However, it has also generated new tensions, not least between countries with large trade surpluses and those with growing trade deficits. Such tensions are equally palatable in international negotiations such as the ones dealing with climate change.

Meanwhile, the number of hungry people is estimated to have reached one billion in 2009, catapulting food security back to the top of the political agenda. As growth in demand continues to rise faster than increases in supply – due fundamentally to low productivity growth – food prices are expected to remain high and volatile in the coming years. Several factors have contributed to enhancing price volatility: low stocks resulting from a succession of weather-related production shortfall, growing demand for biofuels feedstock, rising energy prices and a depreciation of the US dollar; however, these have been aggravated by policy responses such as export restrictions.

This rapidly changing environment and the pressing needs for international cooperative action to address concerns around food security, climate change or unsustainable trade imbalances contrast sharply with the current paralysis of the multilateral trading system. The Doha Round of trade negotiations under the World Trade Organization (WTO) has now remained in a limbo for several months with no real perspectives for the near future. While several factors explain the stalemate in the ten-year-old trade talks, this paralysis raises uncertainties about the future of the multilateral trading system.

As a contribution to this discussion, this chapter looks at how the multilateral trading system has sought to address global public policy objectives, and how it can do so in the future. After a short review of current trends in international trade and recent developments which have led to the current crisis in the Doha Round, Section 3 considers possible options for reforming the way in which the WTO conducts negotiations. Finally, Section 4 focuses on how the WTO has sought to respond to specific public policy objectives in the past – using the case of food security as an example – and what this tells us about the way in which the multilateral trading system relates to broader global public policy goals.

2. The international context

2.1. Recent trends in international trade

Following a sharp 12 per cent drop in 2009, the volume of world merchandise exports increased by a record-breaking 14.5 per cent in 2010, allowing global trade to recover to pre-crisis levels. This figure, the largest since data collection began in 1950, accompanied a 3.6 per cent increase in global gross domestic product (GDP). According to the WTO (WTO, 2011a), world trade growth should settle to a more modest 5.8 per cent in 2011, with a 2.5 per cent increase in global GDP (see Figure 9.1). Unsurprisingly, Asia exhibited the fastest real export growth – 23.1 per cent – with Chinese and Japanese exports increasing by 28.4 and 27.5 per cent, respectively. Meanwhile, merchandise trade grew by 10.8 per cent in Europe, and 15.4 per cent in the US. Overall developing countries and economies in transition accounted for 45 per cent of total world exports, the highest share ever (WTO, 2011a).

Rising commodity prices and a depreciating US currency meant that trade growth in dollar terms – at 22 per cent – exceeded the increase in volume terms. In particular, regions that rely on natural resource exports – such as Africa, the Middle East or South America – experienced lower growth in trade volumes but significant increases in the dollar value of their exports. African exports were up by 6.5 per cent in volume terms, but by 28 per cent in dollar terms. Similarly, Latin American exports grew by just 6.2 per cent in volume terms but by 25 per cent in dollar terms (WTO, 2011b).

Figure 9.1 – World merchandise exports and GDP, 2008–11 (in percentage change*)

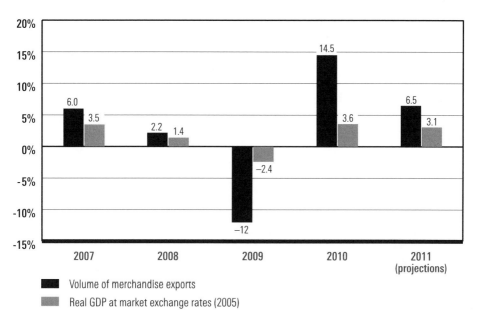

■ Volume of merchandise exports
■ Real GDP at market exchange rates (2005)

* Percentage change compared with same month of the previous year.
Source: WTO (2011b).

Meanwhile, according to the United Nations Conference on Trade and Development (UNCTAD), total foreign direct investments (FDI) increased from US$1.185 to 1.244 trillion in 2010, largely due to increased flow to developing countries which, together with transition economies, accounted for more than half of total FDI (UNCTAD, 2011). Outward FDI from emerging economies also reached record highs, with most of their investment directed towards other countries in the South.

While these figures look impressive, the 2010 increase in merchandise trade did not suffice to return exports to levels consistent with 1990–2008 trends. On the investment front, despite a 5 per cent increase compared to 2009, global FDI flows have remained lower than their pre-crisis average (2005–07), and 37 per cent below their 2007 peak (UNCTAD, 2011). And while emerging economies in Latin America and South-East Asia experienced a rapid growth, FDI flows continued to contract in developed countries, Africa and South Asia.

More generally, as world output in 2009 was depressed, the WTO argues that higher growth in 2010 was to be expected, particularly as GDP growth often reached 4 per cent or more in recent years (WTO, 2011a). Several factors might explain why trade and output grew more slowly than they might have. In 2010, relatively high oil prices raised energy costs for households and business. High unemployment rates also affected domestic consumption and import demand in developed countries. Finally, attempts in Europe, the US and elsewhere to reduce budget deficits led to cuts in spending and revenue, undermining short-term growth prospects. The negative impacts of the financial crisis and global recession are therefore likely to remain for some time despite the record rebound of trade in 2010.

In the US, a low national savings rate and high private consumption as a share of GDP have continued to sustain demand for imported consumer goods, fuelling rapid export-led growth in emerging economies. Over the last 10 to 15 years, these developments have resulted in large imbalances, with sizeable current account deficits accumulating in the US in particular, and large current account surpluses in others, notably China, Germany and Japan. These have in turn

Figure 9.2 – Trade imbalances in selected economies, 2008–10 (in US$ million)

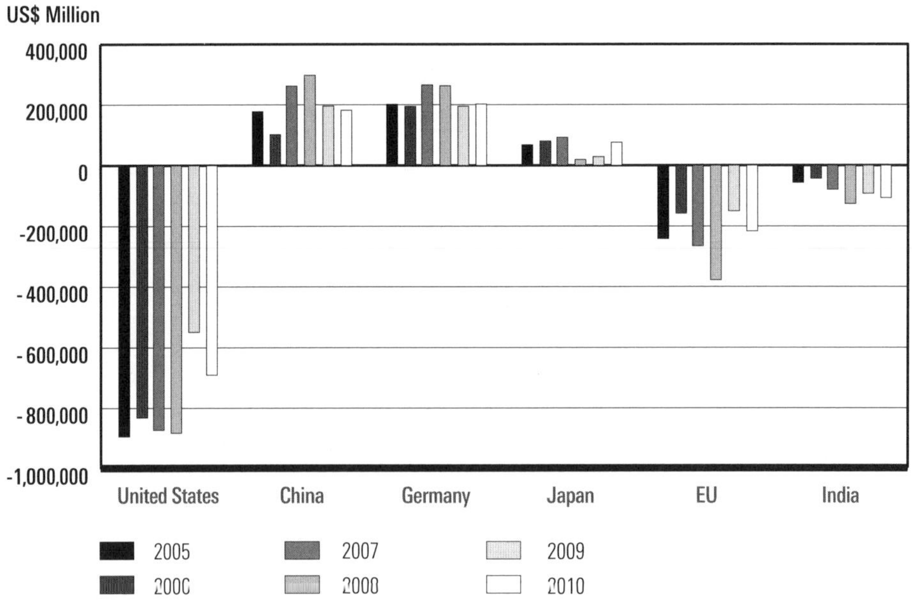

Source: WTO (2011b).

Figure 9.3 – Imports–exports: US and China, 2005–11 (in US$ million)

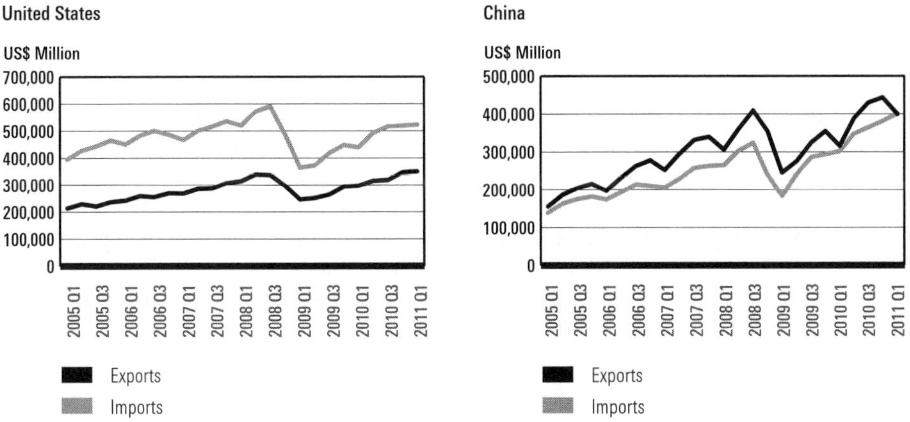

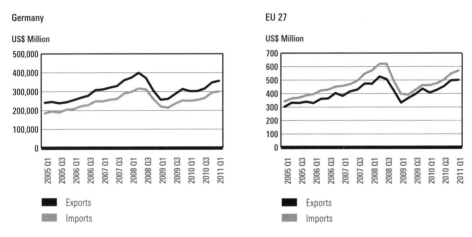

Source: WTO (2011b).

Figure 9.4 – Imports–exports: Germany and the EU, 2005–11 (in US$ million)

generated political tensions, evident in the US–China controversy over exchange rate policies. In 2010, trade imbalances remained smaller than pre-crisis levels, but for most countries, except China, the gap between exports and imports widened compared to 2009 (see Figures 9.3 and 9.4). As Figure 9.2 shows, the US trade deficit increased from roughly US$550 billion to US$690 billion – but remained lower than the US$880 billion seen in 2008. Meanwhile, China's trade surplus fell from nearly US$300 billion in 2008 to just over US$180 billion in 2010. In 2010, the trade deficit of the European Union (EU) widened beyond 2009 levels, despite Germany's US$200 billion trade surplus, even though the overall EU deficit was smaller than in 2008. Japan was an exception to the overall trend towards smaller imbalances, as its trade surplus nearly quadrupled in 2010 compared to pre-crisis levels.

There is widespread consensus that current imbalances are not sustainable in the long term. Persistently high levels of debt-financed household consumption in the US will have to return to slightly lower historical levels (Mayer, 2011). At the same time, low consumption rates and high national savings in China have prompted calls for Beijing to develop its internal market and gradually move from investment and export to consumer-led growth. These trends are likely to affect both the size and composition of global demand in years ahead. This is partly because increased Chinese consumption might not fully compensate a possible decrease in US demand growth, but also because the two economies tend to import different baskets of goods, with China buying more raw material, commodities and food, for example. Unless other trade surplus countries such as Germany or Japan also enhance their domestic consumption, changes in global demand will have major negative repercussions on developing country exports, and also on employment – particularly in manufacturing sectors such as textiles and clothing (Mayer, 2011).

South–South trade has also continued to expand, and now represents roughly 50 per cent of developing country exports. Africa's trade volumes with its emerging partners have doubled in nominal value over the decade and now amount to 37 per cent of the continent's total trade (AFDB et al., 2011). While China represents Africa's leading emerging partner, having surpassed the US in volume terms, the sum of the continent's trade with its other emerging partners (such as Turkey, Brazil, Korea and India) is now even larger than its trade with China. While these developments provide new opportunities – export markets, technology transfer, aid and other forms of cooperation – African exports to other developing countries largely remain concentrated on primary products, with little evidence to date that South–South trade has prompted real structural transformation.

2.2. The collapse of the Doha Round negotiations

Since January 2010, the Doha Round has continued to flounder, with deadlines for concluding the ten-year talks being missed at the end of that year and the next, and now having no end in sight. Over the course of the year, the US repeatedly called for mandatory participation in 'sectoral' agreements for manufactured products, due to slash tariffs across an entire industry. Brazil, China and India rejected US demands for major emerging economies to take on particular responsibilities, and disputed Washington's claim that the December 2008 draft texts disproportionately penalise the US – calling instead on the US to clarify what specific concessions Washington might offer in return for increased market access.

Meanwhile, the G-33 group of developing countries made a series of proposals in favour of a strong 'special safeguard mechanism' that they could use to defend domestic agricultural producers from sudden import surges or price depressions. The US and other exporting countries continued to insist that developing country flexibilities should not undermine growth in normal trade.

After a much-touted but ultimately fruitless 'stocktaking exercise' in March 2010, members met for most of the remaining year in various informal bilateral and plurilateral groups – described as 'variable geometry' by WTO Director-General Pascal Lamy. Trade also featured in discussions on the sidelines of gatherings of the Organisation for Economic Co-operation and Development (OECD) and the Asia-Pacific Economic Cooperation (APEC), and on the agenda of the Toronto and Seoul summits of the G-20 group of leading economies – only for officials to find that the interests of major trading powers were still not close enough for a Doha deal to be struck in the near future. In early 2011, Mexico and Brazil tabled separate proposals on breaking the Doha deadlock, including possible trade-offs between separate negotiating areas such as agriculture and manufactured goods: however, these found little support at the global trade body. Recognising that gaps were increasingly hard to bridge, trade negotiators began discussing options for a 'soft landing'. The release of revised texts or working documents in April 2011 confirmed fears that progress had stymied, with some negotiating group chairs only able to release 'state of play' reports instead of new drafts.

Members then began quiet discussions on what a 'Plan B' might look like. The plan was officially announced in May: members would finalise a mini-package focused on concerns of least developed countries (LDCs) for the December Ministerial, and also establish a work plan to resolve other outstanding issues. At the insistence of the US, the package was broadened to include non-LDC issues too. However, the package quickly began to unravel as members became unable to agree on which LDC and non-LDC items to include. Consensus proved elusive on the four main issues that LDCs sought to include: duty-free quota-free access for their exports; an LDC services waiver, a 'step forward' on cotton, and improved rules of origin. Similarly, trading powers were unable to agree on the growing number of 'non-LDC' issues proposed, which ranged from fishery subsidies to trade facilitation and export competition.

By August, the plan for the December 2011 Ministerial Conference had shifted away from producing an LDC-plus package: members instead decided they would focus on non-Doha issues and on a post-December work plan for concluding Doha, while holding parallel discussions on possible LDC deliverables.

3. Fair and inclusive global trade governance

Several factors explain members' inability to conclude the trade talks. Some point to the fact that the negotiating process has become too politicised and complex, given the growing diversity and varied expectations of the WTO's 153-country membership. Others blame the rise of emerging economies such as Brazil, China and India, together with more assertive developing country coalitions. Others still link it to the global financial crisis and recent domestic difficulties in the EU and the US which have prevented those countries from fully exercising a leadership role in WTO negotiations. Finally, countries' positions and negotiating interests have changed over time reflecting nowadays geopolitical dynamics. All these factors are relevant, but critics are increasingly pointing to a more fundamental flaw in the system, which relates to the way in which negotiations are conducted. Some observers have therefore argued that thorough reform of the system is needed to overcome the current paralysis.

Others remark that it is not necessarily the WTO's institutional procedures that have paralysed the organisation, but rather the way in which members have chosen to use its rules and practices (Rodriguez Mendoza and Wilke, 2011; Rolland, 2010). In fact some experts argue that the WTO has served as a model governance system at the international level, predominantly because of its automatic and enforceable dispute settlement system. Moreover, through its set of rules and disciplines, it is argued, the WTO has also been successful in preventing protectionist tendencies during economic crisis.

Nonetheless debate over institutional reform – whether it is needed, in what form and via what kind of process – has continued ever since the WTO was first established (Deere-Birbeck and Monagle, 2009). In 2003, after the failure of the Cancún Ministerial Conference, Pascal Lamy – then EU trade commissioner – qualified the WTO as 'medieval' and called for its decision-making process to be revamped (Lamy, 2003). In recent years, various actors have proposed reforming virtually every aspect of the WTO's functioning – from management and administration through the conduct of trade negotiations and dispute settlement, to capacity-building and cooperation with other institutions or the public at large (Deere-Birbeck and Monagle, 2009). The objectives behind those proposals and the pace of proposed reforms have been equally diverse, going from incremental improvements to radical changes in the way the institution functions. While some proposals have been introduced by governments, others have been put forward by academia, research institutes, civil society and other international organisations.[1] The multilateral system itself has not been static in the face of these demands. Reforms – or incremental changes – have happened on a number of fronts, including at the management level, in external transparency, public participation in dispute settlement proceedings or in the way in which negotiations are conducted (Deere-Birbeck and Monagle, 2009). There are, however, diverging views on the desirability and impact of these changes and on whether they go far enough.

The debate sparked renewed interest as members prepared for the November 2009 Ministerial Conference. After ten years of complex negotiations, characterised by missed deadlines and few substantive dividends, critics have argued that the body's established rules, principles and practices of decision-making, carried over from the General Agreement on Tariffs and Trade (GATT),[2] are simply ill-suited to the fast changing challenges of our times. Some

---

1   The *Warwick Report*, for example, provides one of the most notable and comprehensive stock-taking exercises produced by non-governmental experts (Warwick Commission, 2007). Another critical milestone in this debate was the report commissioned in 2003 by Dr Supachai Panitchpakdi, then Director General of the World Trade Organization (WTO), to a panel of experts chaired by the former Director General of the General Agreement on Tariffs and Trade (GATT), Peter Sutherland, on 'The Future of the WTO: Addressing Institutional Challenges in the New Millennium'. Despite its comprehensive analysis and concrete recommendations, the *Sutherland Report* was, however, criticised as a defence of the *status quo*, produced by insiders, thus lacking novel approaches (Hufbauer, 2005; Pauwelyn, 2005). As such it did not provide the necessary impetus to initiate a structured discussion among members.

2   When governments launched the Uruguay Round of trade negotiations under the GATT in 1986, the declared aim was not to establish a standing global organisation on trade governance. What later became the WTO, only emerged over the last few months of the almost eight years' lasting negotiations. When members realised that the trade package to be presented at the end of the negotiation round would include new areas such as intellectual property rights and services, the need arose to discuss processes and structures that would ensure the coherence of these different agreements. The decision to establish the WTO finally stemmed from that discussion and other related considerations in the negotiation Group on the Functioning of the GATT (FOGS). Since no systemic, long-term negotiations had taken place on a potential international organisation, most agreements (with the exception of the Dispute Settlement Understanding (DSU) which had been revised completely during the Uruguay Round) thus replicate the principles that have served that GATT for the last five decades. Moreover, when members launched the ongoing Doha Round they referred back to the negotiation principles used during the Uruguay Round, namely the principles of consensus and single undertaking. See Rodriguez Mendoza and Wilke (2011).

even argue that the GATT/WTO's 'golden triangle' of decision-making – the dominance of contracting parties, the consensus principle and the logic of the 'single undertaking' – is unable to meet the challenges of modern global trade governance (Cottier and Elsig, 2009).

Strengthening the WTO's negotiation functioning will require balancing three competing demands: greater efficiency in the conduct of negotiations; enhanced legitimacy including by better addressing public policy concerns; and greater inclusiveness, so as to overcome power asymmetries and foster mutually beneficial outcomes. The following sections review some of the criticism and the proposed reform options for the WTO's conduct of negotiations in light of these objectives.

3.1. The principles of consensus and the single undertaking

WTO negotiations are guided by the consensus principle and by the idea that they represent a *single undertaking*. Consensus is not interpreted as requiring unanimity; however,[3] if no present member state objects, consensus is assumed. The single undertaking, on the other hand, requires that *all areas* are negotiated and adopted by *all parties* at the *same time*.[4] Both principles derive directly from the WTO's nature as a member-driven organisation. With the secretariat assuming an almost marginal role and the consensus principle on the basis of sovereign equality permeating all areas and functions of the organisation, the dominance of contracting parties is its main characteristic.

Each concept can be seen as a double-edged sword. The consensus principle is important for developing countries as, in theory, it guarantees that every member can veto any decisions, irrespective of its political or economic power. The single undertaking, on the other hand, has supported developing countries on numerous occasions, for instance when a group of Latin American members halted the establishment of the WTO until certain concessions of vital interest to developing countries had been made (Croome, 1995).

Both pillars nonetheless need to be seen in the context of the overarching power asymmetries at the WTO. In practice, wealthier nations can hold trade talks hostage more easily than poorer ones, because of the fact that they are better able to withstand political pressure to join a consensus even against great opposition (Steinberg, 2002; Cottier and Elsig, 2009; Low, 2009). The consensus principle is thus less about the actual consensual adoption of a final decision than about the process of consensus-building (Ismail and Vickers, 2011). The largest trading nations therefore bear particular responsibility for helping countries to reach agreement by guiding the process of consensus-building and facilitating an atmosphere of compromise. Ismail and Vickers thus note that, in the Doha round, '[d]eveloped countries also share considerable blame – even responsibility – for frustrating the process of consensus-building. It is [...] disturbing that critics of the consensus principle raise efficiency concerns

---

3   The consensus principle dates back to the International Trade Organization (ITO) and with it the early beginnings of the GATT. See Ismail and Vickers (2011).
4   'With the exception of the improvements and clarifications of the DSU, the conduct, conclusion and entry into force of the outcome of the negotiations shall be treated as parts of a single undertaking. However, agreements reached at an early stage may be implemented on a provisional or a definitive basis. Early agreements shall be taken into account in assessing the overall balance of the negotiations' (WTO, 2001, para. 47).

only when smaller developing countries and larger emerging economies (e.g. Brazil, China, India and South Africa) do not join the consensus of the developed countries' (Ismail and Vickers, 2011).

This is similarly true for the single undertaking and the use of 'linkages' to condition concessions in one area to progress in others. While in principle these could foster compromises by focusing negotiators' attention on the greatest gains, in practice members tend to overemphasise the losses (Van Grasstek and Sauvé, 2006). This is particularly true for the current round, where negotiators do not seek to establish linkages systematically with a view to achieving long-term benefits, but focus instead on achieving short-term gains for tactical reasons (Rodriguez Mendoza and Wilke, 2011). The introduction of linkages prevents certain areas from moving ahead independent of progress in others. As a result, even small deals cannot be reached, as new proposals prompt further linkages.

Proposals to reform those two core negotiating principles (Deere-Birbeck and Monagle, 2009) can be summarised in two categories: those introducing different voting systems, and those relating to 'variable geometry agreements' including so-called 'plurilateral' and 'critical mass' agreements.

Proposals on weighted voting (one suggestion for reforming the consensus principle) and critical mass agreements share a common idea. Power – be it for voting, agenda setting or participation in negotiations – would reflect a country's economic significance. The allocation of votes could thus reflect a country's share in global trade, GDP or the level of market openness. Some experts also suggest taking into account country size or population, arguing that this would ensure power is shared fairly among developed, emerging and other developing countries (Cottier and Takenoshita, 2008; Elsig, 2009). However, experience with weighted voting approaches in the International Monetary Fund (IMF) and World Bank show that the approach can easily manifest real power asymmetries rather than overcoming imbalances (Warwick Commission, 2007).[5]

The current voting system does not suffer from a large group of small countries blocking negotiations, but instead from a handful of powerful countries that are unable to reach agreement among themselves. The alternative, a simple majority vote, could be difficult to introduce as it would undermine the currently powerful position of developed countries by enabling groups of smaller countries to overrule them. Experience in the United Nations (UN) General Assembly indicates that many countries would systematically oppose the introduction of a simple majority vote (Anghie, 2005).

The concept of 'variable geometry' agreements is an alternative to the single undertaking. Plurilateral agreements, for example, have already been used in the past. Here, the participation of all WTO members is not required in order to strike a deal and interested members are free to join the negotiation or not. Several experts have suggested reviving and enhancing this approach (Consultative Board, 2004; Elsig, 2008). The critical 'mass approach' is slightly different in the sense that it requires that participating members represent at

---

5   Note that weighted voting at the World Bank and the International Monetary Fund (IMF) is based on the level of a country's financial contribution to the organisation's budget. Currently the United States holds roughly 17 per cent of the votes, with the G-7 holding a total of 45 per cent. WTO-related proposals certainly differ from this, yet there are important lessons to be learnt from the World Banks' and IMF's experience with 'power-based' voting.

least a critical mass or a certain threshold of a sector under negotiation based on their collective level of economic activity, production, consumption or exports (Jackson, 2001). Supporters argue that the inclusion of import share in the threshold would ensure that critical mass agreements could not be misused by exporters to harmonise their export systems to the detriment of importers – an issue they consider to be of increasing importance as, for instance, high-technology producing countries face shortages in needed raw materials that are extracted in only a handful of countries (ICTSD, 2011d). Proposed thresholds range from 75 to 90 per cent. Proponents argue that the threshold could further be coupled with the requirement to include at least a minimum number of countries. If constructed in a sensitive way, supporters suggest, this second requirement could ensure the legitimacy of a particular critical mass rather than only its efficiency. The Warwick Commission, for instance, notes that 'a positive global welfare benefit, to protect the principle of non-discrimination, and to accommodate explicitly the income distribution effects of rule-making' would need to be part of a critical mass consideration, in particular 'when it relates to the formation of an agenda' (Warwick Commission, 2007, 3).

It needs to be cautioned, however, that most of the proposals for a critical mass approach focus on negotiations on 'downstream' modalities and concessions (basically market access), thus limiting thresholds to purely economic considerations. As the WTO moves towards addressing a greater array of trade-related policies, such a critical mass concept might be inappropriate. Small countries, for instance, may not have a particular export or import trade share in a certain sector and are thus not indispensable for a critical mass, yet they would be critically affected by any new rules – be this on agriculture commodities or new regulation on services trade. This is particularly true as 'trends in rule-making' increasingly serve as a reference for legal interpretation and new regulatory approaches are used as a reference and argument in non-related yet similar negotiations. Each negotiation is thus also about shaping global policy and law trends.

Another aspect that continues to be disputed among the supporters of a critical mass approach is the 'most favoured nation' (MFN) character of the final agreements. Current plurilateral WTO agreements (where no critical mass was required) only apply among the members that have signed them.[6] If further strengthened, this approach has the potential to turn the WTO into an umbrella organisation facilitating group arrangements while losing its multilateral and thus participatory and inclusive character. To meet this concern, alternative proposals suggest extending the rights and benefits deriving from critical mass agreements on an MFN basis to all WTO members (Warwick Commission, 2007). This could preserve the multilateral character of the WTO and thus its integrity while supporting 'fast-track' negotiations.

However, even the latter construct raises certain questions. First, assuming that a given sector was irrelevant for a particular country at the time when a

---

6   'The agreements and associated legal instruments included in Annex 4 (hereinafter referred to as 'Plurilateral Trade Agreements') are also part of this Agreement for those Members that have accepted them, and are binding on those Members. The Plurilateral Trade Agreements do not create either obligations or rights for Members that have not accepted them' (WTO, 1999d, Article II:3).

critical mass negotiation was concluded, it remains unclear how the country could be induced to join the agreement if the benefits already apply on an MFN basis. Also, it is unclear whether a country would be required to join the existing agreement or whether there would be an option to renegotiate the terms (Harbinson, 2009). If no changes were allowed, powerful groups could now conclude agreements that become relevant for developing countries only at a later stage, thus indirectly imposing their terms and conditions. Criticisms regarding a trend towards WTO-plus commitments in Free Trade Agreements (FTAs) and the fear over the Anti-Counterfeit Trade Agreement (ACTA) introducing a new global benchmark for the protection of intellectual property come to mind in this respect (ICTSD, 2008b).

3.2. Redirecting the dominance of member states

While some of the proposals discussed above might be promising, neither a review of the voting procedures nor a critical mass approach *in isolation* of other reforms seem to have the potential to fully achieve the three objectives of WTO reform, namely, efficiency, legitimacy and inclusiveness. Instead, if implemented in their simplest form, both concepts risk excluding smaller countries and exacerbating power asymmetries. Also, none of the proposed reforms would be likely to resolve the current deadlock in the Doha round which results, to a large extent, from political differences rather than weak procedural rules. In this respect, some critics have challenged the 'member-driven' nature of the institution. They argue that a stronger WTO secretariat could be useful, particularly in times where members fail to initiate needed deliberations or where discussions are paralysed by individual member states' political actions. 'If members are not prepared to defend and promote the principles they subscribed to, then the Secretariat must be free to do so', the Sutherland report noted already in 2004 (Consultative Board, 2004).

Such proposals, however, need to be seen in the light of already existing criticism over a too powerful and partial WTO secretariat. The same stakeholders fear that strengthening the secretariat could create a strong institution following its own internal agenda.[7] Consequentially, the challenge would be a strong, yet neutral secretariat. Proponents agree that this could only be guaranteed if member states were to ensure a constant participation and oversight. Efforts on strengthening the secretariat would thus focus primarily on increased political support by member states rather than a budgetary increase or a mandate extension as advocated by others. The idea behind this is to *redirect* but not *replace* the preponderant role of member states, i.e. to strengthen the WTO through increased policy deliberation among its members.

One important starting point could be the election process of the Director General (Consultative Board, 2004; Steger, 2009). This process provides a critical opportunity to reflect on the most pressing challenges facing the organisation. If

---

7   See for instance the 2003 'Memorandum on the Need to Improve Internal Transparency and Participation in the WTO' by the Third World Network, Oxfam International, Public Services International, World Wildlife Fund International, The Center for International Environmental Law, Focus on the Global South, The Institute for Agriculture and Trade Policy, The Africa Trade Network, The International General and Trade Network, and the Tebtebba International Centre for Indigenous Peoples' Rights, 13 July 2003.

candidates were to take a strong position while countries provided them with clear indications on what is expected over the coming term, directors would receive a strong mandate to lead and guide even in critical times (Deere-Birbeck and Monagle, 2009, 74). The current practice of 'nodding through' rather than 'electing' a new Director General, without any internal and external reflection process, on the other hand, weakens the position of the Director General, the member states and the WTO as an institution (Keohane and Nye, 2000). A second point of entry could be the regular Ministerial Conferences. If members used the meetings to reflect on the standing of the WTO, the way forward and the actions expected in the coming years, the secretariat could guide the organisation accordingly over the coming months. In fact Ministerial Conferences were originally meant to provide for such a forum. Only with the launch of the Doha Round they have turned into pure negotiation gatherings. Numerous developing countries have consistently criticised this development.[8]

3.3. Forum and process

As described above, there has been no shortage of thoughtful ideas and recommendations from a variety of different sources and study groups. But some critics argue that these ideas have gone nowhere because they have had no process to feed into. Currently only one set of proposals is being discussed in a formalised manner at the WTO, namely those related to dispute settlement (WTO, 1999b). As foreseen by the original WTO agreements a special session of the Dispute Settlement Body (DSB) has been reviewing related reform proposals since 1997. Formally it proceeds outside of the Doha Round and is not part of the single undertaking. In practice, however, the review is used as a trade-off opportunity in the Doha Round which has prevented any conclusion over the last 14 years. To allow for a proper debate, other reform proposals will also need to be addressed in a formalised process at the WTO. Such a process would probably need to involve and engage trade ministers themselves to generate sufficient credibility and political traction. Ideally, the process should be co-chaired and co-owned by a developing and a developed country trade minister.

At the same time, the experience of the Dispute Settlement Understanding (DSU) review shows that any reform discussion must be de-linked from trade negotiations. Enforcing such an objective and non-concession-based discussion could be easier if various reform proposals were debated in a joint forum with a common objective and a single plan of action. Moreover, a joint process would facilitate the coordination of different reforms ensuring that the executive, legislative and judicial branches of the WTO do not develop in opposite directions but are mutually supportive.

A first opportunity to initiate such a process was missed at the 7th Ministerial Conference, in December 2009, essentially due to a lack of political will to push this agenda through. During the preparatory process and under the leadership

---

8 For instance, during the 7th Ministerial Conference in 2009, the delegation of Uruguay called upon the WTO members to 'not confuse the [...] Ministerial with [various kinds of negotiation sessions]. There would be no justification for continuing to postpone the regular revocation of the topmost body of the WTO, particularly in the current world economic and trade environment, which requires international cooperation, direct political involvement at the multilateral level, and strong credible institutions' (WTO, 2009).

of India, 18 developed and developing countries had proposed to address the need for an institutional reform in a formalised and long-term manner. The coalition, backed by almost the entire WTO membership, called upon the WTO to '[...] periodically engage in a process of review of its functioning, efficiency and transparency' and upon the member states '[to] consider systemic improvements, as appropriate. [...] to establish an appropriate deliberative process to review the organization's functioning, efficiency and transparency and consider possible improvements, while bearing in mind the high priority [...] attach[ed] to the successful conclusion of the DDA [Doha Development Agenda] negotiation' (WTO, 2009).

However, the proposal was dropped from consideration following opposition from Bolivia, Cuba, Ecuador, Nicaragua and Venezuela (ICTSD, 2009). An earlier communication submitted by India in summer 2009, entitled 'Strengthening the WTO', likewise remained without further consideration (Deere-Birbeck, 2009). These missed opportunities further aggravate the dilemma of the WTO as political guidance becomes hampered at the very first stage (Deere-Birbeck, 2009). If the secretariat assumed a more active role in preparing ministerial conferences and guiding towards processes as those called upon by the country coalition, initial opposition might be overcome. As a formal forum for discussing reform proposals continues to be missing, this could be the first step towards reform.

4. The WTO and global public policy goals: the example of food security

Beyond institutional reform, the current paralysis in the Doha Round is affecting the ability of the system to address pressing global challenges. Over the last 17 years, public perceptions of the organisation's relevance and legitimacy have greatly depended on the degree to which it can credibly claim to be responding effectively to broader public policy demands in areas such as food security, environmental protection, labour standards and, more recently, the transition towards a low-carbon economy. However, the difficulty the WTO has experienced in bringing its troubled Doha Round talks to a successful conclusion is arguably hampering its ability to respond and adapt meaningfully to new public policy challenges.

From its inception in 1994 as an organisation outside the UN system, the WTO has consistently been obliged to demonstrate that its decision-making processes, rules and negotiating outcomes are consistent with broader public policy goals – in the areas of health, the environment or development, to name but a few. While calls for greater policy coherence have often come from the governments that constitute the membership of the global trade body, they have also come from civil society groups, the media and even from other inter-governmental agencies concerned with the relationship between trade and public policy objectives.

The evolution in the way in which food security concerns are addressed at the WTO can serve to illustrate the organisation's attempt to take wider public policy goals into account.[9] It also demonstrates the challenges that remain in establishing policy coherence with other global governance mechanisms, and in responding to the scale and ambition of the aspirations and commitments that governments have agreed to in the post-war period (United Nations General Assembly, 1948, art. 25; 1966, art. 11; 2000, goal 1) (FAO, 1996, para. 2).

At the global level, evolving consumption patterns, combined with demographic changes, urbanisation and low agricultural productivity growth, are widely expected to mean that regional and international trade will play an increased role in many developing countries' food security strategies. Combined with increased investment in agriculture, international trade might help offset future climate-induced production decreases in certain regions, ensuring that local populations can purchase food that may be unavailable in sufficient quantities through domestic production.

Two years before the 1996 World Food Summit agreed on a landmark definition[10] of food security that is still widely used and accepted today, the concept was mentioned in the preamble to the Agreement on Agriculture at the end of the Uruguay Round, and in some paragraphs within the text of the accord. These included provisions dealing with export prohibitions and restrictions (article 12), subsidies for public stockholding for food security purposes (Annex 2, para. 3) and a clause permitting exemptions to be made from market access binding and reduction commitments (Annex 5, para. 1d). However, while food security is also related to numerous other aspects of the agreement, such as subsidy reform or market access considerations, it is not explicitly mentioned anywhere else in the text.

As governments concluded the Agreement on Agriculture, they also finalised the Marrakech Decision (WTO, 1999c) on least developed and net-food importing developing countries, supposedly intended to ensure that these countries would remain able to purchase food from external sources 'on reasonable terms and conditions'. The decision has since been widely criticised by developing countries, who have argued that loopholes in the text prevent them from requiring developed countries and the international financial institutions to implement its provisions.[11] Essentially, the decision characterises the challenge that net food-importing countries could face as a trade and balance-of-payments problem rather than a food security problem, and provides a fairly limited set of solutions centring mainly on the provision of food aid.

Arguably, the way in which food security concerns have been approached in the multilateral trading system has evolved considerably since the end of the Uruguay Round, along with the way in which other public policy goals have been treated. In the years running up to the 2001 Doha Ministerial Conference, developing country governments expressed growing concern that they were

---

9   Policies directed at ensuring food security certainly reach beyond the trade arena. Investment in the agriculture sector, land rights and access to water and other natural resources are of equal importance in this context. However, the following discussion will be limited to the interface of the multilateral trading system and food security.

10   'Food security exists when all people, at all times, have physical and economic access to sufficient, safe and nutritious food to meet their dietary needs and food preferences for an active and healthy life' (FAO, 1996).

11   See, for example, proposals from the developing country 'Like Minded Group' (23 June 2000), G/AG/NG/W/13; Kenya (12 March 2001), G/AG/NG/W/136; and Small Island Developing States (29 December 2000), G/AG/NG/W/97, http://www.wto.org/english/tratop_e/agric_e/negs_bkgrnd02_props1_e.htm (accessed on 27 September 2011).

ill-equipped to implement the Uruguay Round agreements, that the provisions of these agreements undermined domestic food security, or – as in the case of the Agreement on Trade-Related Aspects of Intellectual Property Rights (TRIPS) – that they had signed on to texts which affected their food security without fully understanding the practical and legal implications that might result. In some cases, these concerns were also echoed by development agencies and campaign groups, farmers' organisations, research centres, academic experts and the staff of various intergovernmental organisations.

In the summer following the WTO's Seattle Ministerial Conference in 1999, a cross-regional group of 11 developing countries known as the Like-Minded Group submitted a proposal[12] for a 'development box', under the built-in agenda of negotiations foreseen in article 20 of the Agreement on Agriculture. The sponsors called for a development box that would aim to 'increase food security and food accessibility' by allowing developing countries to select which products would be disciplined under the rules of the Agreement on Agriculture; allowing developing countries to re-evaluate and adjust their tariff levels; provide greater flexibility for developing countries to use limited amounts of trade-distorting support under the *de minimis* provision (WTO, 1999a, art. 6.4); and allowing developing countries to use the special safeguard clause. Measures to reform developed country subsidies and tariffs were also included as part of the same proposal. The Indian government echoed many of these proposals in an early 2001 submission[13] calling for the establishment of a 'food security box', which also contemplated measures to reform rules on 'green box' subsidies.[14] Several of the elements outlined in the development box proposal were later to appear, in modified form, in subsequent negotiating submissions and texts.

The Doha declaration launching a new round of trade talks – dubbed the 'Doha Development Agenda' by the WTO – also made explicit reference to food security goals. It stated that developing countries would be accorded special and differential treatment so as to enable them to take account effectively of their development needs, 'including food security and rural development' (WTO, 2001, para. 13). Such treatment was to be an 'integral part' of all elements of the negotiations, the declaration said, in language that was to be echoed in a large number of negotiating proposals submitted in the years that were to follow.

The dozens of proposals that invoked food security during the Doha Round, and in the years immediately before its launch, can be roughly divided into a handful of broad, non-exhaustive categories, largely reflecting the emphasis of the agriculture negotiations on four main areas:[15]

- On market access, many developing countries sought to be granted greater flexibility on tariff commitments, and access to an agricultural safeguard

---

12 Cuba, Dominican Republic, Honduras, Pakistan, Haiti, Nicaragua, Kenya, Uganda, Zimbabwe, Sri Lanka and El Salvador (23 June 2000), G/AG/NG/W/13, http://www.wto.org/english/tratop_e/agric_e/negs_bkgrnd02_props1_e.htm (accessed on 27 September 2011).

13 India (15 January 2001), G/AG/NG/W/102, http://www.wto.org/english/tratop_e/agric_e/negs_bkgrnd02_props1_e. htm (accessed on 27 September 2011).

14 Domestic support measures that are exempt from reduction commitments on the basis that they cause not more than minimal distortion of trade or production, set out in Annex 2 of the Agreement on Agriculture.

15 'Substantial improvements in market access; reductions of, with a view to phasing out, all forms of export subsidies; and substantial reductions in trade-distorting domestic support' (WTO, 2001, para. 13).

that would allow themselves to shield producers from the effects of import surges or price depressions.

- Food security concerns were discussed in relation to trade-distorting support in general, but were also given particular attention in proposals for reform of the WTO's green box, and for maintaining or expanding article 6.2 of the Uruguay Round Agreement on Agriculture.[16]
- The issue of food security also arose in negotiations on proposed new disciplines governing the provision of food aid, and in debates on export credits and other export competition issues.
- Finally, importing countries in particular raised questions and concerns over food security in proposals on export restrictions (including export taxes and export prohibitions).

In each of these areas, different political constituencies and country grouping were active in seeking concessions.

On special products and the special safeguard mechanism, a group of import-sensitive developing countries that came to be known as the G-33 argued in favour of greater flexibility on market access disciplines, on the basis that this was needed to safeguard the livelihoods, food security and longer-term development of their rural populations, including large numbers of small-scale producers that would be ill-equipped to compete with industrialised (and often also subsidised) agriculture elsewhere in the world.[17] Analysis by the Food and Agriculture Organization (FAO), the International Centre for Trade and Sustainable Development (ICTSD) and the South Centre – including country level studies – helped contribute to the evolution of countries' negotiating positions on these issues (Mably, 2007; Wolfe, 2009; ICTSD/FAO, 2007; Matthews, 2011).

The G-33 proposed allowing developing countries to designate a limited set of products as 'special' based on objective indicators of food security, livelihood security and rural development. Such indicators included, for example, the share of local income spent on a particular product, employment by product, productivity levels, rates of self-sufficiency, or the contribution of a product to local nutrition. Based on this country-specific analysis the tariffs of the selected products would then qualify for gentler reduction under the Doha Round, or would even be exempt from any cuts. The G-33, however, encountered opposition to their proposals from developed countries seeking greater access to developing country markets, such as the US, but also from exporting developing countries, such as Argentina, Paraguay and Uruguay.[18] Controversy over the special safeguard mechanism played a significant role in the breakdown of talks in July 2008 (ICTSD, 2008a).

Despite the disagreements in this area, the debate over special products in particular probably represents the most sophisticated attempt at defining

---

16 A provision allowing developing countries to exempt some input and investment subsidies from reduction commitments.
17 See, for example, G-33 proposals: 1 June 2004 (JOB(04)/65); 3 June 2005 (JOB(05)/91); 12 Oct 2005 (JOB(05)/230); 22 Nov 2005 (JOB(05)/304); 22 Nov 2005 (JOB(05)/303); 11 May 2006 (JOB(06)/143); 7 June 2006 (JOB(06)/173); 16 June 2006 (JOB(06)/189/Rev.1); 28 Mar 2007 (JOB(07)/35); 3 June 2008 (JOB(08)/47); 28 Jan 2010 (TN/AG/GEN/30).
18 See, for example, various exporting country proposals: 2 May 2006 (JOB(06)/135); 3 May 2006 (JOB(06)/137); 20 February 2008 (JOB(08)/6); 8 April 2008 (JOB(08)/24).

food and livelihood security concerns in the WTO and how they relate to international trade. It is also symptomatic of how the discussion evolved over time in the trade body from a fairly narrow understanding of food security to a highly complex and differentiated approach based on indicators.

Food security concerns were also given particular attention in the review of the criteria for green box subsidies, as well as in the negotiations on domestic support more generally. The African Group (a group of developing countries that seeks reform of developed country agriculture), along with the G-20, has sought to expand the flexibility that the green box allows developing countries in being able to use domestic support to pursue national development goals.[19] Among other things, these proposals would involve modifying the language on support for public stockholding for food security purposes so as to remove the existing requirement that developing countries count purchases from low-income or resource-poor producers towards their 'aggregate measure of support' (AMS) – an upper ceiling which would be reduced as part of the Doha Round negotiations.

In addition to proposals favouring greater flexibility for developing countries to subsidise their own agriculture sectors, two other main trends can be identified in the discussions on green box reform and in the debate over domestic support more generally (Hepburn and Bellmann, 2009). The first of these is the concern expressed by the G-20[20] and by efficient agricultural exporters in the Cairns Group, which have argued that trade-distorting support undermines competitiveness and food security in countries that do not subsidise their agricultural sectors.[21] These countries have also argued that green box programmes may be causing more than minimal trade distortion, and called for the criteria for these payments to be tightened.[22] The other major trend is characterised by the proposals of countries with highly protected and heavily subsidised agricultural sectors, which have resisted such demands. These countries – which include Japan[23] and others in the G-10 coalition, as well as, to a lesser extent, the EU[24] – have instead historically called for greater flexibility to allow WTO members to address 'non-trade concerns', including food security.

Food security was also debated extensively in the negotiations over new rules on food aid. In exchange for agreeing, at the WTO's Hong Kong Ministerial Conference in 2005, to the elimination of export subsidies, the EU had pressed trading partners to adopt 'disciplines on all export measures with equivalent effect' – including food aid.[25] At the heart of the debate was the notion that in-kind

---

19   See African Group proposal, 20 Nov 2007 (JOB(02)/187).
20   16 May 2006 (JOB(06)/145).
21   Arguably, civil society organisations also played an important role in highlighting some of these connections. See, for example, Oxfam (2002).
22   See, for example, proposals dated 27 Sept 2002: Cairns Group (JOB(02)/132) and Canada (JOB(02)/131).
23   21 Dec 2000 (G/AG/NG/W/91), http://www.wto.org/english/tratop_e/agric_e/negs_bkgrnd11_nontrade_e.htm (accessed on 27 September 2011).
24   14 Dec 2000 (G/AG/NG/W/90), http://www.wto.org/english/tratop_e/agric_e/negs_bkgrnd11_nontrade_e.htm (accessed on 27 September 2011).
25   See WTO (2005), para. 6. The text further specifies: 'On food aid, we reconfirm our commitment to maintain an adequate level and to take into account the interests of food aid recipient countries. To this end, a "safe box" for bona fide food aid will be provided to ensure that there is no unintended impediment to dealing with emergency situations. Beyond that, we will ensure elimination of commercial displacement. To this end, we will agree effective disciplines on in-kind food aid, monetization and re-exports so that there can be no loop-hole for continuing export subsidization.'

food aid or practices such as monetisation have sometimes disrupted local food markets and affected local producers. While members agreed that a 'safe box' would cover *bona fide* emergency situations, they also agreed to introduce rules that would prevent aid from undermining local producers in non-emergency situations. A proposal from the African and LDC groups[26] formed the basis for negotiations, with further contributions from the European Community[27] and the US[28] – the world's major provider of in-kind food aid (ICTSD, 2006).

While the impact of export restrictions on food security has been a concern of various WTO members since the start of the Doha Round,[29] debate and controversy over this issue has recently intensified, as two episodes of unusually high food prices and predictions of a long-term upward price trend for agricultural products increase the pressure on food importing countries, especially in the developing world (ICTSD, 2010, 2011b, c). While net-food-importing countries have drawn on analysis (FAO et al., 2011) by FAO staff and other experts to argue that export restrictions endanger food security by exacerbating shortages and volatility on world markets, exporting countries have thus far resisted any attempts to introduce more systemic disciplines in this area that go beyond the relatively limited disciplines set out in the Agreement on Agriculture or contemplated in the latest draft Doha agriculture accord. In part, this may be because of the role such measures play in supporting a strategy of enhancing value-addition in the exporting countries' agriculture sector, and partly because of concerns that they could serve a useful role in responding to potential domestic food shortages. However, possibly more important is a more generalised reluctance on the part of exporting countries to make concessions in the absence of more far-reaching disciplines on trade distortions on the import side.

Despite the post-2008 stalemate in the WTO's Doha process, the same price trends and projections have helped to push food security back towards the top of the agenda in a number of political and policy-making processes, with the role of trade receiving some attention in this context. A series of high-level meetings – the G-8's meeting in L'Aquila in 2008, the FAO's World Summit on Food Security in 2009 and the G-20 gathering of agriculture ministers in 2011 – reflected the increased political importance being accorded to the question. However, while heads of state and ministers reaffirmed the importance of access to markets and pledged their commitment to raise agricultural productivity by boosting aid and investment, the WTO continues to be seen as the sole forum where concrete market access and subsidy commitments can be made. Even where agreement on trade-related measures has been reached, such as the G-20's June 2011 accord on exempting humanitarian food purchases from export restrictions, governments have recommended that further action be taken at the WTO (ICTSD, 2011a). Other trade-related issues such as biofuel subsidies have proven to be too controversial to be addressed meaningfully by the G-8 or

---

26   6 March 2006 (TN/AG/GEN/13).
27   25 Apr 2006 (JOB(06)/122).
28   7 Apr 2006 (JOB(06)/78).
29   Cairns Group, 21 Dec 2000 (G/AG/NG/W/93); Japan, 15 Nov 2002 (JOB(02)/164); Mauritius, 19 Nov 2002 (JOB(02)/182); Cuba, 20 Jan 2003 (JOB(02)/190/Corr.1; Korea, 18 Dec 2002 (JOB(02)/220); Japan, 28 Feb 2003 (JOB(03)/41; G-20), 18 May 2006 (JOB(06)/147); Japan and Switzerland, 30 Apr 2008 (JOB(08)/34); Net Food-Importing Developing Countries, 6 Apr 2011 (JOB/AG/18).

G-20 (Tangermann, 2011), leaving their food security implications unresolved for the time being.

The establishment of the UN's High Level Task Force on the Global Food Security Crisis, the elaboration of its Comprehensive Framework of Action and the reform of the Committee on World Food Security (CWFS) were significant steps in the effort to improve global governance and enhance policy coherence in this area. The WTO, FAO and eight other relevant bodies also collaborated around the inter-agency report to the G-20 in the first half of 2011 (FAO et al., 2011). However, much more could still be done in this regard. Recent suggestions have included ensuring that the WTO Committee on Agriculture takes a more active role in reviewing food security issues related to trade, and strengthening the collaboration between the CWFS, the WTO, the World Bank and the Rome-based institutions (Ahmad, 2011). Reforming and improving the international governance framework is a necessary step towards overcoming current shortcomings on trade and food security, even though by itself it will not be sufficient to do so.

Measures to enhance policy coherence and to reform governance structures at the international level will, however, need to be accompanied by similar moves at the domestic level, especially in key countries. The disconnect between governance mechanisms responsible for development and aid, for the environment and for agricultural policy can mean that, for example, EU or US policies on farm subsidies may be at odds with policies pursued on related issues such as climate or poverty. Furthermore, to a great extent, the geopolitical tensions between countries and blocs that have thwarted progress on international trade issues are mirrored by similar tensions on climate change, food security and development issues more generally. Behind these lie configurations of domestic interests and political constituencies at the national and sub-national level. The shifting global economic landscape of the last decade has thrown up new opportunities and threats for different actors, in developed countries as well as in the so-called 'emerging' countries of the developing world, and created new challenges for the world's poorest people – whether they live in the group of countries that the UN officially recognises as LDCs, or elsewhere.

Even among trade negotiators, there is a growing awareness that the multilateral trading system is proving increasingly incapable of demonstrating that it is flexible and adaptable enough to prove its relevance in a changing world. At the same time, negotiators are reluctant to abandon the investment that has been made in elaborating a package of farm trade disciplines that are perceived to go some way towards restructuring an agricultural trading system that has been heavily criticised for failing to deliver on a range of global public policy goals, including food security. Any decision to abandon the Doha talks, or place them in deep freeze, would arguably leave a large 'Doha-shaped hole': current patterns of trade-distorting support and tariff protection would remain unchanged, in addition to the new trade and food security challenges that are emerging. Until countries are able to resolve the growing contradictions between domestic policies on trade, food security, climate and international development, there is little prospect of achieving greater policy coherence in these areas at the global level.

5. Conclusion and the way forward

The WTO is not what it used to be a decade or so ago. Many new developing countries have since joined, and shifts in the balance of global economic and political power have transformed the playing field. Accordingly, new needs and different expectations have emerged, including demands on the decision-making processes, and their fairness and transparency. As described above, modern global trade governance requires a careful balance between greater efficiency, legitimacy and inclusiveness. These objectives are not incompatible, but would require WTO members to move from essentially promoting their individual short-term mercantilist interests to developing a shared vision to effectively advance global public policy goals. Numerous proposals have been put forward to strengthen the multilateral trading system. But as for any intergovernmental institution, change must come, and be agreed to, from the inside. This calls for the establishment of an inclusive and bottom-up process, one that seeks input from all WTO members, as well as seeking submissions from the different actors in the international trade community. Only with such a process will ideas have a realistic chance to be considered, and be transformed into agents for strengthening the system.

Years of near-exclusive focus on the Doha Round have inhibited institutional evolution and even diminished some of the WTO's permanent, non-negotiating functions such as the work of the regular committees. Beyond the WTO negotiating function, there might be therefore merit in strengthening the work of the regular WTO committees. In the run-up to the 2009 Ministerial Conference, several such proposals were put on the table, notably by India.[30] These covered a variety of issues such as the need to enhance the WTO trade information system by including data on non-tariff barriers; monitor developments in regional trade agreements (RTAs) and develop non-binding best practice guidelines for negotiating new RTAs; establish an 'omnibus legal system' that would address all forms of preferential market access for LDCs in a coherent way; address the increasing role of standards and standard-setting bodies in international trade. Many of these proposals are still relevant today.

Finally, in parallel with efforts to revive the Doha Round, members could undertake work on a number of pressing global challenges. These could include concerns around the trade dimension of food security, food prices and export restrictions; the potential trade impacts of emerging domestic policies designed to combat climate change; or highly controversial matters around exchange rate policies and current trade imbalances. This is not to say that the WTO should become the sole or even primary body to deal with these matters. Several other institutions such as the United Nations Framework Convention on Climate Change (UNFCCC), FAO or IMF have indeed a major role to play in this area. The WTO, as the main organisation dealing with trade rules, should nevertheless contribute to addressing them insofar as they are linked to trade. Willingness to do so has already been expressed by a wide and cross-cutting segment of the WTO membership, but as a first step it might be more realistic to address these

---

30   See WT/GC/W/605, July 2009, http://www.wto.org/english/thewto_e/gcounc_e/meet_jul09_e.htm (accessed on 27 September 2011).

issues in a non-negotiating setting. In doing so, members could assess whether the WTO rule book is properly equipped to deal with emerging challenges or whether existing disciplines need to be clarified or amended. Existing institutional structures such as the Committee on Agriculture could be used for such an exercise. Precedents for doing so already exist. Singapore, for example, has recently made a submission to the regular session of the Committee on Trade and Environment to embark on work examining possible trade applications of border tax adjustment as a way to address competitiveness and carbon leakage concerns in climate change. Such an approach would enable the system to address challenges of the twenty-first century and prepare the ground for future negotiations when the political situation is ripe.

REFERENCES

AFDB (African Development Bank), OECD (Organization for Economic Co-operation and Development), UNDP (United Nations Development Programme), UNECA (United Nations Economic Commission for Africa) (2011) *African Economic Outlook 2011* (Paris: OECD).

Ahmad, M. (2011) *Improving the International Governance of Food Security and Trade* (Geneva: International Centre for Trade and Sustainable Development).

Anghie, A. (2005) *Imperialism, Sovereignty and the Making of International Law* (Cambridge: Cambridge University Press).

Consultative Board to the Director-General (2004) *The Future of the WTO: Addressing Institutional Changes in the New Millennium* (Geneva: World Trade Organization).

Cottier, T. and M. Elsig (2009) *Reforming the WTO: The Decisions-Making Triangle Re-Addressed*, paper presented at the World Trade Forum, World Trade Institute, University of Bern.

Cottier, T. and S. Takenoshita (2008) 'Decisions-Making and the Balance of Powers in WTO Negotiations: Towards Supplementary Weighted Voting', in Griller, S. (ed.) *At the Crossroads: The World Trading System and the Doha Round* (Vienna: Springer).

Croome, J. (1995) *Reshaping the World Trading System* (Geneva: World Trade Organisation – WTO).

Deere-Birbeck, C. (2009) *Momentum Builds for Discussion of Reform at WTO Ministerial Conference*, Global Economic Governance Programme's blog, 20 November, http://www.globaleconomicgovernance.org/blog/2009/11/momentum-builds-for-discussion-on-wto-reform-at-wto-ministerial-conference/ (accessed on 27 September 2011).

Deere-Birbeck, C. and C. Monagle (2009) *Strengthening Multilateralism: A Mapping of Selected Proposals on WTO Reform and Improvements in Global Trade Governance*, discussion draft (Geneva/Oxford: ICTSD and Global Economic Governance Programme).

Elsig, M. (2008) *The World Trade Organization at Work: Performance in a Member-Driven Milieu*, paper presented at the Annual Convention of the International Studies Association, New York, 15–18 February.

Elsig, M. (2009) 'WTO Decisions-Making: Can We Get a Little Help from the Secretariat and the Critical Mass', in Steger, D.P. (ed.) *Redesigning the World Trade Organization for the Twenty-first Century* (Waterloo: Wilfrid Laurier University Press).

FAO (Food and Agriculture Organization), IFAD (International Fund for Agricultural Development), IMF (International Monetary Fund), OECD (Organisation for Economic Cooperation and Development), UNCTAD (United Nations Conference on Trade and Development), WFP (World Food Programme), World Bank, WTO, IFPRI (International Food Policy Research Institute) and the UN HLTF (High-Level Task Force) (2011) *Price Volatility in Food and Agricultural Markets: Policy Responses* (Rome: FAO), http://www.fao.org/fileadmin/templates/est/Volatility/Interagency_Report_to_the_G20_on_Food_Price_Volatility.pdf (accessed on 27 September 2011).

FAO (1996) *Rome Declaration on Food Security and World Food Summit Plan of Action*, W3613 (Rome: FAO).

Harbinson, S. (2009) *The Doha Round: 'Death-Defying Agenda' or 'Don't Do it Again?'*, ECIPE (European Centre for International Political Economy) Working Paper no. 10 (Brussels: ECIPE).

Hepburn, J. and C. Bellmann (2009) 'Doha Round Negotiations on the Green Box and Beyond', in Meléndez-Ortiz, R., C. Bellmann and J. Hepburn (eds) *Agricultural Subsidies in the WTO Green Box: Ensuring Coherence with Sustainable Development Goals* (Cambridge: Cambridge University Press).

Hufbauer, G. (2005) 'Inconsistencies Between Diagnosis and Treatment', *Journal of International Economic Law*, 8 (2), pp. 291–7.

ICTSD (International Centre for Trade and Sustainable Development) (2006) 'EU Food Aid Paper Proposes Strict Disciplines to Prevent Commercial Displacement', *Bridges Weekly*, 10(15), 3 May, http://ictsd.org/i/news/bridgesweekly/7394/ (accessed on 27 September 2011).

ICTSD (2008a) 'Agricultural Safeguard Controversy Triggers Breakdown in Doha Round Talks', *Bridges Weekly*, 12(27), 7 August, http://ictsd.org/i/news/bridgesweekly/18034/ (accessed on 27 September 2011).

ICTSD (2008b) 'Concern Grows over New IP Agreement', *Bridges Monthly*, 12(5), November, http://ictsd.org/downloads/bridges/bridges12-5.pdf (accessed on 27 September 2011).

ICTSD (2009) *WTO Ministerial Conference Opens in Geneva: Expect No Surprises*, Bridges Daily Update, 30 November, http://ictsd.org/i/wto/geneva/daily-updates-2009/geneva-2009-bridges-daily-updates/62462/ (accessed on 27 September 2011).

ICTSD (2010) 'Under Threat of Higher Food Prices, WTO Members Debate Export Restrictions, Subsidies', *Bridges Weekly*, 14(41), 24 November, http://ictsd.org/i/news/bridgesweekly/96974/ (accessed on 27 September 2011).

ICTSD (2011a) 'G-20 Agriculture Ministers Unveil Plan to Tackle High Food Prices', *Bridges Weekly*, 15(24), 29 June, http://ictsd.org/i/news/bridgesweekly/109720/ (accessed on 27 September 2011).

ICTSD (2011b) 'OECD, FAO: No End for High Food Prices in Upcoming Decade', *Bridges Weekly*, 15(23), 22 June, http://ictsd.org/i/news/bridgesweekly/109150/ (accessed on 27 September 2011).

ICTSD (2011c) 'Agricultural Export Restrictions Spark Controversy at the WTO', *Bridges Weekly*, 15(12), 6 April, http://ictsd.org/i/news/bridgesweekly/103579/ (accessed on 27 September 2011).

ICTSD (2011d) 'Tensions Build over Chinese Rare Earth Quotas', *Bridges Trade BioRes*, 11(16), 25 July, http://ictsd.org/i/news/biores/111203/ (accessed on 27 September 2011).

ICTSD/FAO (2007) *Indicators for the Selection of Agricultural Special Products: Some Empirical Evidence* (Geneva: ICTSD).

Ismail, F. and B. Vickers (2011) 'Towards Fair and Inclusive Decision-Making in WTO Negotiations', in Deere-Birkbeck, C. (ed.) *Making Global Trade Governance Work for Development* (Cambridge: Cambridge University Press).

Jackson, J. (2001) 'The WTO "Constitution" and Proposed Reforms: Seven "Mantras" Revisited', *Journal of International Economic Law*, 4(1), pp. 67–78.

Keohane, R. and J. Nye (2000) *Between Centralization and Fragmentation: The Club Model of Multilateral Cooperation and Problems of Democratic Legitimacy*, paper presented at the American Political Science Convention, Washington, DC, 31 August–3 September.

Lamy, P. (2003) *After Cancun*, Statements by Pascal Lamy, EU Trade Commissioner, at the Press Conference Closing the 5th WTO Ministerial Conference in Cancun on 14 September, http://www.eurunion.org/news/press/2003/2003057.htm (accessed on 27 September 2011).

Low, P. (2009) *WTO Decision Making for the Future*, paper presented at Thinking Ahead on International Trade (TAIT) Inaugural Conference, Geneva, 17–18 September.

Mably, P. (2007) *The Role of Research on Trade Policy Changes Affecting the Developing World: Group of 33 Influence at the World Trade Organization*, Latin American Trade Network Working Paper no. 77 (Buenos Aires: Latin American School of Social Sciences), http://www.latn.org.ar/web/wp-content/uploads/2010/06/wp-77-Mably.pdf (accessed on 27 September 2011).

Matthews, A. (2011) *The Impact of WTO Agricultural Trade Rules on Food Security and Development: An Examination of Proposed Additional Flexibilities for Developing Countries*, IIIS (Institute for International Integration Studies) Discussion Paper no. 371 (Dublin: IIIS, Trinity College), http://www.tcd.ie/iiis/documents/discussion/pdfs/iiisdp371.pdf (accessed on 27 September 2011).

Mayer, J. (2011) *Structural Change, Global Imbalances, and Employment in the Least Developed Countries*, Policy Brief no. 1 (Geneva: ICTSD).

Oxfam (2002) *Rigged Rules and Double Standards. Trade, Globalisation and the Fight Against Poverty* (Brussels/Geneva/New York/Washington: Oxfam), http://www.maketradefair.com/assets/english/report_english.pdf (accessed on 27 September 2011).

Pauwelyn, J. (2005) 'The Sutherland Report: A Missed Opportunity for Genuine Debate on Trade, Globalization and Reforming the WTO', *Journal of International Economic Law*, 8(2), pp. 329–46.

Rodriguez Mendoza, M. and M. Wilke (2011) 'Revisiting the Single Undertaking: Towards a

More Balanced Approach to WTO Negotiations', in Deere-Birbeck C. (ed.) (2011) *Making Global Trade Governance Work for Development* (Cambridge: Cambridge University Press).

Rolland, S. (2010) 'Redesigning the Negotiation Process at the WTO', *Journal of International Economic Law*, 13(65), pp. 65–110.

Steger, D. (ed.) (2009) 'Why Institutional Reform of the WTO is Necessary', in *Redesigning the World Trade Organization* (Waterloo: Wilfrid Laurier University Press), pp. 3–11.

Steinberg, R. (2002) 'In the Shadow of Law or Power? Consensus-Based Bargaining and Outcomes at the GATT/WTO', *International Organizations*, 56(2), pp. 339–74.

Tangermann, S. (2011) 'Securing Food in Volatile Markets: From Rhetoric to Action?', *The Daily News Egypt*, 17 July, http://thedailynewsegypt.com/global-views/securing-food-in-volatile-markets-from-rhetoric-to-action.html (accessed on 27 September 2011).

UNCTAD (2011) *World Investment Report 2011, Non-Equity Modes of International Production and Development* (Geneva: UNCTAD).

United Nations General Assembly (1948) *Universal Declaration of Human Rights* (New York: United Nations), http://www.un.org/en/documents/udhr/ (accessed on 27 September 2011).

United Nations General Assembly (1966) *International Covenant on Economic, Social and Cultural Rights* (New York: United Nations), http://www2.ohchr.org/english/law/cescr.htm (accessed on 27 September 2011).

United Nations General Assembly (2000) *United Nations Millennium Declaration*. A/RES/55/2 (New York: United Nations).

Van Grasstek, C. and P. Sauvé (2006) 'The Consistency of WTO Rules: Can the Single Undertaking be Squared with Variable Geometry', *Journal of International Economic Law*, 9(4), pp. 837–64.

Warwick Commission (2007) *The Multilateral Trade Regime: Which Way Forward?* (Coventry: Warwick University).

Wolfe, R. (2009) 'The Special Safeguard Fiasco in the WTO: The Perils of Inadequate Analysis and Negotiation', *World Trade Review*, 8(4), pp. 517–44.

WTO (1999a) 'Agreement on Agriculture', in *The Legal Texts: The Results of the Uruguay Round of Multilateral Trade Negotiations* (Cambridge: Cambridge University Press).

WTO (1999b) 'Decision on the Application and Review of the Understanding on Rules and Procedures Governing the Settlement of Disputes', in *The Legal Texts: The Results of the Uruguay Round of Multilateral Trade Negotiations* (Cambridge: Cambridge University Press).

WTO (1999c) 'Decision on Measures Concerning the Possible Negative Effects of the Reform Programme on Least-Developed and Net Food-Importing Developing Countries', in *The Legal Texts: The Results of the Uruguay Round of Multilateral Trade Negotiations* (Cambridge: Cambridge University Press).

WTO (1999d) 'Marrakech Agreement Establishing the World Trade Organization', in *The Legal Texts: The Results of the Uruguay Round of Multilateral Trade Negotiations* (Cambridge: Cambridge University Press).

WTO (2001) *Doha Ministerial Declaration*, WT/MIN(01)/DEC/1 (Doha: WTO).

WTO (2005) *Hong Kong Ministerial Declaration*, WT/MIN(05)/DEC (Hong Kong: WTO).

WTO (2009) *Strengthening the WTO*, WT/MIN(09)/W/1, Communication from Australia, Brazil, Canada, China, Hong Kong China, European Communities, India, Japan, Korea, Malaysia, Mauritius, Mexico, Norway, South Africa, Switzerland, Turkey, United States and Uruguay (Geneva: WTO).

WTO (2011a) *World Trade Report 2011. The WTO and Preferential Trade Agreements: From Co-existence to Coherence* (Geneva: WTO).

WTO (2011b) *Quarterly World Merchandise Trade by Region and Selected Economies* (Geneva: WTO), http://www.wto.org/english/res_e/statis_e/quarterly_world_exp_e.htm (accessed on 8 November 2011).

10
FINANCE AND
ECONOMIC DEVELOPMENT

Ugo Panizza

Abstract

This chapter reviews the literature on finance and economic development. It starts with a description of the roles of finance, a definition of financial efficiency, and a discussion of whether countries may have financial sectors that are 'too large' compared to the size of the domestic economy. Next, the author describes several indicators of financial development and reviews the literature on the relationship between financial development and economic growth. In the literature review, he discusses in detail some recent evidence indicating that the marginal contribution of financial development to gross domestic product (GDP) growth becomes negative when credit to the private sector reaches 110 per cent of GDP. The chapter concludes with some policy conclusions targeted to developing countries.

Author's note

I would like to thank Mackie Bahrami, Gilles Carbonnier and the Editorial Board for their helpful comments and suggestions. This chapter draws on joint work with Jean Louis Arcand and Enrico Berkes (Arcand et al., 2011) and on an unpublished background paper prepared for Chapter 3 of the 2009 Trade and Development Report (UNCTAD, 2009). Thus there are some overlaps between Sections 2.2, 3.2 and 4 of this chapter and Arcand et al. (2011) and UNCTAD (2009). The views expressed in this contribution are my own and need not reflect, and should not be represented as, the views of the United Nations. The usual caveats apply.

'If such a man [a banker] is very busy, it is a sign of something wrong. Either he is working at detail, which subordinates would do better…or he is engaged in too many speculations.'

Bagehot (1873, 214)

'The lesson I take from this experience is not that financial regulation and supervision are ineffective for controlling emerging risks, but that their execution must be better and smarter.'

Bernanke (2010)

1. Introduction

On 26 July 2011, Alan Greenspan published an Op Ed criticising regulatory reforms aimed at increasing capital buffers in the financial sector. According to the former chairman of the US Federal Reserve, such policies will lead to the accumulation of 'idle resources that are not otherwise engaged in the production of goods and services' and are instead devoted 'to fending off once-in-50 or 100-year crises' resulting in an 'excess of buffers at the expense of our standards of living' (Greenspan, 2011).

Greenspan's Op Ed was followed by a debate on whether capital buffers are indeed idle resources or if they can make the system safer without having a negative effect on credit availability (e.g. Krugman, 2011; Cowen, 2011). To the best of my knowledge, there was no discussion on Greenspan's implicit assumption that larger financial sectors are always good for economic growth and that policies that lead to a reduction in total lending may have a negative effect on standards of living. The objective of this review essay is to discuss whether this assumption is correct or not. The essay, instead, will not discuss the costs and benefits of financial globalisation and capital account liberalisation. There is a vast empirical literature on this subject and a semi-consensus on the fact that that capital account liberalisation does not have a statistically significant effect on economic growth.[1]

The main message of this chapter is that while financial development is generally good for economic growth, there is a threshold above which finance starts having negative returns, possibly because it increases macroeconomic volatility. As most developing countries are below the threshold at which finance starts having a negative effect on economic growth, these countries could benefit from financial deepening. However, developing countries should be careful in implementing reforms aimed at liberalising their financial systems, because rapid changes may alter the incentives of both bankers and regulators and lead to financial crises. Gradualism dominates big-bang reforms.

This chapter is organised as follows: Section 2 summarises the roles of finance, defines financial efficiency and discusses why financial systems may become 'too large'. Section 3 discusses several indicators of financial development and reviews the literature on the relationship between financial development and economic growth. Section 4 draws implications for developing countries. Section 5 presents some policy conclusions.

2. Why does finance matter?

The financial system is the central nervous system of modern market economies. Without a functioning banking and payment system, it would be impossible to manage the complex web of economic relationships that are necessary

---

1   The most comprehensive survey is Kose et al. (2006). Rodrik and Subramanian (2009) criticise Kose et al. and provide an even more sceptical view arguing that there are no clear benefits from financial globalisation. Henry (2007) instead argues that capital account liberalisation stimulates growth. Further evidence based on industry-level data is in Eichengreen et al. (2011).

for a decentralised economy characterised by a high degree of division and specialisation of labour.

2.1. The roles of finance

Finance can promote economic development through four channels (Levine, 2005): (i) by pooling savings through risk diversification and risk management; (ii) by facilitating the exchange of goods and services through the reduction of transaction costs; (iii) by improving capital allocation through the production of *ex ante* information about investment opportunities; and (iv) by increasing investors' willingness to finance new projects through *ex post* monitoring and corporate governance.

With respect to the first channel, the focus is on 'mobilising' rather than 'generating' savings. While the neoclassical literature on economic growth focuses on the primacy of savings, Bagehot (1873) pointed out that the main constraint to a country's ability to finance large projects is not the saving rate *per se*, but the financial system's ability to pool and allocate resources. Profitable investment projects often have two key characteristics: they require a large amount of capital and they tend to be risky. Few single investors own the capital necessary to finance these projects, and even those who do have the capital might be reluctant to invest a considerable share of their wealth in a single, risky, project. Therefore, without a mechanism that allows diversifying risk across many projects, individual investors would prefer to allocate their money to low-risk, low-return projects. Such an investment strategy would have a negative effect on growth and innovation. An efficient financial system provides a mechanism that allows big and small investors to hold risk (in form of debt or equity) in several projects. If the probability of failure of one project is uncorrelated with the probability of failure of other projects, diversification allows reducing the total risk assumed by each individual investor and provides incentives for investing in high-return projects.

The second channel relates to the fact that specialisation and division of labour, which are at the core of modern market economies, would be impossible without a well-working payment system.

The third channel has to do with the fact that credit is an information intensive activity. There are substantial fixed costs involved in collecting information about the viability of a given project or the creditworthiness of a given borrower, and financial intermediaries that pool many small investors spread around these fixed costs. This mechanism, together with risk diversification, led Joseph Schumpeter to state:

> He [the banker] has either replaced private capitalists or become their agent; he has himself become the capitalist par excellence. He stands between those who wish to form new combinations and the possessors of productive means. He is essentially a phenomenon of development...He is the ephor of the exchange economy. (Schumpeter, 1911, 74)

While information is costly to collect, it is easy to reproduce. Thus, even large economic agents may have limited incentives to collect information if they think that their actions may reveal their private information and thus generate positive externalities. Liquid stock markets may provide the right incentive to collect information, because market participants will be able to conduct transactions without causing large price movements and thus revealing their information.[2]

The fourth channel relates to the ability and incentives of the individuals who supply the capital to monitor firm managers. A system that provides managers with the right incentives is more likely to maximise the *long run* value of the firm and thus mobilise capital towards growth-inducing productive investment. However, information asymmetries and lack of expertise limit shareholders' ability to supervise managers. Moreover, since shareholders do not internalise all the benefits of overseeing managers, monitoring may be suboptimal.

Not all channels have the same relevance for all types of countries. For instance, the first two channels are relatively more important for developing countries with bank-based incipient financial systems, where companies tend to be family owned, and where large investment projects may receive direct financing from the public sector. In fact, in very poor countries a key role of the financial system is to provide the poor with a safe place to store their savings. The third and fourth channels, instead, tend to be more important in advanced economies with market-based financial systems and where companies are owned by large groups of small shareholders.

2.2. What is an efficient financial system?

Up to now I have discussed the benefits of an 'efficient financial system' without supplying a definition of efficiency. Tobin (1984) provides four definitions: (i) information arbitrage efficiency; (ii) fundamental valuation efficiency; (iii) full insurance efficiency; and (iv) functional efficiency. A fifth possible form of efficiency is transactional efficiency.

Information arbitrage efficiency relates to the idea that prices reflect all available public information. Therefore, only insider information would allow earning returns that constantly outperform the market. In technical parlance, in an informational efficient market the best asset pricing model is a random walk (a random walk pricing model implies that today's price of a given asset is the best predictor for the future price of that asset).

Fundamental valuation efficiency refers to a situation in which the price of a financial asset is completely determined by the present value of the future stream of payments generated by that asset. Such a definition of efficiency rules out bubbles and requires that asset prices are always driven by fundamentals. Under this definition of efficiency, the price of assets is always 'the right one' and it is impossible to have periods of financial manias during which prices of stocks (or houses, or any other type of assets) become 'too high' because of excessive optimism or periods of financial panic in which asset prices become 'too low' because of excessive pessimism or liquidity shortages.

Full insurance efficiency refers to the presence of state-contingent contracts. According to this definition, a market is efficient if agents can buy

---

2   This leads to the Grossman and Stiglitz (1980) paradox showing that in the presence of an efficient market all relevant information is reflected in the current price and no single agent has any incentive to acquire the information on which prices are based.

and sell insurance covering all possible states of nature (often referred to as Arrow-Debreu contracts).

Functional efficiency relates to the social value added of the financial industry. Since financial markets do not provide services that directly enter in the utility function, the social return of financial intermediation boils down to two things: consumption smoothing and economic growth. In the words of Bodie, Merton and Cleeton, the ultimate function of a financial system is to 'satisfy people's consumption preferences, including all basic necessities of life, such as food, clothing, and shelter' (Bodie et al., 2009, 2).

Transactional efficiency refers to the market's ability to process a large number of transactions at a low cost. According to this definition, liquid markets or markets with low bid–ask spreads are more efficient than illiquid markets or markets characterised by high bid–ask spreads.

2.3. The dark side of financial development

Financial regulation should maximise functional efficiency. Tobin (1984) evaluated the functional efficiency of the US financial market and worried about the fact that a large financial sector may 'steal' talents from the productive sectors of the economy and therefore be inefficient from society's point of view.[3] He also pointed out that possible benefits in terms of higher liquidity could be more than compensated by the creation of useless or even harmful financial instruments. He argued for stricter regulation and for the introduction of transaction taxes aimed at limiting the incentives to use financial instruments for pure speculative purposes.

The recent crisis is consistent with the idea that some countries may have financial systems which are 'too large' compared to the size of the domestic economy. Two years before the collapse of the US sub-prime mortgage market, Rajan (2005) argued that financial markets can become victims of their own success. The longer they prove to be reliable, the more demands will be placed on them and, if they do not continue to improve, there will be a point in which these demands will exceed the market's ability to deliver and reveal the vulnerabilities accumulated during the periods of rapid growth. Rajan's conclusion that large and complicated financial systems increase the probability of a 'catastrophic meltdown' was controversial in 2005 (Kohn, 2005; Summers, 2005) but looks almost prophetic now.

A large financial sector could also capture the political process and push for policies which may bring benefits to the sector but not to society at large. Political capture is partly driven by campaign contributions but also by the sector's ability of promoting the worldview that what is good for finance is also good for the country. In an influential article on the lobbying power of the US financial industry, Simon Johnson argued that:

> The banking-and-securities industry has become one of the top contributors to political campaigns, but at the peak of its influence, it did not have to buy favours the way, for example, the tobacco companies or military contractors might have to. Instead, it benefited from the fact that Washington insiders

---

3 There are two distortions that may create a wedge between private and social returns: bank bailouts and the remuneration structure of bank managers (Rajan, 2010; Crotty, 2009). The second distortion may also lead to a reduction of shareholder value.

already believed that large financial institutions and free-flowing capital markets were crucial to America's position in the world. (Johnson, 2009)

According to Johnson this political and intellectual influence was at the basis of a set of deregulatory policies that: (i) promoted capital account liberalisation; (ii) repealed regulations that separated the activities of commercial and investment banks; (iii) prohibited the regulation of certain derivative instruments, such as credit default swaps; (iv) allowed banks to increase leverage; (v) allowed banks to measure their own riskiness.

Recent work by Igan et al. (2011) finds that financial institutions that lobbied more against the tightening of laws and regulations on mortgage lending and securitisation were also engaged in riskier lending practices. These authors conclude that lobbying was a key factor driving the deterioration of credit quality in the years prior to the crisis and argue that in 2009 the financial industry intensified its lobbying activities in an effort to limit the regulation of derivative contracts. Along similar lines, Mian et al. (2010) found that politicians who received campaign contributions from the finance, insurance and real estate industry were more supportive of the Emergency Economic Stabilization Act of 2008.

3. What do the data say?

The discussion of Section 2 suggests that there may be a threshold above which a further expansion of the financial sector is no longer beneficial for society at large. However, measuring functional efficiency is more difficult than measuring the other forms of efficiency.

Some may argue that the fact that the US financial system had to be bailed out three times in three decades (the first time after the Latin American debt crisis, the second time with the Savings and Loans collapse, and the third time during the current crisis) is enough evidence that financial sectors can grow too large. Others may suggest that crises are a necessary price to pay for a financial system that promotes risk-taking and leads to high growth: Rancière et al. (2008) make this point in an empirical paper that covers the period 1960–2000 and thus excludes the recent crisis. The ultimate test has to do with the relationship between financial development and economic growth.[4]

3.1. Measuring financial development

A test of the relationship between financial development and economic growth requires a precise measure of financial development. Ideally, one would like a set of indicators that capture the channels described in Section 2.1. However, indicators which capture a financial system's ability to allocate credit, extract and use information and exert governance are hard to define, let alone quantify (Beck et al., 2008). While it is plausible that the structure of the financial sector matters

---

4   A full evaluation of the welfare effects of finance would also require an analysis of the relationship between financial development and each of income distribution and consumption smoothing at the individual level.

and that a financial system endowed with retail banks with a wide geographical coverage able to provide credit to small and medium enterprises may have a larger impact on economic growth than a system concentrated in urban centres, we simply do not have enough cross-country data to test this hypothesis.[5]

Most of the empirical research aimed at capturing the relationship between finance and growth has therefore focused on the size of the financial sector. While different authors experimented with various measures of the size of the financial sector, there is now an agreement that the best indicator is credit to the private sector as a share of gross domestic product (GDP).[6] The rationale for using this measure is that financial systems that collect deposits and then channel credit to the government or state-owned enterprises may provide a payment system and some services in terms of mobilising savings but are less likely to exert the other roles of finance (credit allocation, risk management, corporate control) discussed in Section 2.1.

Bank credit to the private sector has grown rapidly over the past 50 years in both developing and developed countries. In 1960, its cross-country (simple) average was 33 per cent of GDP in the advanced economies and 14 per cent of GDP in the developing and emerging market economies (Figure 10.1).

Figure 10.1 – Bank credit to the private sector, 1960–2010 (as a share of GDP)

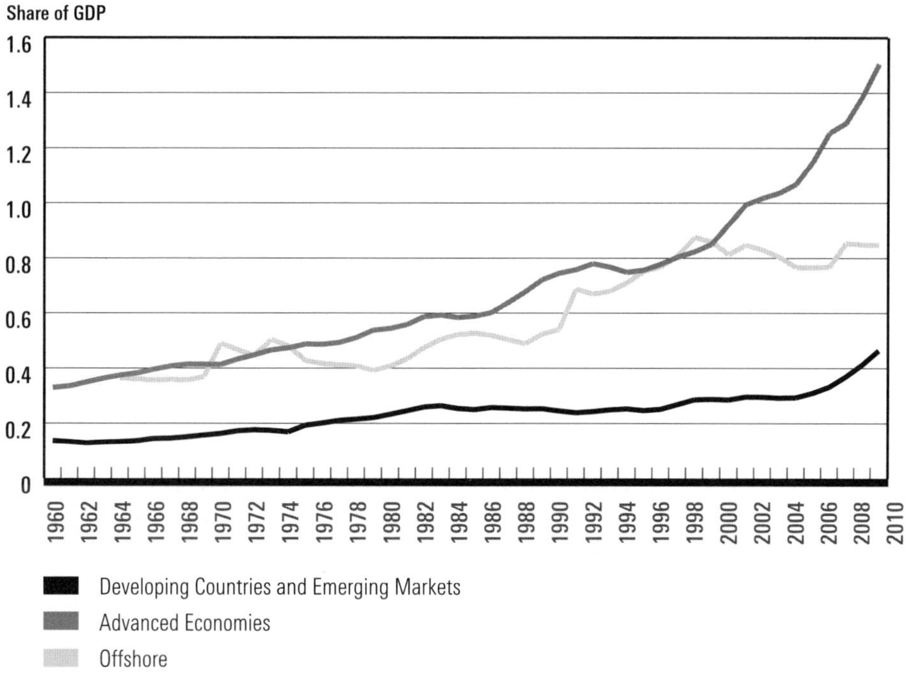

Share of GDP

Developing Countries and Emerging Markets
Advanced Economies
Offshore

Source: own elaborations based on data from Beck et al. (2010).

5 There is, however, evidence for India that this is indeed the case (Burgess and Pande, 2005).
6 Alternative measures are liquid liabilities of the financial system (M2 or M3) over gross domestic product (GDP) and bank credit as a share of bank credit plus central bank domestic assets (Levine, 2005).

By 2009, these cross-country averages where 150 and 45 per cent of GDP, respectively (with offshore centres somewhere in the middle).[7] Credit extended by deposit-taking banks only captures part of total credit provided to the private sector. A broader measure of financial development (claims on the private sector by deposit-taking institutions and other financial intermediaries) shows a similar pattern (Figure 10.2).

Figure 10.2 – Total credit to the private sector, 1960–2010 (as a share of GDP)

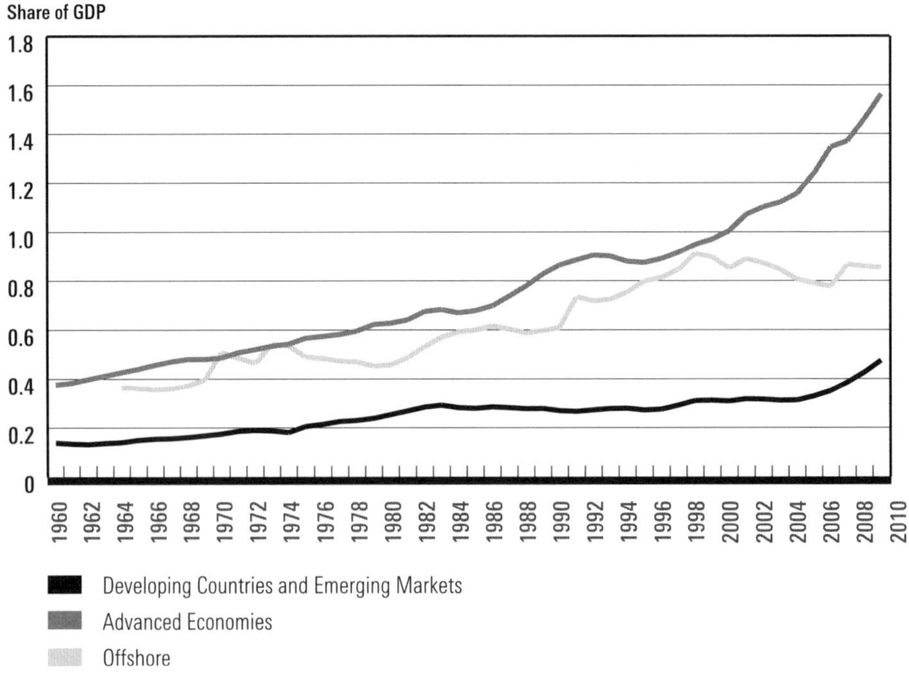

Share of GDP

- Developing Countries and Emerging Markets
- Advanced Economies
- Offshore

Source: own elaborations based on data from Beck et al. (2010).

While there are no large differences between the cross-country averages of the two indicators, there are several countries for which the broader measure is much larger than the one that concentrates on deposit-taking institutions. In the case of the US, for example, bank credit to the private sector ranges between 40 and 60 per cent of GDP, but total credit to the private sector is well above 200 per cent of GDP (Figure 10.3).

The empirical literature aimed at evaluating the relative benefits of bank-based and market-based financial systems does not find any evidence that one system

---

7   Advanced economies are defined as the countries that were members of the Organisation for Economic Cooperation and Development (OECD) in the 1980s (Australia, Austria, Belgium, Canada, Denmark, Finland, France, Germany, Greece, Iceland, Ireland, Italy, Japan, Luxembourg, Netherlands, New Zealand, Norway, Portugal, Spain, Sweden, Switzerland, UK and US). Offshore centres are: Andorra, Aruba, The Bahamas, Barbados, Bermuda, Cayman Islands, Channel Islands, Hong Kong, Isle of Man, Liechtenstein, Macao, Monaco, Netherlands Antilles and Singapore. All other countries are classified as emerging markets and developing countries.

Figure 10.3 – Credit to the private sector in the USA, 1960–2010 (as a share of GDP)

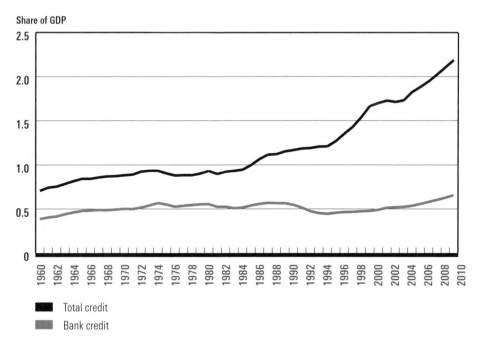

Share of GDP

Total credit

Bank credit

Source: own elaborations based on data from Beck et al. (2010).

outperforms the other in terms of GDP growth (Levine, 2005). However, it is plausible that market-based financial systems characterised by a large number of arm's-length transactions are not well suited for poor countries with incipient financial systems (see Section 4, below).

Within developing countries there are large regional differences in the size of the financial sector (Figure 10.4).

Countries in sub-Saharan Africa and South Asia tend to have small financial sectors (in 2009, average credit to the private sector was below 40 per cent of GDP). Countries in the East Asia and Pacific, Latin America and Caribbean, and East Europe and Central Asia regions have financial sectors that hover around 50 per cent of GDP, and the Middle East and North Africa region has an average index of financial development which is close to 60 per cent of GDP.

While most empirical work on the relationship between financial and economic development focuses on credit, there is also some work that concentrates on the size and liquidity of equity markets (Levine and Zervos, 1998). Over the last 20 years, stock market capitalisation has grown rapidly in both advanced and emerging economies (Figure 10.5).

In the former group of countries, it went from approximately 40 per cent of GDP in 1991 to 150 per cent of GDP in 2009. In the latter group it went from 22 to 80 per cent of GDP.

However, theory does not suggest any direct link between the size of the stock market and resource allocation and growth (Beck and Levine, 2004). There are,

Figure 10.4 – Credit to the private sector by region, 1981–2009 (as a share of GDP)

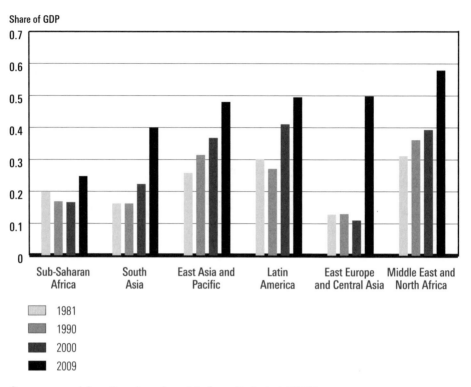

Source: own elaborations based on data from Beck et al. (2010).

instead, theoretical models that predict that the presence of a liquid stock market provides an exit option for investors and hence fosters growth by reducing the risks of long-term investment (Bencivenga et al., 1995; Holmstrom and Tirole, 1993). Figure 10.6 shows that over the last 20 years, stock markets in advanced economies (and offshore centres) have become much more liquid. However, there has been no improvement in liquidity in the average developing country.

3.2. Financial development and economic growth

While Bagehot (1873) and Schumpeter (1911) wrote extensively about the importance of finance for economic development, Goldsmith (1969) was the first to actually prove the existence of a positive correlation between the size of the financial sector and long-run economic growth. 'Correlation' is the key word here. In his pioneering work, Goldsmith assembled data on financial intermediaries' assets for 35 countries over the 1860–1963 period, and graphically showed that there was a positive correlation between the value of these assets (scaled by GDP) and economic growth.

Goldsmith was aware that his analysis was not suited for assessing whether financial development had a causal effect on economic growth. As a consequence, he stood clear from drawing any such conclusion from the results of his study and his work was not successful in changing the mainstream perception that a

Figure 10.5 – Stock market capitalisation, 1991–2009 (share of GDP)

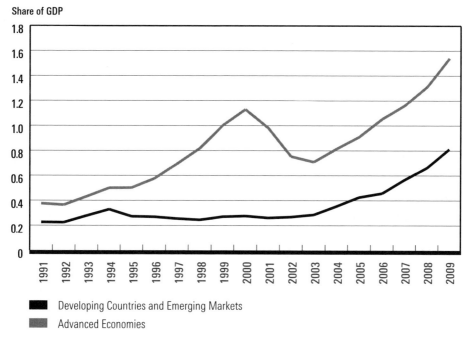

Source: own elaborations based on data from Beck et al. (2010).

well-developed financial system is just one of the many outcomes of the overall process of economic development. A position summarized by Robinson's (1952) claim that: 'where enterprise leads, finance follows'.

This perception started to change in the early 1990s when King and Levine (1993) first showed that the size of the financial sector is a predictor of economic growth. These authors collected data for 77 countries for the period 1960–89 and showed that the size of the financial sector in 1960 predicted economic growth, investment and productivity growth over the following 30 years, even after controlling for initial income, school enrolment, government consumption and trade openness. Successive work by Levine and Zervos (1998) focused on equity markets and, in line with the theoretical models discussed above, showed that stock market liquidity (but not the size of the stock market, liquidity is defined as turnover divided by capitalisation) predicts GDP growth.

Although King and Levine (1993) and Levine and Zervos (1998) showed that financial development *predicts* growth, their results could not be used to argue that financial development *causes* growth. Evidence in this direction can instead be found in successive work by Levine et al. (2000) and Beck et al. (2000). In the first paper, the authors look at a cross-section of 71 countries over the period 1961–95 and use legal origin (La Porta et al., 1998) as an instrument for financial development. They find a strong effect of the exogenous component of financial development on long-run growth and conclude that their results

Figure 10.6 – Stock market turnover, 1991–2009 (share of capitalization)

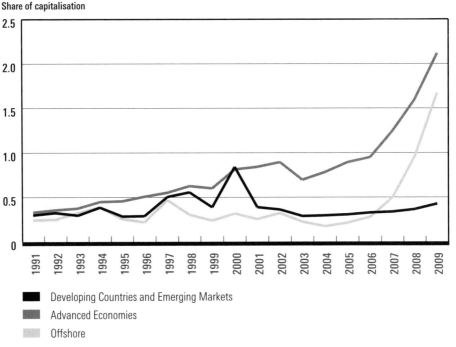

Share of capitalisation

Developing Countries and Emerging Markets
Advanced Economies
Offshore

Source: own elaborations based on data from Beck et al. (2010).

are consistent with the idea that financial development has a causal effect on economic growth.[8]

In the second paper, Beck et al. (2000) use panel data and various Generalised Method of Moments (GMM) estimators to look at the determinants of seven five-year growth spells for 77 countries over the period 1960–95.[9] Their results corroborate the cross-sectional findings of Levine et al. (2000) and provide further evidence in support of a causal link going from financial to economic development.

An influential paper by Rajan and Zingales (1998) addresses the causality issue by looking at the performance of different industrial sectors across countries. Rajan and Zingales start with the observation that industries that, for technological reasons, need more external (to the firm) financial resources should do relatively better in countries with more developed financial sectors. Next, they build an index that captures this industry-level need for external resources and show that the interaction between this index and financial development is positively correlated with industry-level value added growth,

---

8 Aghion et al. (2005) object to this result and argue that financial development accelerates the speed of convergence but has no effect on steady-state growth.
9 This methodology allows one to control for time-invariant country-specific fixed effects and, under certain conditions, to establish causality by using lagged values of the explanatory variables as instruments (for details see Arellano and Bond, 1991; Arellano and Bover, 1995; Blundell and Bond, 1998).

even after controlling for all country and industry-specific factors which may influence the growth rate of a specific industry or country. By checking whether financial development relaxes financing constraints, the approach of Rajan and Zingales tests a specific mechanism through which finance may affect growth. This approach also rules out reverse causality because there is no reason why the deviation between the average growth rate of the manufacturing sector and a given industry's growth rate should affect financial development in the country as a whole.

Loayza and Rancière (2006) recognise that there is a contradiction between the empirical growth literature that studies the effects of financial depth on economic development, and the literature that has found that credit growth is one of the best predictors of banking and currency crises (e.g. Kaminsky and Reinhart, 1999). They try to reconcile these two findings by using a panel error correction model to jointly estimate the short- and long-run effects of financial development. Their results show that a positive long-run relationship between financial development and economic growth coexists with a negative short-run relationship between these two variables, and that this negative short-run relationship is mostly driven by financial crises.

Although most of the literature finds a positive relationship between financial development and long-run growth, there are some papers that challenge this semi-consensus. Demetriades and Hussein (1996) use time series techniques for a sample of 16 countries and find no evidence of a causal relationship from finance to growth. In about half of the countries studied, however, they do find bi-directional causality. Along similar lines, Arestis et al. (2001) use a time series approach to look at the relationship between the development of equity markets and economic growth and conclude that the findings of cross-country studies may exaggerate the contribution of stock markets to economic growth. Arestis and Demetriades (1997) use the examples of the US and Germany to highlight how institutional factors may affect the relationship between finance and growth and warn against the one-size-fits-all nature of cross-sectional exercises. The importance of institutions is also highlighted by Demetriades and Law (2006) who look at 72 countries for the period 1978–2000 and find that financial development does not affect growth in countries with poor institutions. Similarly, Rousseau and Wachtel (2002) find that finance has no effect on growth in countries with double-digit inflation (their exact threshold is 13 per cent).

Rousseau and Wachtel (2011) find that the positive effect of finance on growth is not robust to using more recent data. In particular, they consider pure cross-sectional data and panel estimations and find that credit to the private sector has no statistically significant impact on GDP growth over the 1965–2004 period. De Gregorio and Guidotti (1995) find that, while in high-income countries financial development is positively correlated with output growth over the 1960–85 period, this result is not robust if one does not take into account the data concerning the 1960s. They suggest that this finding may be driven by the fact that high-income countries have reached the point in which financial development no longer contributes to increasing the efficiency of investment. Next, De Gregorio and Guidotti look at a panel of 12 Latin American countries and find a negative correlation between financial development and growth. In their view, this result was the outcome of a rapid expansion of the financial sector in the absence of a proper regulatory framework (see also Díaz-Alejandro, 1985).

Surprisingly, there is limited work that considers a non-monotone relationship between financial and economic development. Deidda and Fattouh (2002) use King and Levine's (1993) cross-country data and a threshold regression model and find that financial development does not have a statistically significant impact on output growth in countries with small financial sectors. Rioja and Valev (2004) use a panel of 72 countries and find that the relationship between finance and growth is particularly strong for countries at the intermediate level of financial development.

In recent work with Jean-Louis Arcand and Enrico Berkes (Arcand et al., 2011) we use different types of data (at the country and industry level) and estimators (simple ordinary least squares, Panel GMM, semi-parametric, differences in differences) to check whether the relationship between financial development and economic growth is non-monotone. We find strong evidence in that direction. In particular, all our datasets and estimators suggest that the marginal effect of financial development on GDP growth becomes negative when credit to the private sector reaches 110 per cent of GDP.[10] Although we do not look at the channels through which a large financial sector may reduce GDP growth, we note that there is evidence that output volatility has a negative effect on growth (Ramey and Ramey, 1995) and that large financial sectors increase macroeconomic volatility (Easterly et al., 2000). It is thus possible that large financial sectors decrease growth by increasing macroeconomic volatility.

Table 10.1 shows a set of summary statistics for credit to the private sector over the 1960–2009 period. Until the early 1990s, less than 5 per cent of countries had an index of financial development which was above the 110 per cent of GDP threshold.

Table 10.1 – Credit to the private sector, 1960–2009 (in percentage of GDP)*

Year	Average	Median	St. dev.	5th pct	95th pct	Min.	Max.	N. obs
1960	24.7	18.7	20.1	7.0	61.1	1.3	101.1	46
1965	25.4	18.2	21.3	3.9	69.3	1.4	103.5	63
1970	28.2	20.7	22.6	3.3	80.0	1.1	103.1	73
1975	30.8	24.1	24.7	4.0	80.5	2.9	115.6	89
1980	35.0	27.9	24.2	5.6	87.2	2.1	117.2	98
1985	37.3	30.0	27.7	2.0	88.1	1.5	132.8	111
1990	39.4	29.3	34.0	4.2	111.6	0.5	168.6	116
1995	39.1	23.2	37.2	3.7	111.4	1.4	180.5	143
2000	43.8	27.7	40.9	4.4	125.5	1.1	195.3	149
2005	48.4	31.5	44.6	5.4	151.7	1.6	197.4	153
2009	65.3	51.1	55.8	9.7	208.6	2.7	265.9	137

* The table includes all countries (advanced and developing) for which there is available data concerning the size of the financial sector.
Source: own elaborations based on data from Beck et al. (2010).

10   These results differ from those of Rioja and Valev (2004) because these set their threshold for the 'high region' at a level of financial development which is much lower than the level for which Arcand et al. (2011) find that finance has a negative effect on growth.

However, the number of countries with large financial sectors increased rapidly over the last two decades and by 2006, there were 17 countries with financial sectors above the 110 per cent of GDP threshold (Figure 10.7) and another six countries with credit to the private sector above 100 per cent of GDP. According to the estimates of Arcand et al. (2011) this is the threshold above which the positive relationship between financial development and growth is no longer statistically significant.[11]

Figure 10.7 – Credit to the private sector, selected countries, 2006 (in percentage of GDP)

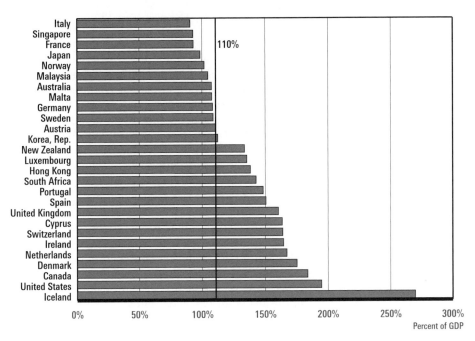

Source: own elaborations based on data from Beck et al. (2010).

It is thus possible that Rousseau and Wachtel's (2011) finding of a vanishing relationship between financial development and growth is due to the fact that there are now many countries that have reached the point at which financial development starts having a negative effect on growth. This would be consistent with the idea that nothing has changed in the fundamental relationship between financial development and economic growth but that models that do not allow for a non-monotone relationship between financial development and economic growth are 'mis-specified'. Past empirical work that used data up to the 1990s could not pick up this 'mis-specification' because the sample included few (or

---

11   The list of countries with the largest financial sector includes almost all the countries which have been most affected by the current crisis. The exception is Greece, which has a relatively small financial sector but serious public finance problems.

no) countries with a level of financial development above the point at which finance starts having a negative marginal effect.

These results have important implications for financial regulation. While the Op Ed by Alan Greenspan, mentioned in the introduction, implicitly assumes that stricter regulation will have a negative effect on financial intermediation and depress future GDP growth, the results by Arcand et al. (2011) imply that there are many countries for which tighter credit standards could actually increase growth.[12]

4. Lessons for developing countries

The majority of developing countries are well below the point at which financial development starts having a negative effect on output growth (Figures 10.1 to 10.3). Therefore, they are right in their aspirations of building deeper and larger financial systems. However, policymakers in developing countries should be aware that in the absence of a proper regulatory framework even relatively small financial sectors can lead to devastating crises and have a negative effect on output growth (Díaz-Alejandro, 1985; De Gregorio and Guidotti, 1995).

Rajan (2005) has a lucid discussion of the costs and benefits of financial development. He acknowledges that non-competitive domestic financial systems are a burden for economic development, but he also points out that such systems limit the incentives for excessive risk-taking, and therefore increase systemic stability.

In his discussion, Rajan (2005) considers the case of a country characterised by a non-competitive financial system in which banks pay low interest on deposits and charge high interest rates on loans. This country may also have a non-competitive brokerage industry in which investment banks charge high fees to book trades for their customers. As a result, credit will be limited and so will the development of the country's bond and stock markets. In such an environment, financial resources will not flow to high-return investment projects and the financial sector is unlikely to contribute to economic growth. However, a non-competitive system is also relatively easy to supervise. As there is no need to offer performance-based compensations, bank managers have no incentives to engage in high-risk/high-return activities. As a consequence, they act conservatively, making the life of supervisors easy.

Next, Rajan (2005) considers the possible outcome of a reform process aimed at increasing the competitiveness of the financial system. He argues that in more competitive environments, the compensation of bank managers depends on their ability to generate profits and, since compensation is bounded at zero, bank managers face less downside and more upside from taking risk. This may increase financial fragility because bankers used to operating under the '3-6-3 risk management rule' (borrow at 3 per cent, lend at 6 per cent and be on the

---

12   A possible criticism to the results of Arcand et al. (2011) is that the relevant market may not be the domestic one. London and New York provide financial services to the whole world and Singapore, Hong Kong and Johannesburg are regional financial centres. This could lead to cross-country positive (or negative) externalities that cannot be captured by simple regressions.

golf course by 3 pm) are ill-equipped to evaluate risk and may end up taking risk that they (and the supervisory authorities) do not fully understand.

Rajan (2005) also points out that financial development often goes hand in hand with a process of disintermediation in which arm's-length transactions replace traditional banking activities. As deregulation, technical innovation and the development of deeper markets continually increase the types of 'standardisable' risk, traditional banks search for new forms of non-standard risk. The consequences of this disintermediation process are an increase in total risk and a stronger link between different parts of the financial market, adding to the systemic importance of non-bank financial institutions. As a consequence, regulators can no longer evaluate credit creation and the stability of the financial system by only observing banks and they need to be able to monitor a vast range of financial intermediaries (Brunnermeier et al., 2009).

5. Policy conclusions

Finance can do wonders for economic development, but like all powerful tools, it can also cause great damage. While developing countries should not refrain from policy reforms aimed at expanding the size and efficiency of their financial sectors, policymakers should be aware that such a reform process needs to be paired with a strong and comprehensive regulatory apparatus. This is not an easy task, the current crisis shows that financial regulation is far from being perfect even in the most sophisticated financial systems, and may be seriously lacking in countries with incipient financial markets.

There are at least three problems with the assumptions at the basis of modern financial regulation (Brunnermeier et al., 2009). The first relates to the idea that the only institutions subject to systemic risks are deposit-taking banks. This narrow focus on deposit-taking banks has led to massive regulatory arbitrage and to the creation of a lightly regulated shadow banking system. The second has to do with the assumption that micro-prudential regulation (i.e. regulation that guarantees the soundness of individual institutions) is sufficient to prevent systemic crises. It is now clear that financial regulation needs to be macro-prudential. However, the implementation of macro-prudential regulation is ripe with several technical and political obstacles. The third relates to the fact that regulators often adopt models of risk similar to those used by the financial industry. However, regulation is necessary because markets sometimes do not work. It is difficult to address market failures by using the same evaluation instruments used by market participants (Persaud, 2008).

Countries interested in expanding their financial system face complicated trade-offs between speed and stability. As a consequence, there are no one-size-fits-all financial reform policies. Countries which are able to absorb shocks and that have good regulatory and institutional capacity may be ready for an aggressive process of financial liberalisation. Other countries may even lack the capacity to regulate and supervise traditional banks and thus may decide to rely on state-owned banks. In fact, recent research has shown that state-owned banks may play a useful role, especially during crises or in low-income countries (Levy Yeyati et al., 2007; Micco and Panizza, 2007; Detragiache et al., 2005).

In particular, there is evidence that credit supply by state-owned banks is less pro-cyclical than credit supply of private banks. Private banks may frustrate expansionary monetary policy because they have limited incentives to lend during periods of economic downturns and low interest rates as they do not internalise the fact that, by increasing lending, they would push the economy out of recession. During the current (and past) crisis, state-owned banks were essential for channelling funds into the real economy and for implementing counter-cyclical policies.

As deposit insurance and regulation do not work well in poor developing countries that are plagued by high levels of corruption and poor institutional quality, direct state ownership could increase the trust of the public in the banking system and lead to deeper financial markets (this was the original view of Gerschenkron, 1962; see Andrianova et al., 2008, for a formal model and empirical tests). Moreover, direct state participation would be warranted to compensate for market imperfections that leave socially profitable (but financially unattractive) investments in infrastructure and public goods underfinanced. Alternatively, state intervention may be justified by big-push theories like the one originally formulated by Rosenstein-Rodan (of course state-owned bank are not a panacea because they are also subject to serious political failures, Levy Yeyati et al., 2007).

These arguments seem to contradict the World Bank's (2001) view that 'state ownership tends to stunt financial sector development, thereby contributing to slower growth' (this is a somewhat ironic statement, given that the World Bank is itself a state-owned bank). After all, the recent crisis has shown that, at the very end, all banks are public.

REFERENCES

Aghion, P., P. Howitt and D. Mayer-Foulkes (2005) 'The Effect of Financial Development on Convergence: Theory and Evidence', *The Quarterly Journal of Economics*, 120(1), pp. 173–222.

Andrianova, S., P.O. Demetriades and A. Shortland (2008) 'Government Ownership of Banks, Institutions, and Financial Development', *Journal of Development Economics*, 85(1–2), pp. 218–52.

Arcand, J-L., E. Berkes and U. Panizza (2011) *Too Much Finance*, unpublished paper (Geneva: The Graduate Institute of International and Development Studies).

Arellano, M. and S. Bond (1991) 'Some Tests of Specification for Panel Data: Monte Carlo Evidence and an Application to Employment Equations', *Review of Economic Studies*, 58(2), pp. 277–97.

Arellano, M. and O. Bover (1995) 'Another Look at the Instrumental Variables Estimation of Error-Components Models', *Journal of Econometrics*, 68(1), pp. 29–51.

Arestis, P. and P.O. Demetriades (1997) 'Financial Development and Economic Growth: Assessing the Evidence', *Economic Journal*, no. 107, pp. 83–99.

Arestis, P., P.O. Demetriades and K. Luintel (2001) 'Financial Development and Economic Growth: The Role of Stock Markets', *Journal of Money, Credit and Banking*, 33(1), pp. 16–41.

Bagehot, W. (1873) *Lombard Street: A Description of the Money Market* (Hamilton: McMaster University Archive for the History of Economic Thought) http://ideas.repec.org/b/hay/hetboo/bagehot1873.html (accessed on 5 December 2011).

Beck, T. and R. Levine (2004) 'Stock Markets, Banks, and Growth: Panel Evidence', *Journal of Banking and Finance*, 28(3), pp. 423–42.

Beck, T., R. Levine and N. Loayza (2000) 'Finance and the Sources of Growth', *Journal of Financial Economics*, 58(1–2), pp. 261–300.

Beck, T., E. Feyen, A. Ize and F. Moizeszowic (2008) 'Benchmarking Financial Development', Policy Research Working Paper no. 4638 (Washington, DC: The World Bank).

Beck, T., A. Demirgüç-Kunt and R. Levine (2010) *A New Database on Financial Development and Structure*, unpublished dataset, http://go.worldbank.org/X23UD9QUX0 (accessed on 7 November 2011).

Bencivenga, V., B. Smith and R.M. Starr (1995) 'Transactions Costs, Technological Choice, and Endogenous Growth', *Journal of Economic Theory*, 67(1), pp. 153–77.

Bernanke, B. (2010) *Monetary Policy and the Housing Bubble*, speech delivered at the Annual Meeting of the American Economic Association, Atlanta, January 3, http://www.federalreserve.gov/newsevents/speech/bernanke20100103a.htm (accessed on 26 September 2011).

Blundell, R. and S. Bond (1998) 'Initial Conditions and Moment Restrictions in Dynamic Panel Data Models', *Journal of Econometrics*, 87(1), pp. 115–43.

Bodie, Z., R. Merton and D. Cleeton (2009) *Financial Economics* (London: Pearson Prentice Hall).

Brunnermeier, M., A. Crockett, C. Goodhart, A. Persaud and H. Shin (2009) *The Fundamental Principles of Financial Regulation* (London: Centre for Economic Policy Research).

Burgess, R. and R. Pande (2005) 'Do Rural Banks Matter? Evidence from the Indian Social Banking Experiment', *American Economic Review*, 95(3), pp. 780–95.

Cowen, T. (2011) *Does Boosting Bank Capital Requirements Limit Output or Growth?*, http://marginalrevolution.com/marginalrevolution/2011/07/does-boosting-bank-capital-requirements-limit-output-or-growth.html (accessed on 26 September 2011).

Crotty, J.R. (2009) 'The Bonus-Driven "Rainmaker" Financial Firm: How These Firms Enrich Top Employees, Destroy Shareholder Value and Create Systemic Financial Instability', Working Paper (Amherst: University of Massachusetts Amherst, Department of Economics).

De Gregorio, J. and P. Guidotti (1995) 'Financial Development and Economic Growth', *World Development*, 23(3), pp. 433–48.

Deidda, L. and B. Fattouh (2002) 'Non-Linearity between Finance and Growth', *Economics Letters*, 74(3), pp. 339–45.

Demetriades, P.O. and K.A. Hussein (1996) 'Does Financial Development Cause Economic Growth? Time-Series Evidence from 16 Countries', *Journal of Development Economics*, 51(2), pp. 387–411.

Demetriades, P.O. and S.H. Law (2006) 'Finance, Institutions and Economic Development', *International Journal of Finance and Economics*, 11(3), pp. 245–60.

Detragiache, E., T. Tressel and P. Gupta (2008) 'Foreign Banks in Poor Countries: Theory and Evidence', *Journal of Finance*, 63(5), pp. 2123–60.

Díaz-Alejandro, C. (1985) 'Good-bye Financial Repression, Hello Financial Crash', *Journal of Development Economics*, 19(1–2), pp. 1–24.

Easterly, W., R. Islam and J. Stiglitz (2000) *Shaken and Stirred, Explaining Growth Volatility*, Annual Bank Conference on Development Economics, Washington, DC, The World Bank.

Eichengreen, B., R. Gullapalli and U. Panizza (2011) 'Capital Account Liberalization, Financial Development and Industry Growth: A Synthetic View', *Journal of International Money and Finance*, 30(6), pp.1090-1106, DOI 10.1016/j.jimonfin.2011.06.007.

Gerschenkron, A. (1962) *Economic Backwardness in Historical Perspective* (Cambridge, MA: Harvard University Press).

Goldsmith, R.W. (1969) *Financial Structure and Development* (New Haven: Yale University Press).

Greenspan, A. (2011) 'Regulators Must Risk More and Intervene Less', *Financial Times*, July 26.

Grossman, S. and J. Stiglitz (1980) 'On the Impossibility of Informationally Efficient Markets', *American Economic Review*, 70(3), pp. 393–408.

Henry, P.B. (2007) 'Capital Account Liberalization: Theory, Evidence, Speculation', *Journal of Economic Literature*, 45, pp. 887–935.

Holmstrom, B. and J. Tirole (1993) 'Market Liquidity and Performance Monitoring', *Journal of Political Economy*, 101(4), pp. 678–709.

Igan, D., P. Mishra and T. Tressel (2011) 'A Fistful of Dollars: Lobbying and the Financial Crisis', *NBER Macroeconomics Annual 2011*, 26, http://www.nber.org/books/acem11-1 (accessed on 26 September 2011).

Johnson, S. (2009) 'The Quiet Coup', *The Atlantic*, May.

Kaminsky, G. and C. Reinhart (1999) 'The Twin Crises: The Causes of Banking and Balance-of-Payments Problems', *American Economic Review*, 89(3), pp. 473–500.

King, R.G. and R. Levine (1993) 'Finance and Growth: Schumpeter Might Be Right', *The Quarterly Journal of Economics*, 108(3), pp. 717–37.

Kohn, D. (2005) *Comment to Rajan*, proceedings of the 2005 Jackson Hole Conference organised by the Kansas City Fed.

Kose, A., E. Prasad, K. Rogoff and S. Wei (2006) *Financial Globalization: A Reappraisal*, IMF Working Paper no. WP06/189.

Krugman, P. (2011) 'The Malevolent Ex-Maestro', *The New York Times*, July 30, http://krugman.blogs.nytimes.com/2011/07/30/the-malevolent-ex-maestro/ (accessed on 26 September 2011).

La Porta, R., F. Lopez-de-Silanes, A. Shleifer and R. Vishny (1998) 'Law and Finance', *Journal of Political Economy*, 106(6), pp. 1113–55.

Levine, R. (2005) 'Finance and Growth: Theory and Evidence', in Aghion, P. and S. Durlauf (eds)

Handbook of Economic Growth, vol. 1 (Amsterdam: Elsevier), pp. 865–910.

Levine, R., N. Loayza and T. Beck (2000) 'Financial Intermediation and Growth: Causality and Causes', *Journal of Monetary Economics*, 46(1), pp. 31–77.

Levine, R. and S. Zervos (1998) 'Stock Markets, Banks, and Economic Growth', *American Economic Review*, 88(3), pp. 537–58.

Levy Yeyati, E., A. Micco and U. Panizza (2007) 'A Reappraisal of State-Owned Banks', *Economía* 7(2), pp. 209–47.

Loayza, N. and R. Rancière (2006) 'Financial Development, Financial Fragility, and Growth', *Journal of Money, Credit and Banking*, 38(4), pp. 1051–76.

Mian, A., A. Sufi and F. Trebbi (2010) 'The Political Economy of the US Mortgage Default Crisis', *American Economic Review*, 100(5), pp. 1967–98.

Micco, A. and U. Panizza (2006) 'Bank Ownership and Lending Behavior', *Economics Letters*, 93(2), pp. 248–54.

Persaud, A. (2008) 'The Inappropriateness of Financial Regulation', *VoxEU.org*, 1 May, http://www.voxeu.org/index.php?q=node/1102 (accessed on 26 September, 2011).

Rajan, R.G. (2005) *Has Financial Development Made the World Riskier?*, proceedings of the 2005 Jackson Hole Conference organised by the Kansas City Fed.

Rajan, R.G. (2010) *Fault Lines: How Hidden Fractures Still Threaten the World Economy* (Princeton: Princeton University Press).

Rajan, R.G. and L. Zingales (1998) 'Financial Dependence and Growth', *American Economic Review*, 88(3), pp. 559–86.

Ramey, G. and V.A. Ramey (1995) 'Cross-Country Evidence on the Link Between Volatility and Growth', *American Economic Review*, 85(5), pp. 1138–51.

Rancière, R., A. Tornell and F. Westermann (2008) 'Systemic Crises and Growth', *Quarterly Journal of Economics*, 123(1), pp. 359–406.

Rioja, F. and N. Valev (2004) 'Does One Size Fit All? A Reexamination of the Finance and Growth Relationship', *Journal of Development Economics*, 74(2), pp. 429–47.

Robinson, J. (1952) 'The Generalization of the General Theory', in *The Rate of Interest and Other Essays* (London: Macmillan).

Rodrik, D. and A. Subramanian (2009) 'Why Did Financial Globalization Disappoint', *IMF Staff Papers*, 56(1), pp. 112–38.

Rousseau, P. and P. Wachtel (2002) 'Inflation Thresholds and the Finance-Growth Nexus', *Journal of International Money and Finance*, 21(6), pp. 777–93.

Rousseau, P. and P. Wachtel (2011) 'What is Happening to the Impact of Financial Deepening on Economic Growth?', *Economic Inquiry*, no. 49, pp. 276–88.

Schumpeter, J.A. (1911) *A Theory of Economic Development* (Cambridge, MA: Harvard University Press).

Summers, L. (2005) *Comment to Rajan*, proceedings of the 2005 Jackson Hole Conference organised by the Kansas City Fed.

Tobin, J. (1984) 'On the Efficiency of the Financial System', *Lloyds Bank Review*, 153, pp. 1–15.

UNCTAD (United Nations Conference on Trade and Development) (2009) *Trade and Development Report 2009*, UNCTAD/TDR/2009 (Geneva: UNCTAD).

World Bank (2001) *Finance for Growth: Policy Choices in a Volatile World* (Washington, DC: The World Bank).

11
BEYOND AID: POLICY COHERENCE AND EUROPE'S DEVELOPMENT POLICY

Maurizio Carbone

Abstract

This chapter discusses the evolution of the concept of policy coherence for development (PCD) since the beginning of the twenty-first century. It finds that, despite rhetorical commitments made in various contexts, results have been modest, as governments in the North have found it difficult to go beyond their short-term political and economic interests. This chapter concentrates not only on explanations related to the widened agenda in international development and the domestic structures within individual countries, but also on two additional significant factors. First, the search for PCD can be understood as a rhetorical attempt to shift responsibilities from aid agencies to actors involved in other public policy areas affecting developing countries. Second, the two actors pushing the PCD agenda forward – the Development Assistance Committee (DAC) and the European Commission (EC) – have had other interests beyond development effectiveness. The EC has been concerned with projecting a common European vision in international development and increasing the visibility of the European Union (EU) in international affairs, while the DAC has tried to protect its role and relevance in the field of international development.

1. Introduction

The beginning of the twenty-first century has brought profound transformations in the area of international development, as many of the framework conditions for the relations between developed and developing countries have changed. On the one hand, most of the traditional donors have significantly increased their volume of aid and made major efforts to enhance aid effectiveness, while a group of emerging donors have provided developing countries with more opportunities. On the other hand, a number of global challenges – such as the rise of international terrorism, the failure of the Doha Development Round, and the global financial crisis – have pointed to the fact that aid alone is far from sufficient to achieve the Millennium Development Goals (MDGs) by

2015. For many years, there was a clear division of labour within governments, wherein departments dealing with international development defended the interests of poor countries, whereas other policy departments sought to promote growth at home. This practice reflected domestic political realities: allocating a small percentage of tax revenues to developing countries could be easily justified on both material and moral grounds, but removing barriers to external trade or cutting agriculture subsidies would meet the resistance of small but powerful groups.

Recently, however, developed countries have reiterated a commitment to promoting the concept of policy coherence for development (PCD) as a potential solution to global poverty. Yet, a number of reports have shown that governments in the North have found it difficult to act in contravention to their short-term political and economic interests. This chapter seeks to explain the reasons behind these modest results. To do so, it first unpacks the concept of PCD, and then explores its evolution in policy circles. The case of the European Union (EU) (and its member states) is taken as an example, as Europe is generally seen as the venue in which PCD has received the greatest attention.

2. Understanding policy coherence

The notion of policy coherence often generates confusion, even among scholars. In general, it indicates a 'situation in which different policies are all pulling in the same direction, or at least, not pulling in different directions' (Winters, 2004, 330). Policy coherence may be facilitated by better coordination, but the two are not interchangeable concepts. In fact, coherence can be seen as both a process (how things are done) and an outcome (what is achieved). Moreover, perspective matters: what is coherent from one policy point of view may not be so from another (Di Francesco, 2001). In the field of international development, traditionally the scope of policy coherence was primarily limited to development assistance – the consistency between the means and ends of foreign aid, or 'internal coherence'. Since the early 1990s, policy coherence has come to be understood as the interaction between foreign aid and other policies – referred to as 'horizontal coherence', or, as it is more conventionally known, PCD. This chapter specifically considers the latter case.[1] While there is considerable consensus on what is generally meant by PCD, a common understanding of the specific implications of the initiative remains elusive. For instance, for the Development Assistance Committee (DAC) of the Organisation for Cooperation and Development (OECD), 'policy coherence for development means taking account of the needs and interests of developing countries in the evolution of the global economy' (OECD, 2003). In contrast, in the 2005 European Consensus on Development, the EU committed to 'take account of the objectives of development co-operation in all policies that it implements

---

1   In the existing literature, various other types of coherence are discussed. For instance, 'donor–recipient coherence' points to the synergies between policies of industrialised countries and those of developing countries. In the case of the European Union (EU), 'vertical coherence' refers to the interaction between the development policies of the European Commission (EC) and those of the member states (Carbone, 2009).

which are likely to affect developing countries, and that these policies support development objectives' (EC, 2006, 22).

2.1. Facing obstacles

The promotion of PCD is a difficult task for various reasons. One of the most significant challenges is related to the substance of development policy. The 'decade of conferences' – on environment and development (Rio de Janeiro, 1992), social development (Copenhagen, 1995), and gender equality (Beijing, 1995), among others – and the adoption of the MDGs in September 2000 contributed to a better understanding of the actions required to eradicate global poverty, but at the same time widened the remit of development cooperation. Foreign aid is no longer simply about channelling financial resources for economic and social development, but is also meant to address political, environmental and security issues. It is no longer a government-to-government activity, but involves a larger number of players (e.g. civil society, decentralised authorities and the private sector). But while some aspects of other policies have been gradually integrated in the objectives set for foreign aid – through aid for trade, for example, green aid, or the development–security nexus – the opposite has not happened at the same pace. In fact, policies which in the past were primarily domestic have increasingly acquired an international dimension. This phenomenon has been significantly accelerated by globalisation. This in turn started to have a negative (and more rarely positive) impact on developing countries (Forster and Stokke, 1999; Picciotto, 2005; Ashoff, 2005).

Another major obstacle to PCD concerns the policy and political structures within individual donor countries. Decisions affecting the developing world involve various policy sub-systems – each with its own interests, values and perceptions. When there is a clash between these policy sub-systems, the needs of developing countries generally succumb to domestic interests. Aid bureaucracies and non-governmental organisations (NGOs), which constitute the development constituency, are far too weak, in comparison to domestic rent-seeking groups operating, for example, in the fields of agriculture, trade and security policy. To manage these clashes, some form of coordination is required. In most political systems, the leadership at the centre aspires to achieve coherence, attempting to mediate between competing interests, but unless clear and easily enforceable hierarchal mechanisms are in place, a certain degree of incoherence is inevitable (Forster and Stokke, 1999; Ashoff, 2005).

This situation is likely to worsen when the economy is under pressure, particularly during economic and financial crises. Not only are aid budgets often the first to be cut, but other measures aimed at promoting international development more broadly (e.g. favourable terms of trade for developing countries, liberal migration policy) become less palatable to the general public. The electoral cycle does not incentivise policymakers to make unpopular decisions. Politicians do not, or cannot, appreciate the long-term costs of failing to deal with agricultural and trade protectionism, climate change and political instability in developing countries. Finally, even the best intentions may be jeopardised by the lack of adequate information. Absolute policy coherence, in sum, would be predicated upon the possibility of aggregating the preferences of diverse groups without ambiguity (Forster and Stokke, 1999; Picciotto, 2005; Ashoff, 2005).

In the case of the EU, there is a further complication. Within the EU, two broad decision-making methods coexist – some policies remain within the competence of the member states, while others are decided at the EU level. In the so-called supranational realm, the European Commission (EC) is charged with ensuring that development concerns are integrated across policies, while the rotating Presidency performs this role in relation to intergovernmentalist policies. More generally, EU member states have different views on what a comprehensive and coherent development policy might involve. Not only do they differ in the ways they deal with security, migration and foreign direct investment, but their more or less progressive approach to international development also has a substantial impact on trade, agriculture and fisheries policy negotiations and outcomes (Hoebink, 2004; Egenhofer, 2006).

2.2. Measuring progress

The difficulty in quantifying the costs of policy incoherence has significantly hampered the PCD agenda, particularly as supporters believe that evidence-based analyses would help foster political support. At a general level, it is argued that policy coherence is both: 'a political imperative that derives from the threat of appearing inconsistent in the electoral arena, and an economic imperative that arises from the need to organise a large and complex organisation to conserve scarce public resources' (Di Francesco, 2001, 105). Correspondingly, while it has been difficult to accurately estimate the costs of policy incoherence, most of the existing efforts have proved useful tools in raising public awareness. For example, it is argued that tied aid reduces the returns of aid by between 15 and 30 per cent. In contrast, Roodman and Waltz (2010) estimate that eliminating the support OECD farmers and food buyers receive from Northern governments – approximately US$300 billion per year in subsidies – in combination with complete developed world economic liberalisation would, after a 15-year adjustment, increase income in developing countries by about US$100 billion per year in the developing world.

Even more difficult is to assess developed country performance in terms of coherence. Despite its various flaws (Picciotto, 2005), the Commitment to Development Index (CDI), published annually by the Center for Global Development since 2003, offers a good starting point to compare countries across policies (see Table 11.1). In fact, it ranks 22 industrialised countries on seven issues: foreign aid; openness to developing country exports; policies that encourage investment; migration policies; environmental policies; security policies; support for creation and dissemination of new technologies.[2]

Despite its limitations – the CDI does not have scientific ambitions – it highlights two general points regarding development commitment. First, the three EU member states that score highest in the foreign aid index (i.e. Netherlands, Denmark and Sweden) score only average in most other policy areas, and even below average in some cases. The countries that perform poorly

---

2   For a full explanation of how the Commitment to Development Index (CDI) is generated and for annual updates, see www.cgdev.org (accessed 1 November 2011).

in the foreign aid index (i.e. Austria, Italy, Portugal, Greece) also perform below average in most of the other policy areas, but above average in some. As for non-EU countries, the US and Australia perform low in foreign aid, but higher than average in trade and security, whereas Japan scores very low in aid and in almost all other policies areas. Second, and most significant for the purposes of this chapter, the performance of most countries has varied only marginally between 2003 and 2011. This can be taken as an indication of the fact that the various commitments to PCD have had little effect, suggesting that the search for PCD remains more an ideal than a reality.

Table 11.1 – Commitment to Development Index 2011

	Aid	Trade	Investment	Migration	Environment	Security	Technology	Overall	Change 2003–11
Austria	3.9	6.5	4	11.1	6.7	4.2	5.5	6	0.6
Belgium	7	6.3	5.6	4	7.6	1.4	4.7	5.2	0.7
Denmark	11.9	6.2	4.7	5.6	7.4	6.1	6.5	6.9	−0.2
Finland	7.3	6.6	4.9	3.8	8.4	5.9	6.1	6.1	1.1
France	4.3	6.4	5.3	3.4	7.4	3.3	6.1	5.2	0.6
Germany	4	6.3	6.4	4.8	7.2	3.5	4.7	5.3	0.3
Greece	2.3	6.3	4	6.8	6.9	5.1	2.7	4.9	1.1
Ireland	8.6	6.1	3.1	4.1	7.4	5.2	4	5.5	0.4
Italy	2	6.5	5.6	3.7	7	4.7	4.5	4.8	0.5
Netherlands	11.5	6.6	6	4.9	7.3	5.3	5.2	6.7	0.2
Portugal	2.8	6.5	5.4	4	7.3	5.7	7	5.5	1
Spain	4.8	6.4	6	4.6	6.6	2.8	5.9	5.3	1
Sweden	14.9	6.5	5.6	9.2	8.1	4.5	4.9	7.7	1.6
United Kingdom	7	6.3	6.4	3.5	7.7	2.7	4.5	5.4	0.2
Australia	4.1	7.7	6.1	4	4.2	7	5.3	5.5	−0.1
Japan	1.5	3.3	4.9	1.8	5.7	2	6.3	3.7	1.1
Switzerland	5.7	3.2	4.6	7.9	6.3	2.7	5	5.1	0.5
United States	3.1	7.4	5.3	4.9	4.4	13.8	5.6	6.4	2.2

Source: Roodman (2011).

3. The itinerary of a concept

The concept of PCD as such may be relatively new but it existed under other names for decades. In the 1960s some of its principles were incorporated in the notion of 'comprehensive planning'; in the 1970s in 'integrated development'; in the 1980s in the 'structural adjustment programmes'; and in the 1990s in the 'poverty reduction strategy papers'.[3] All these initiatives reflected an attempt

---

3   In the 1960s, 'comprehensive planning' implied focusing on strategic economic sectors and adopting national development plans that resulted from the involvement of experts in various partner ministries. In the 1970s, 'integrated development' represented the answer to the ineffectiveness of project aid, as it brought together planning, design and implementation under a single institutional umbrella. In the 1980s, the 'structural adjustment programmes' (SAPs) were meant to induce aid recipients to reform their macro-economic frameworks, followed by an even more rigorous programme aimed at implementing political reforms. In the 1990s, the 'poverty reduction strategy papers' (PRSPs) reflected donor commitment to aligning their work with local priorities, identified thorough a process of wide consultation (Hydén, 1999).

to apply periodically re-adapted versions of a comprehensive approach to development (Hydén, 1999, 64–73). However, despite notable differences, they shared some common ground in the structure of relative responsibility among states and the distribution of domestic burden. For developed countries, this burden was represented primarily by the financial cost of development assistance, which states attempted to make most effective by imposing economic and political conditionalities ('internal coherence') on the recipients. Correspondingly, the burden was higher for developing countries, as they were required to adopt major reforms of their domestic policies. Moreover, throughout this period, the key actors behind these prescriptions were the Bretton Woods Institutions, which monopolised the agenda of international development. As a result, when the DAC and the EC began to promote the concept of PCD, they seemed to challenge the existing consensus by going beyond development assistance to shift attention from the domestic policies of developing countries to the domestic policies of developed countries. Yet paradoxically, and in a manner similar to that of the Bretton Woods Institutions, they failed to involve developing countries in the process. Of course, it must be acknowledged that attempts to promote some forms of policy coherence were also made by other international organisations. For instance, the World Bank and the International Monetary Fund (IMF) started to pay more attention to trade policy, while the World Trade Organization (WTO) began to acknowledge the role of broad development issues in international trade. This, however, has turned out to be merely a rhetorical exercise, as 'seeking to "mainstream" trade negotiations into development or development into trade negotiations by trading responsibilities is more likely to create confusion than clarity'. More importantly, international organisations have failed to achieve 'middle-level' coherence, the 'concrete collective outcome at the global level' (Winters, 2007, 462).

3.1. PCD and the DAC

The forum that is generally seen as the greatest contributor to a better understanding of PCD is the DAC. When this concept was first discussed in the DAC High-Level Forum in December 1991, the central concerns were, on the one hand, how to tackle poverty and other global challenges in the face of decreasing levels of foreign aid, and, on the other, how to ensure an effective participation of the developing countries in the global architecture for international development. The agreement on the eight MDGs – on the basis of the 'Shaping the 21st Century' paper produced by the DAC in 1996 (DAC, 1996) – further legitimised these views. The international community was correspondingly forced to address major funding gaps in the fight against world poverty, while at the same time a consensus emerged that aid needed to be supplemented with additional efforts in other policy areas, as witnessed by the addition of MDG-8 ('Develop a global partnership for development'). This implied a call for the development of an open trading and financial system committed to good governance, development and poverty reduction, as well as measures to address the special needs of least developed countries through tariffs and quota-free market access for their exports.

The launch of the Doha Development Agenda in November 2001, the adoption of the Monterrey Consensus in March 2002, and the World Summit on Sustainable Development held in August 2002, provided a new momentum for PCD, which the DAC used to further legitimise its role in international development. This became clear at the OECD Ministerial Council Meeting in 2002 when, as part of the 'OECD Action for a Shared Development Agenda', the DAC sponsored its key role in providing policy guidance to, and diffusing best practices among, its members. To support this role, the DAC started to publish both research documents that highlighted the 'development dimension' across a number of policy areas and compendiums that identified tools and mechanisms for the promotion of PCD. Moreover, the DAC included a specific chapter on PCD in peer reviews of its members, which reaffirmed its central role in spreading best practices (OECD, 2009). It should be noted, however, that in this process the two peer reviewers and the DAC Secretariat depend heavily on the information provided by the country being reviewed, which may somewhat compromise the objectivity of the final reports (Picciotto, 2005).

3.2. PCD and the EU

The other actor that has widely promoted the concept of PCD is the EC. Interestingly, the EU is the sole example in which PCD has been 'constitutionalised': Article 178 of the Treaty of Maastricht (1991) established that 'The Community shall take account of the development objectives in the policies that it implements which are likely to affect developing countries.'[4] Despite this codification, however, little, if any, progress was made for the remainder of the 1990s. The EC was paralysed by territorial and ideological clashes between the various Directorates-General (DGs), on the assumption that the needs of developing countries were sufficiently taken care of by development assistance. Some member states (i.e. Denmark, Belgium and the Netherlands) tried in vain to advance concrete proposals. The most vocal actors were actually NGOs, which launched a number of public campaigns on the incoherence of development and agricultural and fisheries policies, particularly in West Africa (Hoebink, 2004).

An unexpected change occurred at the beginning of the 2000s when, thanks to the leadership of the EC, PCD was placed high on the EU's agenda.[5] In the context of a number of measures aimed at boosting the quantity and enhancing the quality of aid, the EU established specific 'coherence for development commitments' in 12 policy areas.[6] The EC managed to garner a leading role in the monitoring process, which it used to produce critical reports in 2007 and 2009. These reports concluded that the importance of PCD was recognised across Europe, and that this was mainly reflected in the many mechanisms put in place. At the same time, however, the reports criticised the member states for the lack of

---

4   Together with the principle of coherence, the Treaty of Maastricht introduced two other policy principles, complementarity and coordination. By complementarity, it was acknowledged that development policy is a shared competence and that the programme managed by the EC complement those of the member states. By coordination, it was intended that member states and the EC would consult on their aid programmes, with a view to speaking with a single voice in the international arena. The EC was given the task to take initiatives to promote such coordination (Hoebink, 2004).
5   Following a decade of declining trends, in light of the 2002 international conference on Financing for Development, in March 2002 the member states committed to jointly increasing their collective volume of aid from 0.33 to 0.39 per cent of their collective gross national income (GNI). In May 2005, they committed to a more ambitious target, that of reaching 0.56 per cent by 2010 and 0.7 per cent by 2015 (Carbone, 2007).
6   The 12 areas were: trade; agriculture; fisheries; environment; climate change; social dimension of globalisation; employment and decent work; transport; energy; security; migration, information society; research and innovation (EC, 2005).

progress in policy outcomes, and urged the EU as a whole to find a better balance between its interests and those of the developing countries – particularly in sensitive areas such as migration and security (EC, 2007, 2009). Similarly, many NGOs that had initially welcomed the new PCD agenda became very critical, and accused the EU of underestimating the negative impact on developing economies of their trade and agriculture policies; overlooking key areas such as food policy and international finance; and failing to consult with civil society actors and governments in developing countries (CONCORD, 2009).[7]

4. Fighting for relevance

The previous paragraphs have identified some obstacles that seem to make the pursuit of policy coherence a sort of 'mission impossible' (Carbone, 2008). The increased complexity of the development agenda and the interplay of interests and values within countries were identified as particularly salient challenges. Now, the discussion turns to two additional but interlinked factors that contribute to explaining the existence of a gap between stated intentions and policy reality. The first factor highlights the fact that the promotion of PCD is, on the one hand, an attempt to shift responsibility from development agencies to other policy actors, which tends to result in mere rhetorical action. The second factor consists of the extent to which PCD has been affected by a form of institutional rivalry between two key actors, i.e. the DAC and the EC, each of which appears more interested in self-preservation rather than the substance of policy.

4.1. Rhetorical action

Over the past decade, development agencies have been under increasing pressure. Some authors have questioned their performance in managing aid (Easterly, 2008; Knack et al., 2010). Others, more fundamentally, have questioned the real added value of foreign aid (Moyo, 2009) and, more generally, the policies adopted by donors to promote broad international development (Chang, 2007). Though each begins from an independent point of critique, all seem to reach the same conclusion: that unless countries in the North stop engaging in 'business as usual', the achievement of the MDGs is unrealistic. To avoid being seen as the sole actors responsible for this failure, development agencies have therefore sought to go beyond their conventional aid-based mandate to become the key proponents of the PCD agenda. However, as argued by Kapstein (2004, 5) 'policy and institutional change often involves a process of articulating and enforcing new rules, and domestic actors who find themselves on the losing end of these changes may try to resist them'. This policy game has resulted in the adoption of

---

7   Interestingly, non-governmental organisations (NGOs) have exercised intense pressure at the EU level, but they have been less vocal at the national level. Of course, exceptions do exist, such as the UK, Sweden, the Netherlands and Denmark. It should be noted, however, that in these cases NGOs raised issues directly with governments rather than in public campaigns. The European Parliament has gradually become more involved in policy coherence for development (PCD), but its role is minimal in the case of supranational policies like trade and agriculture, to say nothing of intergovernmental policies such as security and migration. Over the years, however, it has adopted several resolutions urging the EC and the member states to comply with the principle of PCD as enshrined in the treaties.

various declaratory projects, all of which obscure the diffusion of responsibility, as the more actors involved in a policy, the less the responsibility that lies with any one of them (Chandler, 2007). For this reason, Winters (2004, 329) concludes that 'except in terms of some particular trade-off, coherence is not operational: it begs the critical question of what point to cohere about, i.e. where is "here" in cohere. In practice, the use of "coherence" in the abstract term is rhetorical – as a means of signalling concern and persuading partners to pursue some course of action.' It is therefore unsurprising that both the DAC and the EC have measured success in terms of the increased number of broad policy statements regarding PCD and the attempt to coordinate policy through overly ambitious but generic tools and mechanisms (EC, 2007, 2009; OECD, 2009).

To provide a more specific overview of the policy of member states, among the most proactive countries in the EU are the Netherlands and Sweden, which with their 'Policy for Global Development' have put PCD at the heart of their international development policy. Similarly, the UK has established an overarching plan for policy coherence, but has focused on three key priority areas (poverty reduction and economic growth, climate change and conflict). Moreover, the framework set by the cross-government public sector agreements is meant to reinforce coherence across policies in the UK, though the emphasis has been on 'whole-of-government' mechanisms to deliver the aid programme rather than ensuring that cross-cutting policies support development objectives. Finland and Germany have also made some explicit commitments to PCD in their legislation. Within the Danish government, inter-ministerial discussion and policy coordination occur on an issue-by-issue basis. In France, Greece and Luxembourg, different ministers attempt to find common grounds and reach coherent decisions. Beyond Europe, Australia has also promoted a 'whole-of-government' approach and development issues have been successfully interlinked with broader national priorities, particularly in the case of trade and migration. At the opposite end of the spectrum is Japan, where neither an overall framework nor concrete mechanisms exist to promote PCD. In the case of the United States, there has been an attempt to ensure consistency across all external policies, but limited attention has been paid to the impact of these policies on developing countries (nor has the US attempted to coordinate its efforts with other international actors or to align with developing country priorities).[8]

As a matter of fact, developing countries have been rarely involved in any of these policy discussions. Interestingly, the Cotonou Agreement, which governs the relations between the EU and the African, Caribbean and Pacific (ACP) Group of countries, holds that ACP countries should be consulted when a policy proposal is likely to affect any of its members. Yet in 2007, when the ACP Group requested information on five concrete proposals, the EC did not go beyond a reassurance that any development concerns would be taken into account in the preparation of these proposals and their implementation (EC, 2009).

This type of paternalistic attitude is not the only challenge for developing countries posed by PCD. Picciotto (2005) has pointed to the practice of 'ganging up', in which developed countries and international organisations make joint

---

8   This information is drawn from the peer review of the 15 EU members of the Development Assistance Committee (DAC) and the working papers attached to the EU reports on PCD.

efforts to impose high compliance burdens on developing countries, under the guise of 'donor–recipient coherence'. More radically, Grabel (2007) has argued that the entire coherence agenda serves only to legitimise the view that trade liberalisation is essential to the promotion of global growth and stability. This has not only led to a 'locking in' of neo-liberal policies, but also constrained the policy autonomy of developing countries.

4.2. Institutional rivalry

The two actors that have been actively involved in the promotion of PCD, the DAC and the EC (or rather, its Directorate-General for Development), have engaged in a form of institutional rivalry. This, of course, is not a new phenomenon: 'There will always be competition between institutions in setting the international agenda; taking the lead in policy co-ordination, therefore, serves a self-promotional purpose' (Forster and Stokke, 1999, 27). Since it launched the PCD agenda in the early 1990s, the DAC has sought to ensure a prominent role for itself as part of its mandate of donor coordination. In practice, most of its activities in the 1990s were of limited significance, with the notable exception of a 1996 publication that outlined a number of lessons on general policy coherence drawn from member experience (OECD, 1996). Similarly, in that same decade the EC, and the EU more generally, were generally inactive. This period of passivism ended, however, at the beginning of the 2000s, when the EC became central to the new PCD agenda. The EC's PCD initiatives, as well as those aimed to enhance aid effectiveness, have been part of a wider external relations agenda pursued by the EC, aimed at federalising the development policies of the member states around a common vision and, correspondingly, using development policy to enhance the role of the EU as a global actor (Carbone, 2011).

By engaging in these activities, the EC came to be seen as operating in a field that traditionally had been under the remit of the DAC; Orbie (2008) has even raised the prospect of the 'OECDisation' of the EC. This may be an exaggeration, but the DAC nevertheless felt threatened. For instance, a senior official in the DAC in 2007 stated the following: '[The] OECD's role as a "hub for globalisation" gives our work on PCD an added value and visibility...Interdisciplinary analyses increase the relevance of OECD work in the global context' (Lahnalampi, 2007). Correspondingly, the DAC reacted by launching a number of bold initiatives, suggesting institutional requirements for improving PCD, and attempting to broaden the PCD agenda – working all the while to carve out a central role for itself. More recently, in the introduction to the Development Cooperation Report 2010, the Chair of the DAC, Eckhard Deutscher, wrote: 'The DAC of the future will be much more involved with the global architecture of development finance; with the development dimension of global public goods such as climate change, peace and security; and with an equitable global trading system.' Moreover, he continued, there will be 'a stronger focus on policy coherence for development', but for this, 'the DAC will need better and sharper policy tools' (DAC, 2010, 30).

Interestingly, the most recent policy initiatives demonstrate a convergence between the DAC and the EC in terms of the 'reframing' of PCD. In June 2008, the OECD Ministerial Declaration on Policy Coherence for Development highlighted the fact that PCD is not meant (only) to promote international development, but also has an important role in responding to the global challenges which affect *both* developing and developed countries. Similarly, in September 2009 the EC (2009) proposed 'a-whole-of-the-Union' approach in a limited number of areas: climate change, global food security, migration, intellectual property and security. In doing so, the EC sought to make progress on those issues that were already high on the EU agenda, and for which there was already a high level of political commitment.

Incidentally, it should be noted that the Treaty of Lisbon, which entered into force in December 2009, modified the Treaty of Maastricht by extending the obligation of PCD from 'Community' policies to 'Union' policies. At the time of writing, it is too early to derive a conclusive assessment of this new framing of PCD, but what earlier appeared to be an institutional rivalry may actually result in an improved division of labour between the DAC and the EC. This would involve the former focusing on the technical dimension of PCD, with the latter concentrating on the political aspects. In the case of the EU, this may mean trading some policy autonomy for increased collaboration with other international organisations. As concluded by Holland (2009, 38), however, even if 'this may create a tension with the EU's foreign policy aspirations to be an autonomous global actor, from the perspective of recipient states such global coherence is welcome and long overdue'.

5. Conclusion

Since the early 2000s, it has been recognised that the achievement of the MDGs demands comprehensive and coherent development policies beyond conventional foreign aid. Despite the numerous commitments to promote PCD, however, results have been far below expectations. In general, policy coherence cannot be guaranteed by democratic political systems, as policy-making is less about eliminating incoherence than effectively managing it. In the case of development, both conflicting interests between different domestic policy areas and the broadened agenda of development policy itself have made PCD more difficult. This chapter points to two additional potential explanations for the wide gap between stated intentions and actual policy decisions. First, it is suggested that the search for PCD is only a rhetorical attempt to shift responsibilities from aid agencies to other actors. In light of the slow progress in achieving the MDGs, aid agencies did not want to be held solely responsible for this failure. Second, the EC has promoted PCD as part of its broader external relations agenda, while the DAC has sought to use PCD as a way to safeguard its relevance in the field of international development. This instrumentalisation of PCD has led to a counterproductive institutional rivalry between the two organisations.

Ideally, PCD should not be treated as the newest fad in the international development discourse (Van der Hoeven, 2010), but should be seen as part of a new development paradigm in which developing countries are treated as partners and are able to enjoy the benefits of globalisation.

REFERENCES

Ashoff, G. (2005) *Enhancing Policy Coherence for Development: Justification, Recognition and Approaches to Achievements*, DIE Studies no. 11 (Bonn: German Development Institute).

Carbone, M. (2007) *The European Union and International Development: The Politics of Foreign Aid* (London: Routledge).

Carbone, M. (2008) 'Mission Impossible: The European Union and Policy Coherence for Development', *Journal of European Integration*, 30(3), pp. 323–42, DOI: 10.1080/07036330802144992.

Carbone, M. (ed.) (2009) *Policy Coherence and EU Development Policy* (London and New York: Routledge).

Carbone, M. (2011) 'The EU and the Developing World: Partnership, Poverty, Politicisation', in Hill, C. and M. Smith (eds) *International Relations and the European Union* (Oxford: Oxford University Press), pp. 324–48.

Chandler, D. (2007) 'The Security-Development Nexus and the Rise of "Anti-Foreign Policy"', *Journal of International Relations and Development*, 10, pp. 362–86, DOI: 10.1057/palgrave.jird.1800135.

Chang, H-J. (2007) *Bad Samaritans: Rich Nations, Poor Policies and the Threat to the Developing World* (London: Random House).

CONCORD (2009) *Spotlight on Policy Coherence* (Brussels: CONCORD), http://www.concord.se/page.asp?id=360&lang=EN (accessed on 5 December 2011).

DAC (Development Assistance Committee) (1996) *Shaping the 21st Century, The Contribution of Development Cooperation* (Paris: Organisation for Economic Cooperation and Development – OECD).

DAC (2010) *Development Cooperation Report 2010* (Paris: OECD).

Di Francesco, M. (2001) 'Process not Outcomes in New Public Management? "Policy Coherence" in Australian Government', *The Drawing Board: An Australian Review of Public Affairs*, 1(3) pp. 103–16.

Easterly, W. (ed.) (2008) *Reinventing Foreign Aid* (Cambridge: MIT Press).

Egenhofer, C. (2006) *Policy Coherence for Development in the EU Council: Strategies for the Way Forward* (Brussels: Centre for European Policy Studies).

EC (European Commission) (2005) *Policy Coherence for Development – Accelerating Progress Towards Attaining the Millennium Development Goals*, COM (2005)134, 12 April (Brussels: Commission of the European Communities).

EC (2006) *The European Consensus on Development* (Luxembourg: Office for Official Publications of the European Communities).

EC (2007) *EU Report on Policy Coherence for Development*, COM (2007)545, 20 September (Brussels: Commission of the European Communities).

EC (2009) *EU Report on Policy Coherence for Development*, COM (2009)461, 17 September (Brussels: Commission of the European Communities).

Forster, J. and O. Stokke (1999) 'Coherence of Policies towards Developing Countries: Approaching the Problematique', in Forster, J. and O. Stokke (eds) *Policy Coherence in Development Co-operation* (London: Frank Cass), pp. 16–57.

Grabel, I. (2007) 'Policy Coherence or Conformance? The New World Bank-International Monetary Fund-World Trade Organisation Rhetoric on Trade and Investment in Development Countries', *Review of Radical Political Economics*, 39(3), pp. 335–41, DOI: 10.1177/0486613407305281.

Holland, M. (2009) 'The EU and the Global Development Agenda', in Carbone, M. (ed.) *Policy Coherence and EU Development Policy* (London and New York: Routledge), pp. 21–40.

Hoebink, P. (2004) *The Treaty of Maastricht and Europe's Development Co-operation* (Amsterdam: Aksant).

Hydén, G. (1999) 'The Shifting Grounds of Policy Coherence in Development Co-operation', in Forster, J. and O. Stokke (eds) *Policy Coherence in Development Co-operation* (London: Frank Cass), pp. 58–77.

Kapstein, E.B. (2004) *The Politics of Policy Coherence*, paper presented at the OECD Policy Workshop on 'Institutional Approaches to Policy Coherence for Development', Paris, 18–19 May.

Knack, S., F.H. Rogers and N. Eubank (2010) *Aid Quality and Donor Rankings*, World Bank Policy Research Working Paper Series (Washington, DC: World Bank).

Lahnalampi, R. (2007) *The Policy Coherence for Development Work in the OECD*, presentation at the OECD Workshop 'More Coherent Policies for More Inclusive Growth and Development', Paris, 30 November.

Moyo, D. (2009) *Dead Aid: Why Aid is Not Working and How There is a Better Way for Africa* (New York: Farrar, Straus and Giroux).

OECD (1996) *Building Policy Coherence: Tools and Tensions* (Paris: OECD).

OECD (2003) *Policy Coherence: Vital for Global Development* (Paris: OECD).

OECD (2009) *Building Blocks for Policy Coherence for Development* (Paris: OECD).

Picciotto, R. (2005) 'The Evaluation of Policy Coherence for Development', *Evaluation*, 11(3), pp. 311–30, DOI: 10.1177/1356389005058479.

Orbie, J. (ed.) (2008) *Europe's Global Role: External Policies of the European Union* (Aldershot: Ashgate).

Roodman, D. and J. Walz (2010) *Commitment to Development Index 2010* (Washington, DC: Center for Global Development).

Roodman, D. (2011) *Commitment to Development Index 2011* (Washington, DC: Center for Global Development).

Van der Hoeven, R. (2010) 'Policy Coherence: The Newest Fad in the International Discourse?', in Hoebink, P. (ed.) *European Development Cooperation: In Between the Local and the Global* (Amsterdam: Amsterdam University Press), pp. 25–46.

Winters, L.A. (2004) 'Coherence with No "Here": WTO Co-operation with the World Bank and the IMF', in Nelson, D. (ed.) *The Political Economy of Policy Reform: Essays in Honor of J. Michael Finger* (Amsterdam: Elsevier), pp. 329–51.

Winters, L.A. (2007) 'Coherence and the WTO', *Oxford Review of Economic Policy*, 23(3), pp. 461–80, DOI: 10.1093/oxrep/grm019.

INFOGRAPHIC SECTION

Trends in Development Aid

NORTH-SOUTH FLOWS

1 | Net Flows from DAC Members to Developing Countries, 1990–2010 (in billion USD constant, 2009)

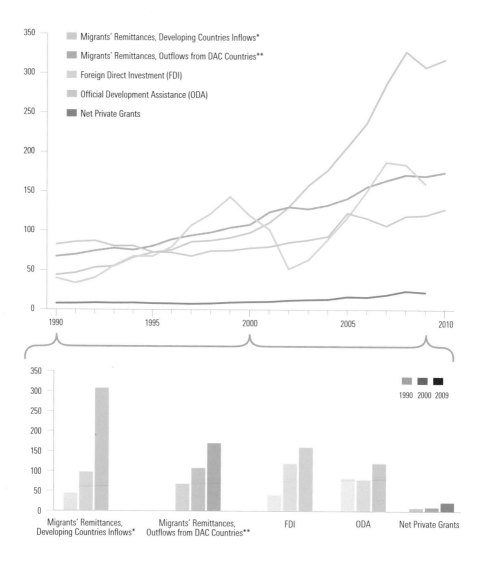

Sources: OECD, *OECD.Stat Extracts*, http://stats.oecd.org/index.aspx; World Bank (2010) *Annual Remittances Data*, Outflows (Washington, DC: World Bank).

* Outflows from DAC countries include transfers to other high-income economies as well.
** Developing Countries Inflows include transfers between developing economies as well. This is the definition of migrants' remittances that will be used in the following figures.

Remittances

2 | Major Developing Country Recipients of Remittances, 2010 (estimates in million USD)

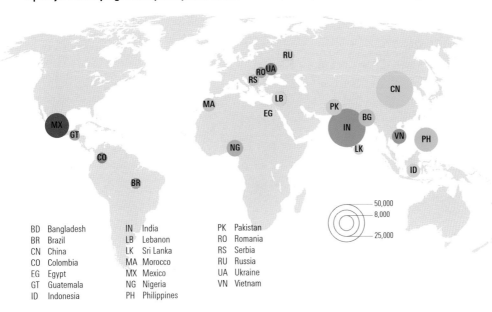

BD Bangladesh	IN India	PK Pakistan
BR Brazil	LB Lebanon	RO Romania
CN China	LK Sri Lanka	RS Serbia
CO Colombia	MA Morocco	RU Russia
EG Egypt	MX Mexico	UA Ukraine
GT Guatemala	NG Nigeria	VN Vietnam
ID Indonesia	PH Philippines	

3 | Migrants' Remittances per Capita, 2010 (estimates in USD)

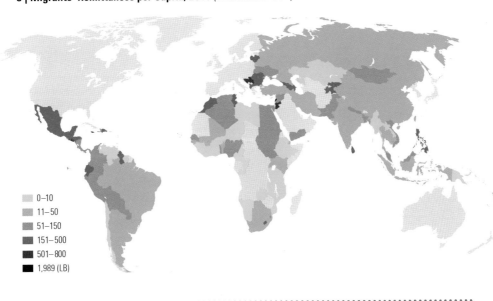

- 0–10
- 11–50
- 51–150
- 151–500
- 501–800
- 1,989 (LB)

Sources: Our calculations based on: World Bank (2010) *Annual Remittances Data*, Inflows (Washington, DC: World Bank); World Bank, *World Development Indicators*, http://databank.worldbank.org.

Foreign Direct Investment (FDI)

4 | Major Developing Country Recipients of FDI, 2010 (in million USD)

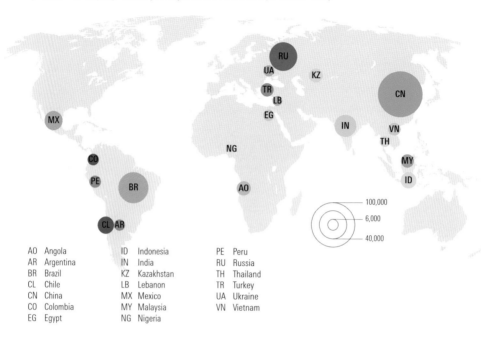

AO	Angola	ID	Indonesia	PE	Peru
AR	Argentina	IN	India	RU	Russia
BR	Brazil	KZ	Kazakhstan	TH	Thailand
CL	Chile	LB	Lebanon	TR	Turkey
CN	China	MX	Mexico	UA	Ukraine
CO	Colombia	MY	Malaysia	VN	Vietnam
EG	Egypt	NG	Nigeria		

5 | FDI per Capita, 2010 (in USD)

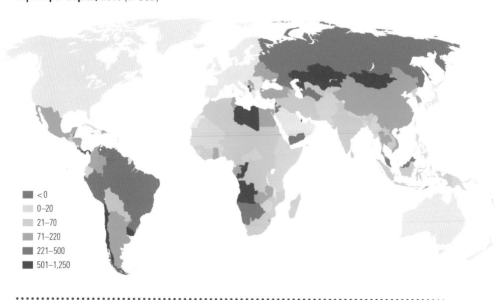

- <0
- 0–20
- 21–70
- 71–220
- 221–500
- 501–1,250

Sources: Our calculations based on: UNCTAD (2011) *World Investment Report 2011* (New York: UNCTAD); World Bank, *World Development Indicators*, http://databank.worldbank.org.

Official Development Assistance (ODA)

6 | Major Recipients of DAC Members' ODA, 2009 (in million USD)

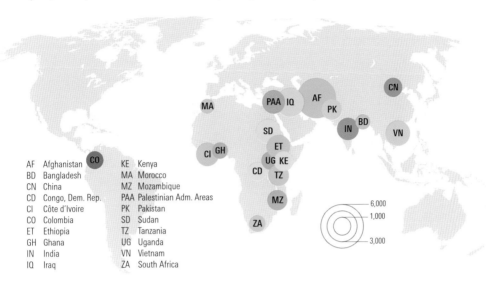

AF	Afghanistan	KE	Kenya
BD	Bangladesh	MA	Morocco
CN	China	MZ	Mozambique
CD	Congo, Dem. Rep.	PAA	Palestinian Adm. Areas
CI	Côte d'Ivoire	PK	Pakistan
CO	Colombia	SD	Sudan
ET	Ethiopia	TZ	Tanzania
GH	Ghana	UG	Uganda
IN	India	VN	Vietnam
IQ	Iraq	ZA	South Africa

7 | Net ODA Receipts per Capita, 2009 (in USD)

- −1.3 (TH)
- 0–10
- 11–30
- 31–75
- 76–200
- 201–450

Sources: Our calculations based on: OECD, *OECD.Stat Extracts*, http://stats.oecd.org/Index.aspx; World Bank, *World Development Indicators*, http://databank.worldbank.org.

Dependence on ODA and Remittances

8 | Net ODA Receipts, 2009 (in percentage of GDP)

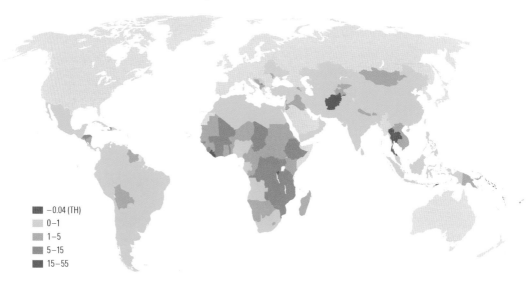

Legend:
- −0.04 (TH)
- 0–1
- 1–5
- 5–15
- 15–55

9 | Migrants' Remittances, 2009 (in percentage of GDP)

Legend:
- 0–1
- 1–5
- 5–15
- 15–45

Sources: Our calculations based on: World Bank (2010) *Annual Remittances Data*, Inflows (Washington, DC: World Bank); World Bank, *World Development Indicators*, http://databank.worldbank.org.

FOCUS ON OFFICIAL DEVELOPMENT ASSISTANCE (ODA)

10 | Evolution of Selected DAC Members' ODA, 1990–2010 (in percentage of GNI)

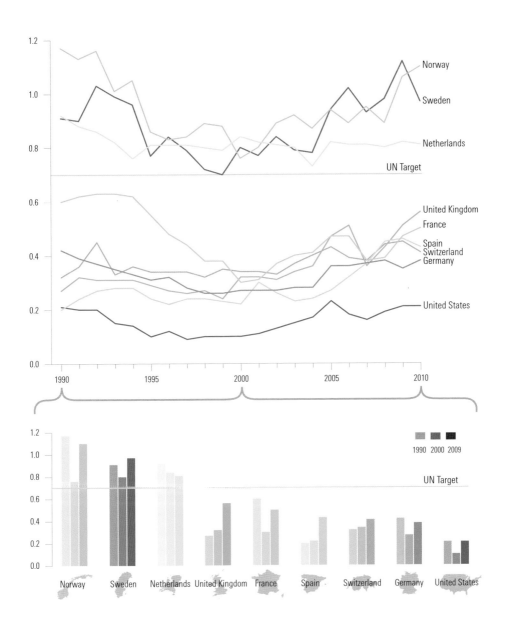

Source: OECD, *OECD.Stat Extracts*, http://stats.oecd.org/Index.aspx.

183

ODA by Donor Country

11 | DAC Members' Net ODA, 2010 (in million USD)

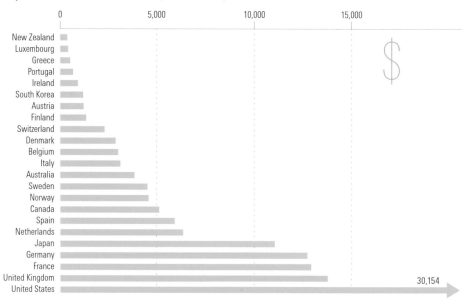

12 | DAC Members' Net ODA, 2010 (in percentage of GNI)

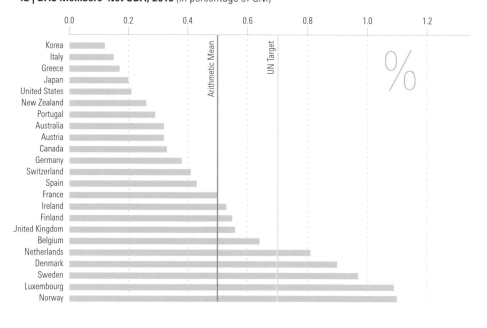

Source: OECD, *OECD.Stat Extracts*, http://stats.oecd.org/Index.aspx.

ODA by Recipient Country

13 | Net ODA by Region, All Donors, 2009 (in billion USD and in percentage of total aid)

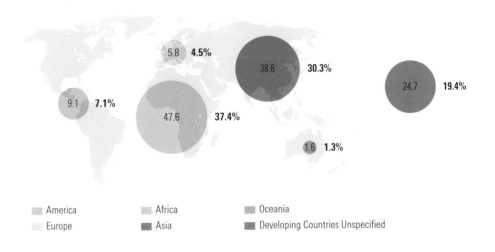

■ America	■ Africa	■ Oceania
■ Europe	■ Asia	■ Developing Countries Unspecified

14 | Net ODA by Income Group, All Donors, 2009 (in percentage of total aid)

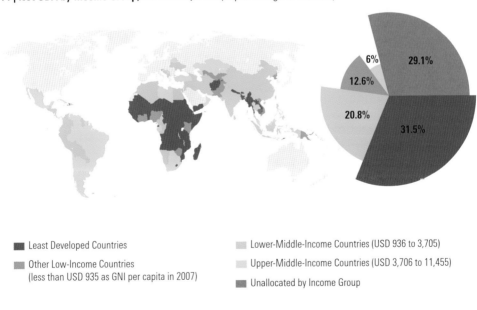

■ Least Developed Countries	■ Lower-Middle-Income Countries (USD 936 to 3,705)
■ Other Low-Income Countries (less than USD 935 as GNI per capita in 2007)	■ Upper-Middle-Income Countries (USD 3,706 to 11,455)
	■ Unallocated by Income Group

Source: OECD, *OECD.Stat Extracts*, http://stats.oecd.org/Index.aspx.

POLICY COHERENCE

Recipient Countries

15 | Net ODA Receipts and Military Expenditures in Selected Countries, All Donors, 2010 (in million USD)

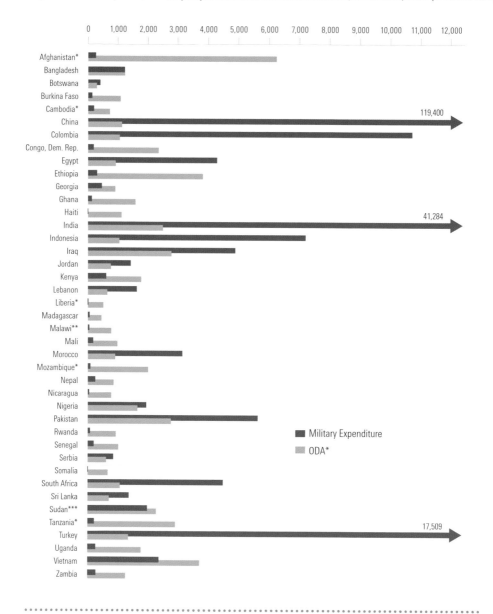

Sources: OECD, *OECD.Stat Extracts*, http://stats.oecd.org/Index.aspx; SIPRI (2011) *SIPRI Military Expenditure Database 2011*, http://milexdata.sipri.org.

* 2009. | ** 2007. | *** 2006.

Donor Countries

16 | Agricultural Support, Military Expenditures and ODA, OECD Members, 2010
(in percentage of GDP)

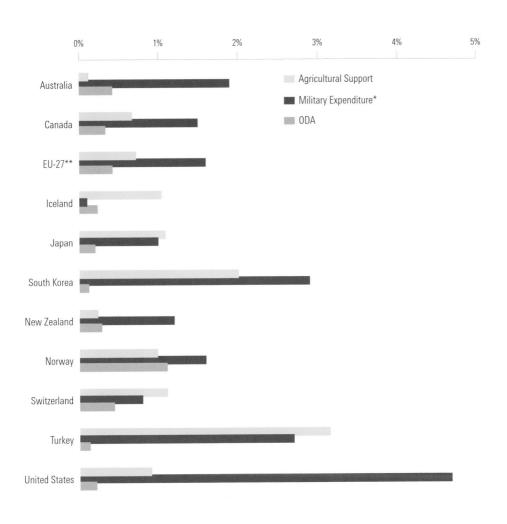

Sources: OECD, *OECD.Stat Extracts*, http://stats.oecd.org/Index.aspx; SIPRI (2011) *SIPRI Military Expenditure Database 2011*, http://milexdata.sipri.org.

* 2009.

** Data concerning agricultural support and military expenditures includes non-OECD EU members as well.

Aid to Refugees

17 | Expenses for In-Country Refugees vs. Contributions to the UNHCR, 2009 (in million USD)

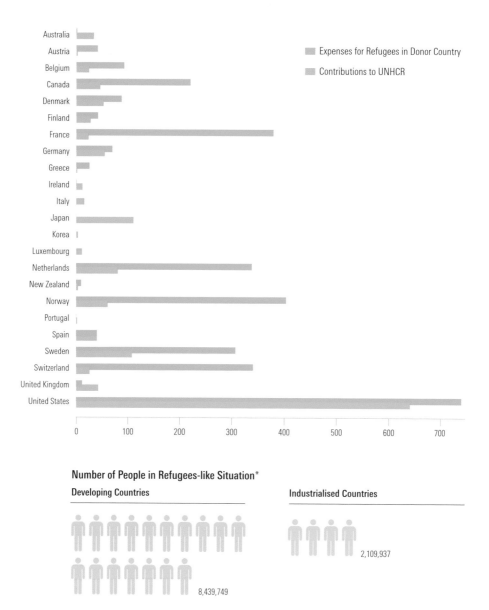

Number of People in Refugees-like Situation*

Developing Countries

8,439,749

Industrialised Countries

2,109,937

Sources: OECD, *OECD.Stat Extracts*, http://stats.oecd.org/Index.aspx; UNHCR (2011) *UNHCR Global Trends 2010* (Geneva: UNHCR); UNHCR (2010) *Contributions to UNHCR Programmes For Budget Year 2009* (Geneva: UNHCR).

* Palestinian refugees assisted by UNRWA are not included.

INFOGRAPHIC SECTION

Aid, Emerging Economies and Global Policies

POVERTY

18 | Poverty Evolution, 1990–2010 (World Bank income categories)

- High-Income Countries
- Upper-Middle-Income Countries
- Lower-Middle-Income Countries
- Low-Income Countries

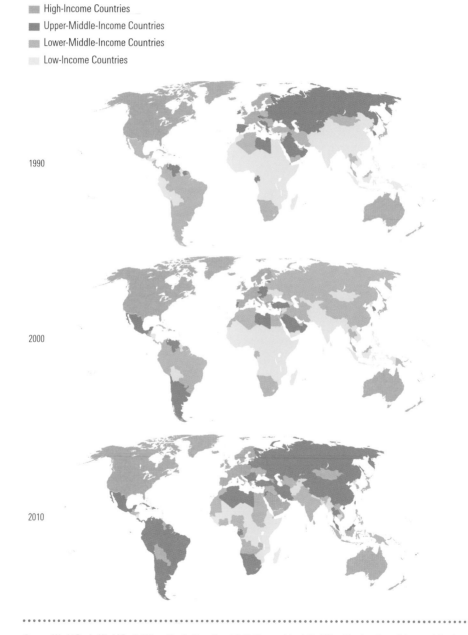

1990

2000

2010

Source: World Bank, *World Bank GNI per Capita Operational Guidelines and Analytical Classifications*, http://data.worldbank.org/
about/country-classifications/a-short-history.

19 | Where the Poor Are, 2007–2008 (million of people living under USD 1.25/day, Purchasing Power Parity)*

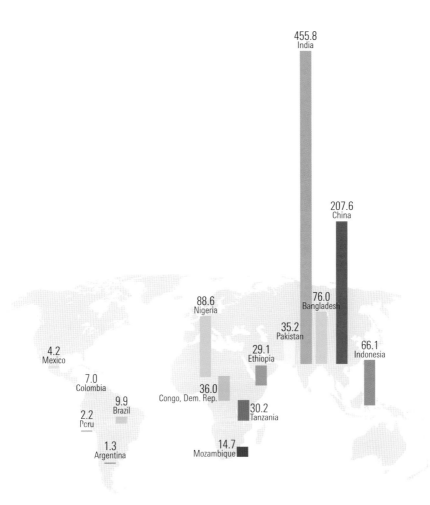

Source: Sumner, A. (2010) *Global Poverty and the New Bottom Billion*, IDS Working Paper no. 349 (Brighton: Institute of Development Studies).

* We selected the five countries with the highest number of poor in Africa, Asia and Latin America.

DEVELOPMENT ASSISTANCE FOR HEALTH (DAH)

20 | Deaths by Disease vs Development Assistance for Health (DAH)*, 2008
(in percentage of total DAH and total deaths by region)

Deaths by Disease

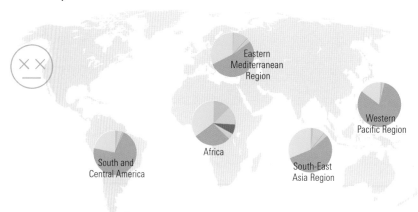

DAH by Health Area

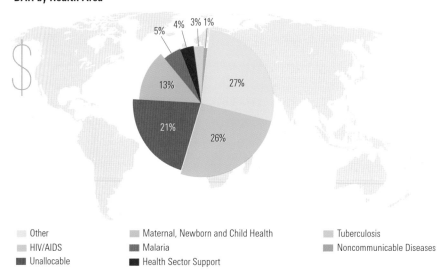

▢ Other	▢ Maternal, Newborn and Child Health	▢ Tuberculosis
▢ HIV/AIDS	▢ Malaria	▢ Noncommunicable Diseases
▢ Unallocable	▢ Health Sector Support	

Sources: IHME (Institute for Health Metrics and Evaluation) (2010) *Financing Global Health 2010: Development Assistance and Country Spending in Economic Uncertainty* (Seattle: IHME); WHO (2011) *Causes of Death 2008 Summary Table* (Geneva: WHO).

* DAH includes both financial and in-kind contributions for activities aimed at improving health in low- and middle-income countries.

DAH Stakeholders

21 | DAH Channels, 1990–2008 (in million USD constant, 2008)

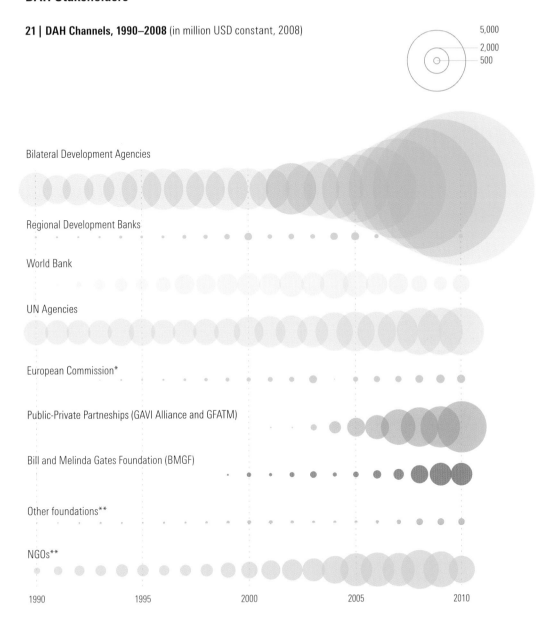

Source: IHME (Institute for Health Metrics and Evaluation) (2010) *Financing Global Health 2010: Development Assistance and Country Spending in Economic Uncertainty* (Seattle: IHME).

* Includes funds from the European Development Fund and the European Commission budget.
** Includes only organisations incorporated in the United States.

Health Budgets

22 | Selected Expenses and Profits in the Health Sector, 2009 (in million USD)

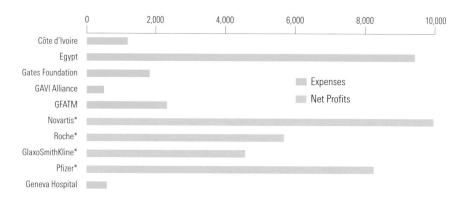

Sources: Annual Reports for corporations and Geneva Hospital (disbursements); OECD, *OECD.Stat Extracts*, http://stats.oecd.org/Index.aspx for Gates Foundation, GAVI and GFATM (disbursements); WHO's website for country data.
* 2010.
Data for Roche, Geneva University Hospital (HUG) and GlaxoSmithKline has been converted at the following average exchange rates: CHF 1 = USD 0.96, GBP 1 = USD 1.55.

23 | WHO, Regular and Extrabudgetary Income, 1990–2010 (in million USD constant, 2008)

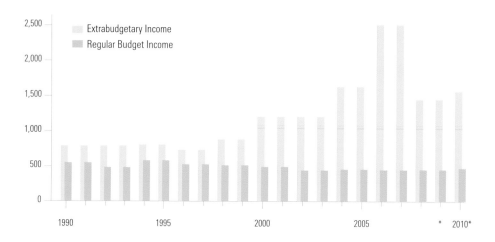

Sources: IHME (Institute for Health Metrics and Evalutation) (2010) *Financing Global Health 2010: Development Assistance and Country Spending in Economic Uncertainty* (Seattle: IHME); WHO (2011) *Unaudited Interim Financial Report on the Accounts of WHO for the Year 2010*, A64/49 (Geneva: WHO), p. 8.

* In line with WHO's two-year budget planning, we assumed the 2009 and 2008 budgets to be equal.

Non-Governmental Actors

24 | GFATM, Gates Foundation, GAVI and WHO Disbursements by Recipient Region, 2009
(in million USD)

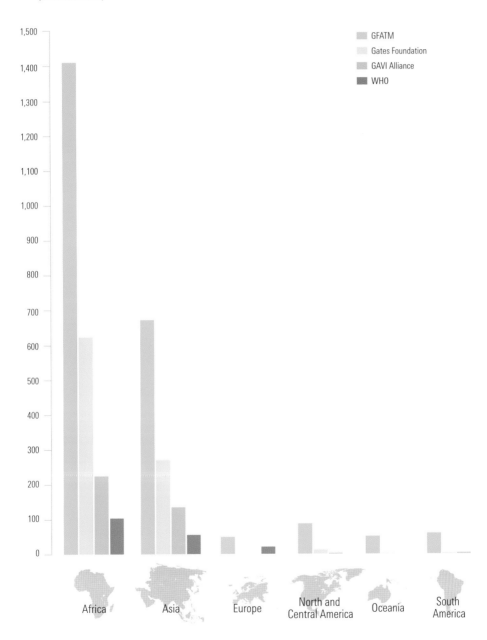

Source: OECD, *OECD.Stat Extracts*, http://stats.oecd.org/Index.aspx.

GLOBAL SECURITY

25 | Peacekeeping Operations Expenditure, Humanitarian Assistance and ODA, 1990–2010
(in billion USD constant, 2009)

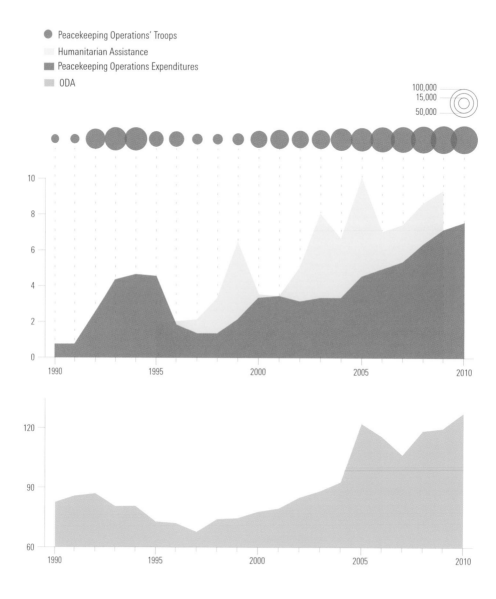

- Peacekeeping Operations' Troops
- Humanitarian Assistance
- Peacekeeping Operations Expenditures
- ODA

Sources: OECD, *OECD.Stat Extracts*, http://stats.oecd.org/index.aspx; UN, *United Nations Peacekeeping*, http://www.un.org/en/peacekeeping; Renner, M., *Peacekeeping Expenditures in Current vs. Real Terms 1947–2005*, http://www.globalpolicy.org; UN documents A/63/5 (Vol. II), A/75/175 and A/64/643.

26 | Payments Owed to the UN by Member States, 1975–2008 (in million USD)*

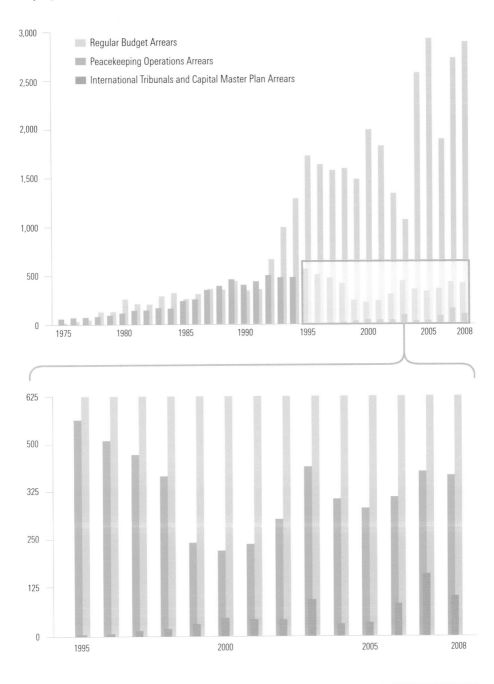

Source: Global Policy Forum, *Payments Owed to the UN by All Member States*, http://www.globalpolicy.org.

* Arrears are equal to payments due on 31 December of each year.

MULTILATERAL AID

27 | Bilateral and Multilateral Aid, DAC Members, 1960–2010 (in million USD constant, 2009)

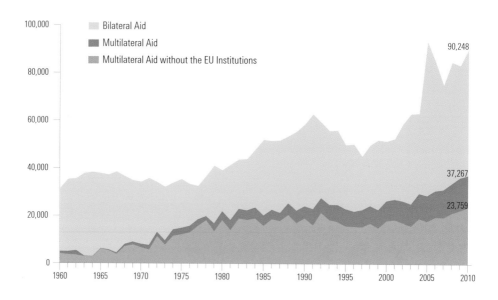

28 | Bilateral and Multilateral Aid by Recipient Region, DAC Members, 2008 (in percentage of total aid by Region)

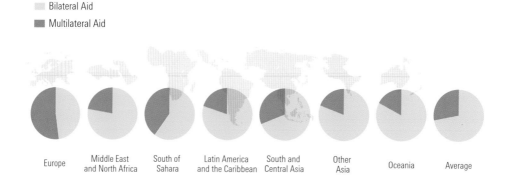

Sources: OECD (2010) *2010 DAC Report on Multilateral Aid* (Paris: OECD); OECD, *OECD.Stat Extracts*, http://stats.oecd.org/Index. asp.

29 | Multilateral and Multi-bilateral* Aid by Recipient Organisation, 2008 (in million USD)

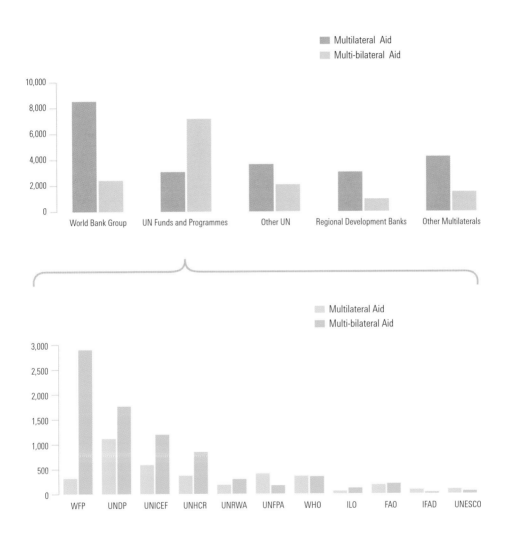

Source: OECD (2010) *2010 DAC Report on Multilateral Aid* (Paris: OECD).

* Multi-bilateral ODA, or non-core multilateral ODA, is bilateral ODA earmarked for a sector, theme, country, or region through a multilateral institution.

PRIVATE ACTORS

30 | ODA and Philanthropy compared by DAC Member, 2009 (in million USD)

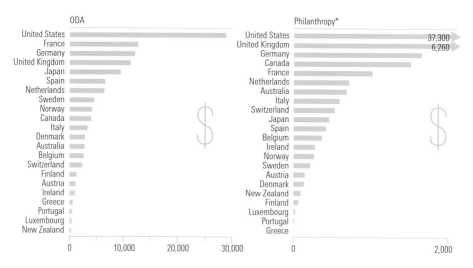

31 | ODA and Philanthropy compared by DAC Member, 2009 (in percentage of GDP)

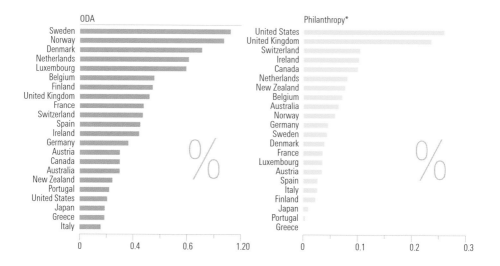

Sources: OECD, *OECD.Stat Extracts*, http://stats.oecd.org/Index.aspx; Center for Global Prosperity (2010), *The Index of Global Philanthropy and Remittances 2010* (Washington, DC: Hudson Institute).

2008.

Philanthropy includes givings by private: foundations, corporations, voluntary organisations, universities and colleges, and religious organisations. For the US the value of volunteer time for developing countries is also included.

EMERGING DONORS

32 | Brazil, China and South Africa at a Glance, 2009

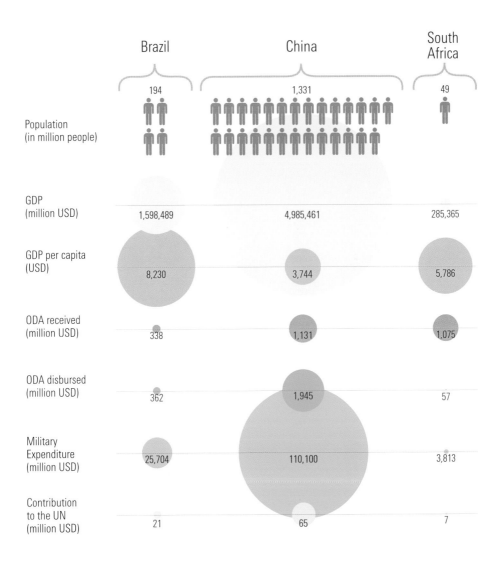

Sources: OECD, *OECD.Stat Extracts*, http://stats.oecd.org/Index.aspx; World Bank, *World Development Indicators Dataset*, http://databank.worldbank.org; SIPRI (2011) *SIPRI Military Expenditure Database 2011*, http://milexdata.sipri.org; ARF (African Renaissance and International Cooperation Fund) (2004–2010) *Annual Financial Statements* (Pretoria: DIRCO); ABC (Agência Brasileira de Cooperação) (2010), *Cooperação Brasileira para o Desenvolvimento Internacional: 2005-2009* (Brasilia: ABC); IOSC-PRC (Information Office of the State Council of the People's Republic of China) (2011) *China's Foreign Aid* (Beijing: IOSC-PRC).

China

33 | Chinese ODA, 1953–2009 (in million USD)

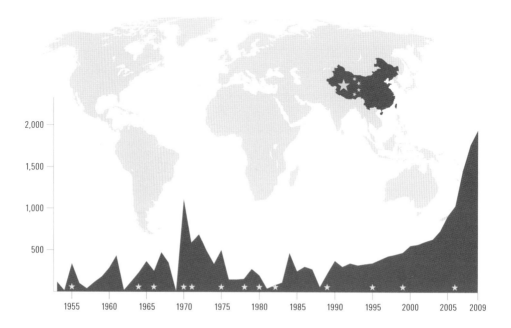

1955 Bandung Conference

1964 Eight Principles of Aid

1966 Beginning of the Cultural Revolution

1970 Beginning of the Tan-Zam Railway Project

1971 Accession to the UN

1975 Completion of the Tan-Zam Railway Project

1978 'Four Modernisations' Policy

1980 Accession to the IMF and the World Bank

1982 Four Principles of Cooperation with Africa

1989 Tiananmen Square protests

1995 Aid policy reform

1999 'Go Out' Policy

2006 First China-Africa Summit

Sources: Lin, T. O. (1996) 'Beijing's Foreign Aid Policy in the 1990s: Continuity and Change', *Issues and Studies* 32(1); Kobayashi, T. (2008), *Evolution of China's Aid Policy*, JBICI Working Paper no. 27 (Tokyo: JBICI); State Statistical Bureau of the People's Republic of China (2003-2010) *China Statistical Yearbook* (Beijing: China Statistics Press) for 2006–2010 data.

34 | Chinese ODA by Type and Recipient Region, 1953–2009 (in percentage of total Chinese aid)

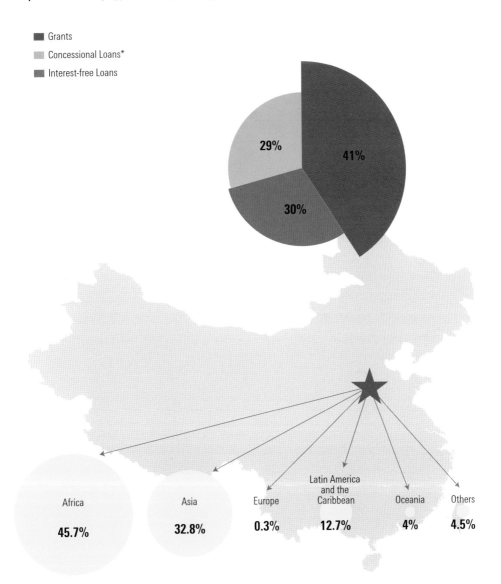

- ■ Grants
- ■ Concessional Loans*
- ■ Interest-free Loans

41%

29%

30%

Africa	Asia	Europe	Latin America and the Caribbean	Oceania	Others
45.7%	32.8%	0.3%	12.7%	4%	4.5%

Source: IOSC-PRC (Information Office of the State Council of the People's Republic of China) (2011) *China's Foreign Aid* (Beijing: IOSC-PRC).

* The annual interest rate of China's concessional loans is between 2 and 3 per cent, and the period of repayment is usually 15 to 20 years (including five to seven years of grace).

Brazil

35 | Brazilian ODA, 2005–2009 (in million USD constant, 2009, and in percentage of GDP)*

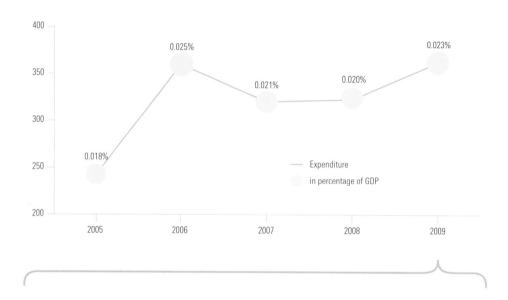

Sectoral Distribution, 2009 (in percentage of 2009 aid)

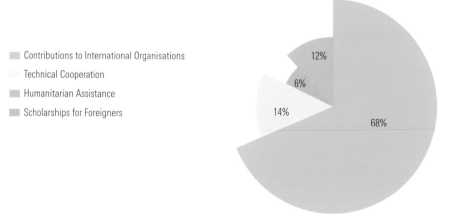

- Contributions to International Organisations
- Technical Cooperation
- Humanitarian Assistance
- Scholarships for Foreigners

Source: ABC (Agência Brasileira de Cooperação) (2010), *Cooperação Brasileira para o Desenvolvimento Internacional: 2005-2009* (Brasilia: ABC).

Brazilian ODA includes bilateral and multilateral aid committed to: technical, scientific and technological cooperation; scholarships for foreigners; humanitarian assistance; refugees in Brazil; peacekeeping operations and contributions to international organisations.

36 | Brazilian ODA by Region, 2005–2009 (in percentage of Brazilian aid*)

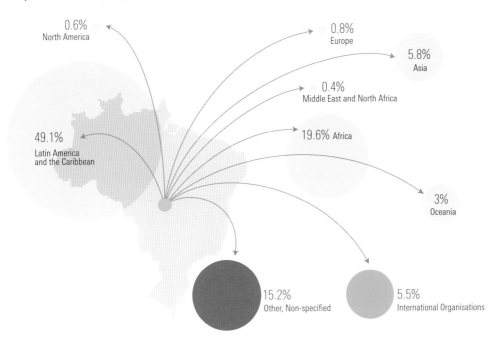

0.6%
North America

0.8%
Europe

5.8%
Asia

0.4%
Middle East and North Africa

19.6% Africa

49.1%
Latin America
and the Caribbean

3%
Oceania

15.2%
Other, Non-specified

5.5%
International Organisations

37 | Top Ten Recipient Organisations of Multilateral Brazilian ODA, 2009 (in million USD)

80.25	Mercosur
39.32	UN
10.81	International Drug Purchase Facility (UNITAID/IDPF)
10.74	Organization of American States
10.00	Pan-American Health Organization (PAHO/WHO)
9.23	Comprehensive Nuclear-Test-Ban Treaty Organization (CTBTO)
9.07	International Atomic Energy Agency (IAEA)
5.70	Food and Agriculture Organization (FAO)
5.28	WHO
4.76	Organización de Estados Iberoamericanos para la Educación, la Ciencia y la Cultura (OEI)

Source: ABC (Agência Brasileira de Cooperação) (2010), *Cooperação Brasileira para o Desenvolvimento Internacional: 2005-2009* (Brasília: ABC).

* Aid here refers to humanitarian assistance and technical cooperation.

South Africa

38 | African Renaissance and International Cooperation Fund's Expenditure, 2003–2010 (in million USD and in percentage of GDP)

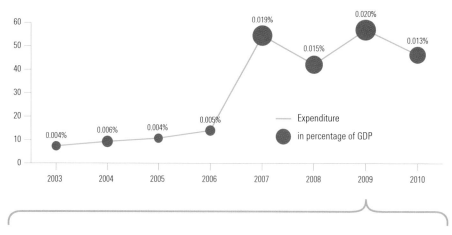

2009 Projects (in million USD)

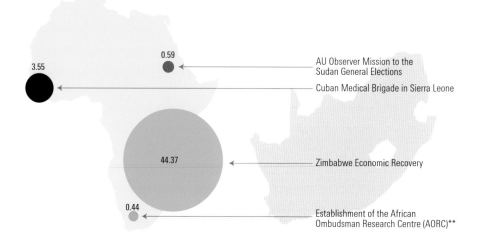

Sources: ARF (2004-2010) *Annual Financial Statements* (Pretoria: DIRCO).
* Although the fund is estimated to represent only 3-4 per cent of total South African aid, it is the only body producing reliable data. ZAR figures were converted into USD at the average exchange rate for each year.
** While located in South Africa, the AORC aims to serve as a focal point for coordination of activities and support of Ombudsman Offices in the entire Africa.

INDEX

Revue internationale de **politique de développement**

The *International Development Policy* is also available in French
under the title *Revue internationale de politique de développement*

POLDEV 2012 | N° 3

Revue internationale de **politique de développement**

L'AIDE
BOUSCULÉE
Pays émergents et politiques globales

THE GRADUATE INSTITUTE | GENEVA
PUBLICATIONS

L'aide bousculée. Pays émergents et politiques globales, *Revue internationale de politique de développement*, No. 3, Genève: Graduate Institute Publications, 2012, ISSN papier 1663-9375 | ISSN en ligne 1663-9391 | ISBN 978-2-940415-82-3